"Franck Cochoy is one of the most theoretically adept scholars working in marketing and consumer research at the moment. This book is a major contribution to the history of marketing theory and practice and is firmly at the cutting edge of research that aims to displace the consumer from the centre of analytic attention. It demands attention."

Mark Tadajewski, *Professor, Durham University, UK*

On the Origins of Self-Service

Most marketing scholars implicitly consider independent merchants as conservative and passive actors, and study the modernization of retailing via department stores, chains and supermarkets. In this innovative study, Franck Cochoy challenges this perspective and takes a close look at the transformation of commerce through the lens of *Progressive Grocer*, an American trade magazine launched in 1922.

Aimed at modernizing small independent grocery stores, *Progressive Grocer* sowed the seeds for modern self-service which spread in small retail outlets, sometimes well before the advent of the large retail spaces that are traditionally viewed as the origin of the self-service economy. The author illustrates how this publication had a highly influential role on what the trade considered best practice and shaped what was considered cutting edge. By displacing the consumer and their agency from the centre of analytic attention, this innovative book highlights the complex impact of social, technical and retailing environment factors that structure and delimit consumer freedom in the marketplace.

This detailed critical analysis of the origins of self-service will be of interest to a wide variety of scholars, not only in marketing and consumer research but also in business history, sociology and cultural studies.

Franck Cochoy is Professor of Sociology at the University of Toulouse, France. He is one of France's most influential economic sociologists and has published extensively in the area of critical marketing and consumer culture, specifically the market mediations between producers and consumers, from marketing to packaging, via advertising and other devices.

Routledge Studies in the History of Marketing
Edited by Mark Tadajewski and Brian D. G. Jones

It is increasingly acknowledged that an awareness of marketing history and the history of marketing thought is relevant for all levels of marketing teaching and scholarship. Marketing history includes, but is not limited to, the histories of advertising, retailing, channels of distribution, product design and branding, pricing strategies, and consumption behaviour – all studied from the perspective of companies, industries, or even whole economies. The history of marketing thought examines marketing ideas, concepts, theories, and schools of marketing thought including the lives and times of marketing thinkers.

This series aims to be the central location for the publication of historical studies of marketing theory, thought and practice, and welcomes contributions from scholars from all disciplines that seek to explore some facet of marketing and consumer practice in a rigorous and scholarly fashion. It will also consider historical contributions that are conceptually and theoretically well-conceived, that engage with marketing theory and practice, in any time period, in any country.

1. **On The Origins of Self-Service**
   Franck Cochoy

On the Origins of Self-Service

Franck Cochoy

Translated by Jaciara Topley-Lira

Routledge
Taylor & Francis Group

LONDON AND NEW YORK

First edition published 2014 in French
by Le Bord de l'Eau, Lormont
Franck Cochoy
Aux origines du libre-service, Progressive Grocer (1922–1959)
All Rights Reserved

First published 2016
by Routledge

2 Park Square, Milton Park, Abingdon, Oxfordshire OX14 4RN
52 Vanderbilt Avenue, New York, NY 10017

Routledge is an imprint of the Taylor & Francis Group, an informa business

First issued in paperback 2019

British Library Cataloguing in Publication Data
A catalogue record for this book is available from the British Library

Library of Congress Cataloging in Publication Data
Cochoy, Franck.
On the origins of self service retail / Franck Cochoy.
pages cm. – (Routledge studies in the history of marketing)
Includes bibliographical references and index.
1. Retail trade. 2. Self-service stores. I. Title.
HF5429.C545 2015
658.8'7–dc23
2015004915

ISBN: 978-1-138-90249-7 (hbk)
ISBN: 978-0-367-87260-1 (pbk)

Typeset in Bembo
by Taylor & Francis Books

Contents

List of figures viii
List of tables x
Acknowledgement xi

Introduction 1

1 How to read *Progressive Grocer* 10

2 Making people do business with words-things 40

3 The beginnings of *Progressive Grocer*: Improving commerce before
   transforming it 61

4 Transforming commerce: A business of pens and brands 131

5 Rolling stores, or the tour of trolleys 166

6 Conclusion 199

Bibliography 204
Index 214

List of figures

1.1   *Buy-at-Home News*, published by the magazine that bans out mail order advertising   18
1.2   Readership map   20
1.3   How to run a retail store   23
1.4   More money every year   27
1.5   The development of sales methods   30
1.6   Between yesterday and today, sales jumped 50%   31
1.7   Pocket size   34
1.8   NRLF at Berkeley, United States, and the author's desk in Toulouse, France   36
2.1   How to build displays that sell   41
2.2   Models   46
2.3   Photonovelas   49
2.4   "How did they know we were coming along?"   52
2.5   "I understand their clean-up man has been drafted"; "Isn't rationing wonderful? Think what it's doing for our figures!"   53
2.6   "I think this store is carrying self-service a little too far"   53
2.7   Will it come to this?; Notice to customers   55
3.1   Credit and delivery, or cash and carry?   67
3.2   Beware of bugs   70
3.3   There is only one Fly-Tox   71
3.4   How to wrap a package neatly   74
3.5   Dayton – A complete line of Store Equipment   78
3.6   The grocer on the phone as front-page news   79
3.7   Forty employees appointed to telephone sales   86
3.8   Staging telephone sales   87
3.9   Number of telephones per inhabitant   91
3.10   "Yes, we always have Jap Rose"   93
3.11   Quaker Oats, "When she telephones …"   95
3.12   Every one of these delivery trucks is an advert   99
3.13   How Fords cut food delivery costs   100
3.14   McCray refrigerators   104
3.15   US Slicer meat slicers   106

3.16 Dayton: the A-B-C of open display   109
3.17 False-bottom baskets   111
3.18 Keep the kitty out of the prunes   112
3.19 The display computing cheese cutter   113
3.20 Panay display cases   114
3.21 The bottled drinks distributer   115
3.22 "Ma wants to know if you'll [...] open this can for her"   117
3.23 The art of can opening   118
3.24 Progress of production of canned foods   120
3.25 List of winners of the "Canned Foods Week" photo competition   125
4.1   Arranging one's shop   134
4.2   One big jump ... from this to this   136
4.3   The development of shop routes   137
4.4   Growth in value of packaged products ($ million)   140
4.5   Food cans and counters   141
4.6   The Monarch way   142
4.7   Can pyramids   143
4.8   Cellophane   145
4.9   Endless Tote-Cart baskets   146
4.10 The Zephyr till prevents check-out errors automatically   148
4.11 A moveable partition   149
4.12 "Your name goes here"   150
4.13 Turnstiles and magic doors   152
4.14 The circularity of magazines   156
4.15 *Life* magazine ... *Life* displays   157
4.16 Is the grocer on your side?   159
4.17 M.C. Escher, "Ascending and Descending"   160
4.18 Shopping cart parks   162
4.19 Flagpole of the Boys Market   163
5.1   From the folding cart to the telescoping cart   169
5.2   Variations of foldable trolleys   172
5.3   Remodeling Narrow Store? Here Are Ideas   173
5.4   Needs no folding, needs no stacking   175
5.5   Automatic cart return   178
5.6   Tunnel check-out   179
5.7   Permanence of service   181
5.8   Children and counters   185
5.9   Weber glass display case   186
5.10 Double welded for double wear   188
5.11 Child seat variations   190
5.12 Shopping is a family affair   193
6.1   Branding, penning ... loading   202

List of tables

5.1   Distribution of trolley types   191
5.2   Distribution of customer types (%)   192

Acknowledgement

This book is the result of two fieldwork sessions, one carried out at the University of California, Berkeley, between 14 July and 8 August 2006, and the other at the Center for Research Libraries of Chicago, between 14 and 18 January 2013, and the subsequent analysis, over several years, of the data collected. It combines a completely original monograph on the beginnings of the magazine *Progressive Grocer* with a series of previously published articles and chapters.[1] All of these previous works were developed, updated and reworked.

I am very grateful to Catherine Grandclément, to whom I owe the discovery of *Progressive Grocer*, the ANR and Education Abroad Program, which provided me with the funding and the material resources needed to carry out this research. I am deeply indebted to Jutta Wiemhoff, Martha Lucerto (NRLF), Steve Mendoza (central library) and three other anonymous librarians from the Business/Economics Library and Environmental Design of the University of Berkeley, and to Michelle Carver from the Chicago Center for Research Libraries. I would like to thank David Vogel for his support, the Haas School of Business of Berkeley for its material support and Carmen Tapia for her administrative assistance. I am extremely grateful to Sandrine Barrey, Anni Borzeix, Roland Canu, Laure Gaertner, Joël Jornod, Martin Giraudeau, Claire Leymonerie and Basile Zimmermann for their comments on some of the texts that contributed to this work. I would like to express my gratitude to all those who gave me the opportunity to test my arguments at workshops, seminars and conferences, too numerous to mention here. The material and intellectual support provided by the Centre for Retailing at the School of Business, Economics and Law of the University of Göteborg in Sweden was extremely useful to me in writing this book.

Finally, I would like to warmly thank *Progressive Grocer* for allowing me permission to reproduce the images upon which this publication rests.

Note

1 Cochoy, 2008c, 2008d, 2009, 2010a, 2010b, 2010c, 2010d, 2010e, 2013.

Introduction

During the nineteenth, twentieth and twenty-first centuries, new forms of commerce emerged, as diverse as they were spectacular: department stores, mail-order houses, cooperatives, chain stores, supermarkets, and more recently shopping centres, online sales or even the "drive-throughs" of current e-commerce. These changes set things and people in motion, thanks to technical innovations, ranging from the mechanised warehouses of the mail-order company Sears which industrialised long-distance product distribution (Strasser, 1989), trains (Chandler, 1977) and lorries (Hamilton, 2008) which unified previously isolated markets (Tedlow, 1990), to the smartphone applications of today, capable of combining e-commerce and mobility (Cochoy, 2011b), via the escalators and lifts that encouraged the expansion of large shops and the movement of consumers (Worthington, 1989), and the automobiles and shopping trolleys that underpinned the emergence of supermarkets (Bowlby, 2001; Daumas, 2006; Grandclément, 2006; Longstreth, 1999; Longstreth, 2000).

By channelling the movement of products as well as people differently, these innovations could have left small businesses far behind, as if abandoned on the banks of the new commercial flows. Small traditional shops and boutiques might have remained inert, eclipsed by the eruption of new commercial scenarios, condemned by the competition of more efficient techniques, forgotten in the shadow of more attractive, innovative and larger forms. By prioritising the study of department stores and supermarkets,[1] and thus somewhat neglecting the commercial spaces of an "outdated" past, many researchers would merely follow the course of history – in the tradition of the famous novel by Émile Zola from which they often draw inspiration and whose title, *The Ladies' Paradise*, features the large mutagenic shop of the enterprising Mouret, whereas it relegates the immutable small business of yesteryear – *The Old Elbeuf* – owned by the unfortunate Baudu, to the recesses of the story (or history?).

> The Old Elbeuf has been known for nearly a hundred years, and has no need for such at its door. As long as I live, it shall remain as I took it, with a few samples on each side, and nothing more!
>
> (Zola, 1886, p. 25)

However, we now know, with 100 years of hindsight, that small business is not dead, particularly in the textile industry, which Zola had nevertheless chosen. What can be said of France and the textile sector applies elsewhere and in the food industry: the advent of supermarkets did not lead to the disappearance of local grocers (Strasser, 1989; Deutsch, 2001). As was highlighted by David Monod (1996), Claire Leymonerie (2006) and Susan Spellman (2009) regarding Canada, France and the United States, respectively, small business did not remain unchanging and immobile; far from settling for resistance, they often got ahead of the competition with new forms of distribution.

In the United States and in the food industry, rather than pitting modernist chains of shops and supermarkets against small conservative businesses, the general movement of commerce instead demonstrates, according to a typically Tourainian[2] pattern, the confrontation between several kinds of actors who, despite going in different directions, were nonetheless all focused on action and looking to the future – movement vs. counter-movement. Small food shops in particular did not wall themselves up in opposition to progress,[3] but were, on the contrary, the location of a powerful reforming current, led by the magazine *Progressive Grocer*, which, as its name suggests,[4] intended to support the modernisation of small independent grocers, confronted by chains of shops (catered for by the magazine *Chain Store Age*) and soon by supermarkets (accompanied by the magazine *Supermarket Merchandising*). The mere fact that *Progressive Grocer* was launched in 1922 – in other words, long before its competitors, *Chain Store Age* (1925) and *Supermarket Merchandising* (1936) – shows to what extent the retail sector's concern to change was the response to a project that was at least as active as it was reactive, by the actors concerned.

It is to this magazine, or rather to the history of self-service from this magazine's point of view, that this book is dedicated. *Progressive Grocer* is a trade magazine targeting grocers, in order to show its audience a thousand ways to change and improve its practices. It is not a magazine for one profession, like the bulletin of an association, but rather an entirely original magazine, founded by a media company that thought there was room, in the United States of the 1920s, for a publication directed towards the modernisation of the retail trade, in the wake of the modernist rhetoric of the "Progressive Era"[5] (to which the title of the magazine is making a clear reference), and by taking advantage of the war at the time between "independent grocer" and new "retail chains" (Deutsch, 2001; Haas 1979; Seth, 2001; Tedlow, 1990). In its early stages, the magazine appeared as a thick pocket-sized booklet,[6] published on a monthly basis and sent to American grocers free of charge – in other words, funded by advertising. From its launch in 1922, the magazine boasted that it reached 50,000 retailers (1922, 05, 1[7]), an audience that grew to 68,000 a few years later (1930, 08, 2–3) – that is to say almost one third of the 250,000 independent grocers at the time (1930, 02, 14–15), a considerable achievement that no other kind of distribution would have had the opportunity to reach.

I shall analyse this magazine for the period 1922–59, in order to examine how specialists of a "progressive grocery sector" attempted to reshape or introduce a considerable amount of commercial equipment – shelves, tills, refrigerators, display fixtures, shopping trolleys, etc. – in order to move products and consumers in a different way, in the hope of thus moving themselves, and with them, in the direction of modernity. The study of small retail grocers, perhaps more so than that of large retailers, is particularly interesting when examining the joint mobility of the different forms of commerce, products and consumers, given that the lack of space and thus the limited nature of the possibilities of the display area and of achieving the sales volumes of supermarkets, makes it possible to isolate, in a particularly striking manner, the contribution of technical innovations to the transformation of distribution spaces.

By borrowing a metaphor from the history of science, I would say that in this work I intend to defend a Pasteurian concept of commercial innovation – in other words, a concept combining the "contagionist" approach of inventions prevailing in most works on the history of business, and a "diffusionist" perspective more sensitive to the conditions for the simultaneous emergence of these same objects (this perspective cannot, therefore, in any way be mistaken for the traditional theory of the diffusion of innovations, which confuses diffusion and contagion; Rogers, 1962).[8] Remember that until the nineteenth century, those involved in public health considered that diseases emerged and spread through spontaneous generation, resulting from local sanitary conditions (miasmas, stains, insalubrity), whereas others believed them to spread through the circulation of invisible agents, spreading contamination from person to person. Louis Pasteur managed to bring together both points of view, by revealing the existence of germs and the contamination of healthy people by those who were sick (contagion), but also by showing how particular sanitary conditions encouraged or inhibited the proliferations of pathogenic agents (diffusion) (Latour, 1988b).

The history of business, by often attempting to identify the "original inventor", supposedly hidden behind each commercial innovation, implicitly promoted a "contagionist" view of the commercial change where, astonishingly, the same accounts, referring to the same sources of innovation, contaminated one work after another. Thus, with one reference referring to another, the shops Piggly Wiggly and Kroger, in particular, were constantly indicated as the places where self-service originated, especially after the publication of certain monographs funded by the companies themselves (Laycock, 1983; Presley, 1984). The first Piggly Wiggly shop opened in 1916, based on a concept patented the following year, whereby customers were instructed to take their goods off the shelves themselves, on a purchasing circuit, with a separate entrance and exit (Bowlby, 2001; Tolbert, 2009); the same year, the Kroger chain promoted a similar solution, founded on low profit margins, a large shopping area, self-service, a car park and an edge-of-town location to reduce the cost of the commercial lease (Bowlby, 2001; Spellman, 2009). Based on these models, whose independent and simultaneous appearance should have led the authors who use them to reason in terms other than that of pure contagion, the literature on the subject tends rather to isolate and establish two types of business, one purely innovative and modernist (chains), the other irreducibly conservative and dated (traditional grocers), and implies that the most advanced in some way "contaminated" the others by forcing them to copy in order to stay in business.[9]

I would, of course, not entirely dismiss the existence of such processes, for several reasons. First, the companies Piggly Wiggly and Kroger, and more generally other chains and innovations introduced by them, effectively preceded the publication of *Progressive Grocer*, whose first issue appeared in 1922. Second, chains were clearly very present and influential on the American business scene: Piggly Wiggly owned as many as 2,600 shops in the 1920s (Grandclément, 2011); the Kroger chain had 1,413 shops at the time *Progressive Grocer* was created, and this figure grew to 5,575 in 1929, before decreasing under the effect of the Great Depression (Phillips, 1936). The largest chain, A&P, went from 7,300 to 15,400 outlets over the same period (Tedlow, 1990, p. 195). Furthermore, the battle between defenders of independent retailers and promoters of chains played a major role in American economic history, with the help of economies of scale obtained through joint purchasing and vertical integration, scientific management of stock and personnel, cash and carry sales, self-service for some, and profit through volume strategy (Deutsch, 2001; Haas, 1979; Lebhar, 1959; Tedlow, 1990; Spellman, 2009; Strasser, 1989).

Progressive Grocer clearly bears the mark of this presence and this battle. Many articles in the magazine refer to the competition from chains, question the pressure on prices attributed to them, sometimes refuting it (1923, 10, 37 sq.), and also in terms of their unfair competition (1922, 07, 13). Several suggest drawing inspiration from the methods of multiple-branch shops, by reducing the variety of products offered in order to lower costs (1922, 09, 7 sq.), banking more on volume and stock rotation than on price (1923, 04, 46 sq.), by improving cleanliness and taking care with the appearance of window displays (1924, 04, 12 sq.), showing prices, keeping up stock levels and being attentive to the customer (1923, 08, 31 sq.), ensuring rigorous accounting (1925, 08, 71), imitating their adverts (1926, 09, 56) and promotional techniques (1927, 02, 23 sq.), and even turning themselves into a joint purchasing syndicate and thus fighting "fire with fire" (Spellman, 2009, p. 198), which proves that there is, of course, a significant element of contagion between chains and independent grocers.

Having said that, the contagionist dynamic deserves to be strongly nuanced, or rather expanded upon. The fact that chains existed before *Progressive Grocer* was launched tells us nothing about the places from where these chains obtained their own ideas – in other words, as was shown by Susan Spellman (2009),[10] these same independent businesses they were nonetheless supposed to have inspired! In fact, it is strange that we often forget that a chain generally has its origins in the model of a successful independent retailer. For that matter, the importance and pressure of chains must be put into perspective. Even in 1930, or when they were considered to be so widespread as to have achieved their maximum expansion, there were at best 57,000 shops of this kind compared with 250,000 independent grocers, according to *Progressive Grocer* estimates (1930, 02, 14).[11] What was even better (or worse for the chains) was that, as a result of the Great Depression, anti-chain store measures[12] and the modernising transformation of small business, the number of grocers owned by chains fell by a quarter between 1929 and 1939, whereas their share in the general sales volume of food products – still very much a minority – contracted from 39.1% to 36.8%, while over the same period, despite the crisis, the number of independent retailers grew by 26% (Spellman, 2009, p. 299).

More fundamentally, one cannot be too careful about later interpretations of history that often judge the importance of historic objects on the basis of their subsequent fate (Grandclément, 2008). As we shall see in the next chapter, the actors, deprived of the extensive and predictive knowledge available to an historian, had a more limited view. It is one thing to have become, like Piggly Wiggly and Kroger, important chains, and to have applied for a patent and/or developed a concept, and another to make them known and to impose them when they are being implemented. Instead of being imitated, copied or reproduced, some of the innovations attributed a little too hastily to chains could just have well have been either, as in the case of the profit-through-volume strategy, accounting improvements or optimised stock management, reinvented everywhere by very diverse actors, or, as in the case of shop layout and merchandising techniques, introduced by "external" suppliers to different sales formats.[13] As we shall see, these suppliers – manufacturers of branded, tinned, bottled or packaged products (Twede, 2012), producers of different equipment (cash registers, slicing machines, refrigerators), and promoters of furniture that made it possible to improve merchandise presentation and therefore soon after to adopt self-service – proposed their solutions regardless of the type of shop, and even to independent businesses first, for the very reason that they represented by far the main outlet for their products.[14] This is evidenced by the fact, highlighted by *Progressive Grocer*, that its first issue benefited from "advertising from some of the leading manufacturers of food products and store equipment in the country" (1922, 08, 3). It is also demonstrated, more generally, by the lack of any noticeable difference between the different types of shops: chains and independent businesses might differ in terms of management model, logistical system, back-office organisation, even production with their own brands, but their shops were surprisingly similar, having obtained their improvements from the same suppliers, as shown by the inability of consumers at the time to distinguish between them (Spellman, 2009).

Nevertheless, above and beyond the simultaneous (but not necessarily imitative) implementation of the same merchandising innovations, the competition from chains, far from pushing independent businesses towards mimicry, often led them, on the contrary, to opt for a strategy of differentiation in order to survive. Symptomatically, it was not Kroger or Piggly Wiggly that *Progressive Grocer* initially referred to as the shops most worthy of interest; on the contrary, the magazine gave pride of place to another sales outlet that history has of course not retained, but which it presented as "the world's finest grocery store" (1925, 09, 9 sq.). This imposing six-storey shop that looked like a "palace of art" and had very recently been inaugurated in December 1923 by the Young's Market Company, a business that had been operating in Los Angeles for thirty-seven years, achieved a turnover of $8 million a year, investing essentially in the quality of service, with the many employees, telephone orders and motorised deliveries. This case is obviously only a symbolic illustration of a more general strategy consisting in avoiding price competition from chains by concentrating on what were considered the distinct advantages of independent business, such as quality and service (1922, 04, 30–31; 1925, 03, 24 sq.), better integration in the community (1924, 11, 25 sq.), and the supply of fresh products not covered by chains such as fruit and vegetables, meat, etc.[15] As summed up by a grocer from Minneapolis, who prided himself on having managed to increase his turnover after attempting to respond to the appearance of a competitor from a chain, the idea was to "develop to the highest efficiency the things which we had and which the other store did not" (1922, 06, 25).

More generally speaking, and as we shall see later on, the observation of and competition from chains took up very little space in the pages of *Progressive Grocer*, which, far from operating purely defensively and reactively, concentrated on the more positive description and promotion of innovations it held dear. What was true for chains was even more so for supermarkets. These were a late development, well after *Progressive Grocer* had set grocers on a path of modernising renovation. The rise of supermarkets might have begun with the Mike Cullen shops in 1930 (of the Kroger chain) and Big Bear in 1932 – in other words two other avatars of these legendary prototypes so beloved of the literature, initially honoured by the promoter of the sector and founder of the competing magazine, *Supermarket Merchandising*, Max Zimmerman (1937, 1955). The success of supermarkets was more definitely assured at the end of the 1930s (Grandclément, 2008), particularly in the very motorised environment of California (Longstreth, 1999; Longstreth, 2000), at the crossroads of innovations that had been tested, at least partially, by chains and independent businesses. Far from being the places where self-service originated, supermarkets were therefore rather its consequence, extension, systematisation, refinement or even more so, its "takeover", to use the expression dear to Catherine Grandclément, the author who has studied them most effectively.

Given these different developments, my concern is therefore neither to state that *Progressive Grocer* lies at the root of self-service (the magazine simply contributes, among other kinds of sale, to its origins, plural), nor to echo existing genealogies, but rather to get away from the vain search for places of exclusive and original invention[16] in order, in the wake of the remarkable works by Thomas Hughes (1983), to examine on the one hand the emergence of multiple, concomitant independent innovations of the same type, and on the other and above all, the dynamics of "lateral" innovations where products and equipment "from outside" entered a large number of different institutions and places, transforming them, until, after successive adjustments, this new form of sale emerged that we call self-service.

After providing some clarifications about the source used, which warrants certain precautions, and defining an appropriate method and way to read it (Chapter 1), I shall present the material, pictorial and discursive techniques through which *Progressive Grocer* intends to mobilise words and to modernise business (Chapter 2).

I shall then show that this modernisation was brought about by two semi-simultaneous, semi-consecutive movements. The first is, paradoxically, the improvement of traditional human service (and not its suppression), with the help of sanitation, the training of the labour force, equipment improving labour productivity and even very "technological" innovations, such as the use of the telephone and motorised transport (Chapter 3). The second movement is the transformation of business, through the gradual introduction of the "open display" and self-service. This transformation consists in very tightly rearranging the free movement of people, by introducing ingenious devices for channelling (pens) and identifying (brands) products and customers (Chapter 4).

Lastly, I shall address the way in which the introduction of shopping trolleys completed the reshaping of business, not only by increasing the capacity to circulate and purchase, but above all, by changing the morphology of those who went around the shops (Chapter 5).

Contrary to and adding to the available literature on my subject, which focuses especially on legal and organisational patterns, overall transformations, social and political regulations, the general introduction of sales techniques into the American economy, I shall opt for a localised and practical approach, at the level of the shelves that predominate in *Progressive Grocer* – an approach implicitly suggesting that in order to understand the history of the retail trade, one must (also? above all?) take an interest in its details. Beyond simply updating the forgotten contribution of the small progressive grocer to the advent of self-service, I hope that my study makes it possible to understand the role played by the business media in the transformation of sales premises; the vital importance of technical innovations in shaping the trade relationship; the dynamics of physically interlocking human and non-human elements to be found in commercial spaces, beyond the traditional paradigm of trade as embedded in society; the central role played by the "market of marketing devices" in bringing markets to life; and above all, the "making people do what they want" – in other words, all the knowledge, techniques and know-how used by sales professionals to arrange carefully our "free movement" in market spaces.

Notes

1 As wonderfully demonstrated by the literary journal by Chatriot and Chessel (2006).
2 Alain Touraine – a major French sociologist and a specialist of social movements – showed that in contemporary post-industrial societies, social struggles do not rest on the classic opposition between progressives who want to move and conservatives

who wish to remain immobile, but rather engage several conflicting movements that fight one another (Touraine, 1977).

3 American grocery stores cannot be suspected of attachment to the past for the good reason that they are themselves quite recent: as James Mayo showed, these retail outlets emerged around the middle of the nineteenth century in the wake of public markets, general stores and country stores, along diverse evolutions that favoured the development of small shops specialising in food trade, i.e. urbanisation, the generalisation of railroads, the decline of self-production, the improvement and transformation of marketing channels, the development of branded products and of new forms of packaging (Mayo, 1993).

4 The play on words is clear: the almost anagrammatical homophone *progressive-grocer* is there to back the idea that the modernisation of the grocer sector is self-evident, is inherent in the very nature of the activity.

5 The "Progressive Era" was a period historians generally consider to date from the second half of the nineteenth century until the 1920s, but which *Progressive Grocer* clearly intended to extend. It corresponds to an important reformist current aiming to spread technical progress and modernisation to all sectors of American society, in particular to the economic world (Alexander, 2008: Buenker and Kantowicz, 1988; Carson, 2011; Diner 1998; Glad, 1966; Gould, 2001; Hofstadter, 1963; Jaycox, 2005, McGerr, 2003; Society for Historians of the Gilded Age and Progressive Era, n.d.; Thompson, 1979).

6 The size of each issue, around 100 pages long in the 1920s, grew to more than 200 in the 1930s, of which about half was filled with advertisements and the rest dedicated to articles on merchandising, the development of and news about the retail trade, etc.

7 Throughout this work I use the pattern "YYYY, MM, pp.", where YYYY refers to the year, MM the month and pp. the pages of the *Progressive Grocer* edition cited.

8 The relationship between distribution and Pasteurism goes far beyond a simple metaphor, given that the heating process for preparing Nicolas Appert's preserves on the one hand helped Louis Pasteur to understand, nearly a century later, the bacteriological mechanisms involved in sterilisation, and on the other hand developed the canned food industry and thus contributed to the advent of mass consumption (Twede, 2012, p. 252).

9 In this book, I merely intend to agree, using additional arguments, with Susan Spellman's point of view, which calls into question the dominant historical view of distribution, in order for Spellman to insist on the organisational innovations of small business, and so that I can reveal the contribution of equipment to change: "There is little doubt that chain stores have received greater attention in popular accounts of the grocery trade. Corporate histories abound, with works such as A&P-Past, Present and Future (1971), The Kroger Story: A Century of Innovation (1983), and Piggly Wiggly Southern Style: The Piggly Wiggly Southern Store, 1919–1984 (1984). These studies illustrate the rise of vertical integration, self-service, and other features generally attributed to chain stores. Often written with celebratory fervor by 'company historians', these works make little effort to analyze critically the grocery trade in the context of larger social, cultural, and economic questions. More important, they make little attempt to link the success of these businesses and their methods to those of independent grocers, despite the fact that many regional and national chains began in the nineteenth century with the opening of a single, owner-run store" (Spellman, 2009, p. 10).

10 The author mentions the case of a shop owned by August Bjorkman, recognised in 1896 as "the Most Modern Grocery Store" in San Leandro, California, with his packaged and tinned branded products arranged on wide wall shelves, which would inspire large chains (Spellman, 2009, p. 1). Even the practice of group purchasing,

despite being considered one of the distinctive attributes of chains, had been started before them by independent retailers (*ibid.*, p. 200).

11 These statistics, put forward by the independent business magazine, are astonishingly favourable to chains, given that Godfrey Lebhar, editor-in-chief of *Chain Store Age*, estimated for his part that the peak reached in 1929 by the number of shops belonging to the twenty largest chains, in all sectors, was 37,000 (Lebhar, 1959, p. 54), whereas Richard Tedlow calculated the number of independent retailers, in the inter-war period, to be 300,000 (Tedlow, 1990, p. 203).

12 Taxation for chains in relation to the number of shops, legalised in 1931 by the Supreme Court, Robinson–Patman Act of 1936, limiting their discriminatory price practices (Deutsch, 2001). Incidentally, one should note the focus of the national political battle against chains, on issues of prices and organisational patterns: this approach allowed for the possibility of fighting them, with landslide success, in a less collective and more individual way, based less on accounting and more on quality, by investing in the art of shop layout and presentation – an entire strategy promoted by *Progressive Grocer*.

13 In both cases, innovation appears almost like spontaneous generation, by virtue of favourable local conditions.

14 The case of cash registers, excellently analysed by Susan Spellman, is particularly significant: independent businesses were the first to acquire this tool and constituted the main market for the National Cash Register. Better still, demand for them was largely voluntary, given that almost 30% of the cash registers sold by the company were done so without the intervention of a sales representative being necessary (Spellman, 2009).

15 This strategy made sense, as revealed in a survey carried out in 1939, involving 2,798 consumers: although 84% of people interviewed believed that chains offered the lowest prices, 85% of them said that independent shops gave them personalised service, and 62% that independent shops offered better-quality products (Bader, 1939, p. 60).

16 The quest for origins, although very instructive, is endless: whereas everyone agrees that Piggly Wiggly and Kroger were the ultimate pioneers of self-service, Susan Spellman points out that this way of selling had been inaugurated by restaurants around 1900, and mentions that a shopkeeper in Ohio was already running a self-service shop long before the first chain patented the system (Spellman, 2009, p. 276). We can bet that other historians will soon be able to find even earlier examples. However, isolated cases are never enough to establish lineage or a movement and, as such, remain of anecdotal interest only. Therefore, I believe that what should draw our attention, more than the first initiatives, is the more collective dynamic leading to one solution being multiplied and generalised at a given time. The hybridisation of contagion- and diffusion-based hypotheses specifically helps to set us on this path.

1   How to read *Progressive Grocer*

Archeology is the story of man through long ages, and we as men are interested in that story. But it is a story; it is not a series of detached extracts from notebooks. Our attempt to see the story as a whole will not always be successful. We are certainly fallible, and in our fallibility we shall make mistakes which will give the cosmic sweep of history an air of the comic. But this time we should be able to see the story in the large as well as in its parts, and we have a duty to try to present it in comprehensive intelligibility, in the expectation that our errors will be corrected by future generations. If archeology is to be a tool useful to other disciplines and meaningful to the lay public, we must attach plain label to the various levers, gearshifts, and gadgets, and we must group them around some central operating position. Thus we may escape the danger of suffocation from our own exhaust fumes and thus we may find the opportunity to take our brothers and neighbors traveling to ever new frontiers of research.

(Wilson, 1942, p. 9)

The magazine *Progressive Grocer* is a wonderful source for describing the history of self-service but it must nevertheless be handled with care. As we shall see, the source is impressive by virtue of its documentary and pictorial wealth, the theories it conveys on commerce, the actors it spotlights – grocers, competing types of commerce, suppliers of all kinds of materials – its ability to understand self-service in places other than supermarkets, where this type of sale was eventually copied, and for a thousand other reasons that we shall discover in this book, without claiming to be exhaustive. Despite the quality of the source, however, it must nonetheless be handled with care.

A medial focalisation

Is my intention, with this warning, to question the nature of the source, to criticise its discursive and journalistic nature? Not really. Of course, it is common knowledge that the media misrepresent reality, retain certain elements, forget others, etc., and we shall see that *Progressive Grocer* is no different. However, this kind of criticism is based on a double hypothesis: first, that the world is apparently split in two, with reality on one side, and its social and cultural construction on the other; and second, that there are other means of accessing the former without the help of the latter, in order, possibly, to denounce the radical difference between them. I intend to refute both hypotheses in preference for an alternative view of the elements involved.

Thanks to more than thirty years of anthropology of sciences and techniques, we now know that reality is not the starting point, but rather the result of a long process of interpreting, writing and rewriting the world, consisting in selecting certain elements within it, linking them together and showing them in different ways, so that the referent can be transported remotely, interpreted and "re-presented" (Latour and Woolgar, 1979; Latour, 1995). In this regard, the media are only one mediator amongst many whose task or effect is, like them, to produce reports on reality. Just as Barbara Czarniawska (2011) recently showed, based on an enlightening study carried out at the heart of news agencies, the media work hard to "arrange"[1] (rather than construct) the facts that correspond to their objectives; they sort, choose, classify, underline and conceal the many elements they collect, move, produce and transform. However, for all that, this does not mean either that the "whole" truth, "in its entirety", could be known, in other words, that apart from the media, reports, archives, statistics, testimonies or other historical works, an irrefutable and directly accessible referent exists, or on the contrary, that the reality resulting from these operations is merely "constructed", whether involving a figment of the imagination or a performative artefact, meaning that media representations of what is real can be reduced to pure effects of discourse.

The discursive and tangible elements are very rigorously rearranged: "facts (les faits) are made (faits)", as is beautifully highlighted by Bruno Latour, echoing a pun used by Bachelard (Latour, 1993): facts are objective data but they are manufactured. In *Progressive Grocer*, new ways of marketing grocery products are not invented but articulated by intelligently selecting and combining hard facts with more conceptual arguments. In this chapter, the idea that facts and discourse are produced simultaneously is therefore used as a reason to avoid a debate on the "veracity" of what is reported in *Progressive Grocer*.

Is the command to handle *Progressive Grocer* with care therefore intended to question whether it is reasonable to retrace the development of food distribution based on a single source, no matter how rich it is and how systematic it renders the analysis? Paradoxically, this is not my main concern either. I would even go as far as to claim that approaching the subject from a (virtually) single source is an intentional bias, by turning a mistake that all historians, even beginners, try their hardest to avoid, into the central principle of the method. In order to justify this choice, I could mention a problem that is so endemic to the daily practice of historical research as to generally go unnoticed: the permanent risk of drowning that creeps up on the historian – submerged by the overflow of materials available, incapable of embracing it all (Fellman and Popp, 2013)[2] – and his need to find subterfuges, if he is to remain afloat in the sea of materials, either by selecting data on the basis of more or less explicit principles, or by limiting the number of sources. In other words, I could justify the decision to use a single source as making a virtue out of necessity, as the lesser of several evils but one that would have its advantages given that it would consist in replacing the impressionist examination of many chronological series, secretly serving as the basis for many historical records, by an investigation of one of them that is more sensible, rigorous and systematic. However, the choice of one source goes well beyond these very mundane constraints, imposed by the concern to overcome the recurrent incompatibility of the limited cognitive and temporal resources of the researcher and the abundance of data he intends to represent.

The issue at hand can be understood in terms of the methods of focalisation dear to Gérard Genette (1972). Genette distinguished three ways of narrating a story: the "internal focalisation", consisting in restricting the narration to one character's subjective point of view; the "external focalisation", consisting, on the contrary, in imagining the tale from the point of view of an outside observer, such as a camera that follows the protagonist; and the "zero focalisation", consisting in adopting an "omniscient" point of view, overlooking the whole, equipped with an absolute knowledge of both the objective events and the subjective views involved, as the story unfolds. We might think that the ideal position for an historian inevitably lies in the search for zero focalisation, supposedly providing an exhaustive, exact and quasi-divine knowledge of history. However, the quest for maximum realism ironically ends in a total lack of realism, given that none of the actors of history is endowed with such a view; in fact, we misunderstand history if we ignore the fundamental uncertainty that inspires its actors, both in terms of what is afoot around them and what awaits them in the future. Must one then, conversely, seek an internal or external focalisation? Both of these are preferable, but whereas the first requires the adoption of a single witness's point of view[3] and here it is more a question of collecting the opinions of thousands of them, the second deprives us of the subjectivity that nevertheless conditions the actors' real experience.

However, approaching the subject through *Progressive Grocer* seems especially suited, in my opinion, to overcome both of these difficulties, by offering us the means to experiment with a new type of focalisation, which I propose to call "medial" focalisation. Paradoxically, recourse to this terminology is intended less to bother the reader with new jargon and more to provide clarity. I have borrowed the adjective "medial" from grammar, where it refers to a letter located in the middle of a word, in order to give it another meaning, similar to "media-based" but which cannot be replaced by this term which I believe has too many connotations. I would therefore say that medial focalisation is one suitable for use by a form of media – nothing more, nothing less. Using *Progressive Grocer* gives us access to what is certainly a particular point of view but one which cannot be reduced to that of a single body, as was the case with an internal focalisation. In fact, the point of view of one media outlet is an observation point shared by many others. In other words, a medial focalisation consists less in changing the position than in changing the way in which we see things: it leads us to adopting the effect produced by using the same artificial eye, accessible to a great number of actors, rather than adopting the view of one particular actor. Everything happens as if we were looking at something not "with the eyes" of a given character (as with internal focalisation), not from above (as with zero focalisation) or from the side (as with external focalisation), but instead with a certain type of "spectacles" that he himself, but many others too, might wear. It is not a question of putting yourself in this or that person's place, nor in that of God or an outside observer, but rather in that of all those who use the same viewing mode, and of seeing "what it does" to consider the world from this angle.

By looking at the history of commerce from the point of view of *Progressive Grocer*, we thus obtain a very different image from those that would be provided by the "internal", "external" or "omniscient" focalisations, intended to offer a subjective, objective or all-round point of view (respectively) on the course of events. More specifically, adopting the "medial" point of view of *Progressive Grocer* allows us to consider the course of business development through the only major prism available to actors at the time, if one wishes to obtain an overall view, thus to picture what could be observed, understood and felt by far and away the largest and most interested group of professionals and to comprehend the effect on them of looking through the spectacles of *Progressive Grocer*, to the extent of laying the foundations of the self-service of the future.

In order to understand the targeted nature of a given mediation and experience the impact of seeing differently, one must be aware of this "differently", and thus resort to a reference that is, if not external, at least at one remove: it is clearly impossible to be aware that we are adopting a particular view if we do not relate it to what is produced or could have been produced had we adopted another point of view. The viewing deficit, in the sense of something missing rather than imperfect, is due to the activation of a single type of vision where two modes of cognition were, however, available. Specialists in perception in fact distinguish between two means of visually accessing reality: central vision, focusing the eye on a particular point to which the subject's entire attention is directed, as opposed to peripheral vision, providing the same subject with overall impressions of the rest of the field of vision (Neville and Lawson, 1987; Smith, 2012; Campbell and Wright, 2012). In order to reduce the viewing deficit, one should therefore adopt a stereoscopic view, which looks at both "the centre of" and what is "around" its object, as is clearly brought out by the American sociologist David Stark:

> [I]n the preface [of my book, *The Sense of Dissonance*; Stark, 2009] where I briefly mention a *sociological double vision*. I like this notion. Of course, double vision is a kind of malady, things are out of focus. But "focus" can be overrated, especially if it's the single-minded variety. We so often hear advice, whether it is to organizations or, for example, to our students: "Get focused!" But, continuing with this visual metaphor, there is also something to be said about the importance of *peripheral vision* […] If the strategy horizon is foreshortened, meaning that the future is not far away and it is

highly unpredictable, then you should not be locked-in looking ahead but must also be attentive to the movement that is happening around you. Peripheral vision achieves awareness of that movement.

(David Stark, quoted in Brooke, 2010)

Promoting peripheral vision, in order to understand the particular contribution of the medial focalisation, is not to propose seeing another world, nor to suggest looking at things from an angle different from that of the actors, nor even to request that "preference" be given to the peripheral rather than central vision. It is simply an appeal to combine them both, to couple research and serendipity, associate rationality and curiosity (Cochoy, 2011a). Whereas the medial (central) focalisation consists in adopting one medium's point of view to follow the action from the point of view on the vision of reality offered by this medium to a group of actors, the peripheral vision allows one to extract from it the effects of particular perspectives.

In other words, paradoxically, the medially focalised view makes sense by resorting to other "points of view" making it possible to identify and contrast their effects. Without such additions, we would in fact risk not noticing the extent to which this vision can lead the actors (and us) to neglect parallel developments, ignore silent information in the source studied, even to make chronological mistakes, by dating the appearance of certain objects that already existed elsewhere, to when they first occurred in the resource considered. My recourse to medial focalisation will therefore be reasonable: it will give priority to but will not concern exclusively *Progressive Grocer*. I shall use other sources and references "to provide a second look" every time this helps me to identify some of the distorting effects of the publication considered.[4]

Having said that, paradoxically, the element needed to identify these distorting effects does not necessarily have to be found "outside": as we shall see in the following pages, what allows us to avoid being completely absorbed by the medial focalisation is often provided by the media organ itself. I mentioned earlier that *Progressive Grocer* contains a number of reports and that it is through them that we can "understand" the history, its possible manifestations and the different issues behind its publication. One of the original aspects of the magazine is precisely that it links statistics on the state of commerce, militant articles, adverts, personal testimonies, reports, photographs, etc., in such a way that the "discrepancies" of which we accuse the press, far from requiring a detour via a utopian and inaccessible "reality", or even far from necessarily demanding the use of alternative or secondary sources, can, on the contrary, be traced to the diversity inherent in my core material. To understand it better, I suggest taking a detour via a more detailed presentation of the magazine, its origins, how it works and its objectives.

The origins of *Progressive Grocer*

Progressive Grocer was founded by a publishing house, the Butterick Publishing Company, whose managers one day decided to launch a new publication, aimed at the modernisation of the small retail trade, by adopting the modernising rhetoric of the Progressive Era. Why this decision? Why enter this market?

To answer these two questions, it should first be noted that the Butterick Publishing Company was not just any publishing house: it was certainly a media company ("Publishing Company"), but it stemmed from an older company, completely different in nature ... which is still very active today ("Butterick"). My readers will have a better sense of its sector and importance if I remind them that Butterick directly contributed to the success of the world famous magazine *Vogue*, by adding to the journalistic coverage of fashion the provision of patterns for making textile articles at home. The tiny company was in fact founded by a couple from Massachusetts, the tailor Ebenezer Butterick and his wife Ellen, who had developed a business for designing and marketing patterns based on two innovations. In 1863 Ellen had the first idea, creating patterns of different sizes, more easily adaptable to female clients' needs, while her husband tried his hardest to print these patterns on flexible and bendable tissue paper rather than on stiff pieces of cardboard, thus making it easier to send them by post and subsequently handle at home. These were by no means minor innovations, given that the introduction of Butterick patterns in several sizes contributed to democratising fashion throughout the United States and then the world, and thus to spreading a cultural production that had previously been reserved for a cosmopolitan and wealthy elite.

In order to develop their enterprise, the fashion business founded the Butterick Publishing Company which then specialised in publishing "magazines of small page size and big circulation" (1923, 04, 1). The first of these magazines was the *Ladies' Quarterly of Broadway Fashions*, launched in 1867, to which was added, a year later, *The Metropolitan Monthly*, itself renamed in 1875 as *The Delineator*.[5] The latter, initially designed simply to sell the company's patterns, soon grew into a women's magazine, aimed more specifically at housewives, to whom it offered not only patterns but photographs and pictures of embroidery and knitting, fiction, articles on fashion and interior decoration. This magazine enjoyed considerable success, reaching a million and a half copies in 1922 (1922, 08, 1), making it one of the main American women's magazines at the time. This first portfolio of publications was enhanced with the acquisition, in 1887, of an analogous magazine, *The Designer* (*The New York Times*, 1926).

A second expansion occurred thirty years later, when Butterick diversified its portfolio of publications to include retail trade professionals. This expansion was initially very modest and discreet with the launch, in February 1917, of a one-page bulletin entitled *Buy-at-Home News*, dedicated to different ways of improving the retail trade. This bulletin was distributed with the help of large traders, in exchange for promoting their name on the cover, to a readership of grocers, dry goods retailers and chemists. *Buy-at-Home News* soon increased in volume and dissemination, going from one to four, then to eight, and soon sixteen pages, and from 20,000 to 100,000 copies a month. In the summer of 1920, in light of this success and the diversity of target audiences, it was decided that *Buy-at-Home News* should be split into *Good Hardware* (aimed at non-food goods) and … *Progressive Grocer* (specialising in the retail grocery trade), the first issue of which appeared in January 1922 (1922, 08, 1).

However, how can we make sense of this development? What can justify the Butterick company's choice to move from the world of tailors and patterns to that of retailers and clients (or patrons)? Were I a linguist, I could confine myself to recalling the very troubling relationship between these two worlds, because of their common etymology: the word retail in fact comes from the old French word "*retaillier*" (1365), meaning to "cut, trim, attach". The meaning of retail as "sale in small quantities", dates from 1433, from the medieval French word "*retail*" meaning "cut piece, scrap, fragment, offcut" (Cochoy, 2006).[6] However, as a sociologist I must take into consideration both the opinion of the actors on the one hand, and the more immediate circumstances directing their action on the other. Regarding the actors' opinion, *Progressive Grocer* itself puts forward other more obvious and contemporary reasons to justify its founder's investment in the world of the retail trade. In an article retracing its origins, the magazine thus presents "The development of Progressive Grocer" as "part of a broad constructive program" launched a few years earlier (1922, 08, 1 sq.). More specifically, the publication *Buy-at-Home News* would be one initiative, amongst others, adopted by Butterick in order to support the domestic universe, the neighbourhood, the community group, linking, within a single local area, a population and its traders:

> Butterick had committed itself to a policy of community development, of helping to build up the smaller town and city, and the importance of this action as the first step in such a program was immediately evident from the thousands of letters from retailers and jobbers that immediately began to come in. Butterick was heralded as a true friend and champion of the retailer and his community.
>
> (1922, 08, 1)

By launching *Buy-at-Home News*, the prototype of *Progressive Grocer*, Butterick had done nothing more than defend a world in line with his values – that is to say, a universe based on a mix of tradition and modernity, or more precisely, on the modernisation of the traditional model of local domestic life, for example, by opening it up to fashion and by improving patterns, then by supporting innovations likely to preserve small, independent grocers.

Actually, the first issue of *Buy-at-Home News*, reproduced in support of this argument, clearly reflects this concern: it echoes a campaign launched by *The Delineator* entitled "Save the Seventh Baby". This campaign was meant to contribute to "interest women in community needs and welfare" and a "lower baby death rate". In order for this effort to be successful, the magazine appointed the "well-known authority Dr. Terry and corps of field nurses", and funded "10,000 to 40,000 services of trained field nurses and bacteriologists". In addition, *Buy-at-Home News* echoed the initiative of McClelland Grocer Company, a wholesaler from Decatur Illinois, which published a full-page advert in the press encouraging the public to "buy from retail grocers" and thus support "local" business. Lastly, a third section at the front of the issue tackled mail order sales. Thanks to a study carried out by *The Delineator*, we learn that in 1916, mail order companies spent more than $1 million in fifteen women's magazines and more than $2 million in all the available magazines put together. *Buy-at-Home News* concludes this information by proudly announcing, without any other justification, that *The Delineator* and associated publications "stand alone among women's magazines in refusing mail order advertising". In fact, this commitment is so dear to *Buy-at-Home News* that the bulletin posts it as a motto on the cover: "PUBLISHED BY THE DELINEATOR, The Magazine That Bans Out Mail Order Advertising."

Boycotting mail order companies appears as a form of action helping to support the declared general objective of backing local communities. Long-distance sales, because of their ubiquity and because of the competitive advantages gained from centralised purchases, in fact unquestionably and fiercely competed against local businesses, the food trade included (Mayo, 1993), thus weakening small, close-knit American communities by exposing them to intervention by distant partners.[7] Incidentally, this concern is clearly stated in the article's title: "Meeting mail order competition."

However, what applies "on the actors' side" deserves to be completed by paying greater attention to what was happening regarding the circumstances moving them to take action. For those who know about Butterick's business, "there is something not quite right". The title is ambivalent: mail order sales clearly compete with local communities but also with the company's own activity, its business being based on selling sewing patterns also from a distance. As Butterick reminds us, "[t]he weapon of the mail order house is the catalog. ... Catalog must go to live list of names. Magazine advertising is used to build up live list". Butterick knows what it is talking about, given that it published *The Delineator* in order to increase his own client list and sell its patterns! Thus, supporting local communities and the boycotting of (other) mail order companies was also a means of protecting its own commercial interests.

The threat of mail order sales was a real one. Since 1893, Sears, Roebuck & Company had not only added sewing machines to its catalogue, making it possible to make textile articles at home (a market favourable to that of Butterick), but also "ready-to-wear" clothes, liable to cannibalise the former solution and thus limit the potential for selling patterns (Strasser, 1989, pp. 212–213). Even more worrying was the fact that there was at least one mail order clothing sales competitor: the National Cloak and Suit Company, which had launched this activity in 1880 (Tedlow, 1990). Generally, textile items represented a considerable and ever increasing portion of the turnover of American mail order

Figure 1.1 Buy-at-Home News, published by the magazine that bans out mail order
   advertising
Source: 1922, 08, 2

companies, given that this share had risen from 23% to 33% between 1902 and
1907 (according to Emmet and Jeuck, 1950, p. 111).

Now we have a better understanding of the reasons why *Progressive Grocer*
was founded: boycotting mail order companies, backing communities and
supporting retailers meant attempting to contain customers' recourse to a
method of distribution that promoted alternative products to the sewing patterns sold by Butterick. In other words, if the communities received backing
from business, the latter was indivisible from the business of the communities.
By publishing *The Delineator* on the one hand and *Buy-at-Home News* on the
other, Butterick ran the entire distribution chain. Lastly, it could complete the
advertising of the former, addressing female consumers, with advertising aimed

at the retailers meant to serve them. This concern to "seal off" the distribution chain is very clearly visible in the many adverts for *The Delineator* that we find in *Progressive Grocer* (1922, 08, 62–63; 1922, 09, 62–63; 1922, 10, 50–51; etc.). Admittedly, these adverts were certainly meant to occupy the empty advertising space when the magazine was first issued, in other words, at a time when it still had to build its reputation and advertising clientele. However, they were also intended very explicitly to align Butterick's interests with those of both magazines, for consumers and for grocers, by presenting *The Delineator* to the latter as "The Retailer's Silent Salesman" (1922, 08, 62–63). In the end we can clearly see that Butterick's cultural bias in favour of local communities and the economic interest of the media company are at one. *Progressive Grocer* bases its identity on a mixture of modernity ("progressive") and an attachment to the past ("grocer"), on preserving the making of clothes at home and on promoting modern business, on anchoring female consumers in their role as housewives and on introducing them to the innovative world of fashion. The Butterick company is protecting its rear as a manufacturer of fashion patterns and looking to the future by becoming a media company. The magazines defend ideas and actors linked to local communities and are simultaneously part of an original project involving a portfolio of deliberately linked publications, which brings them in line with economic modernity.

A doubly reflected strategy

From its inception, the economic model of *Progressive Grocer* was subject to a doubly reflected strategy, given that on the one hand it consisted in attentively (in a carefully reflected manner) defining the forms of action used, and on the other, in making these public (reflecting them outwards), with a view to making an impression, demonstrating its professionalism and thus increasing its effectiveness. Therefore, it is in the advertising *for* the magazine, published *in* the magazine, that we learn that *Progressive Grocer* journalists have travelled 30,000 miles and visited twenty-nine states, "From Maine to California", to collect information (1923, 12, 1). We can see especially how the readership, far from being gradually won over, as the magazine's reputation grew, was formed and defined straightaway, to guarantee dissemination to advertisers, thanks to the establishment of a list of about 50,000 professionals and grocers to whom the publication was sent directly in an envelope (1922, 05, 1; 1925, 70, 1 sq.).

It is in an advertorial entitled "Questions and answers", that we discover that these targets, far from having been chosen at random, were in fact "handpicked", by using the Dun's and Bradstreet telephone directories, and that this list was drawn up and constantly updated with the cooperation of professional associations, based on carefully designed sampling principles, in order to cover all of the states of the union (1925, 07, 2) (as a map published in 1924 (1924, 09, 3) intended to demonstrate, similarly to maps showing the coverage of contemporary mobile networks) and represent around 45% of total food sales. The recipients of the magazine comprised 46,029 grocers, 3,104 jobbers and

1,008 brokers, meaning a total of 50,141 potential readers (the average for the first six months of 1924) (1925, 07, 1 sq.). Therefore the magazine covered almost the entirety of its target audience, at least the most advanced, given that its readership was nearly equivalent to the 65,000 grocers who made at least $1,000 in annual turnover and equal to one third of the 155,000 general stores with a food aisle (1923, 04, 1). The fact that the selection principle was exclusive, restricted to grocers with the highest volume of sales, shows that in the mind of the magazine's promoters, "progress" was measured not only in terms of the ability to innovate but also in financial terms, incidentally in line with the identifiable lead-in posted in boxed text at the top of the first page of the very first issues: "The Progressive Grocer is a clearing house of good ideas that retail grocers are using to get more business and make more money" (1922, 04, 4; 1922, 05, 5).

As another publication from 1925 sums it up:

> Half our population still lives in rural America and another big percentage in towns under 25,000 [...] We have selected 50,000 substantial retailers, jobbers and brokers that do a big percentage of the total volume of the grocery business. We have chosen live, big volume grocers from Maine to California, well balanced between city and country.
>
> (1925, 06, 2–3)

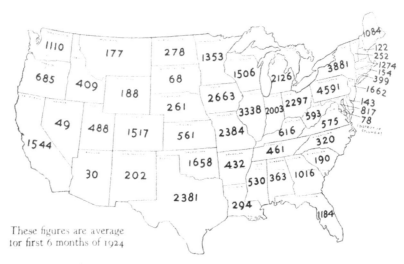

These figures are average for first 6 months of 1924

Established Communication with 50,000 Important Grocery Distributors

Figure 1.2 Readership map
Source: 1924, 09, 3

Lastly, the magazine was careful to highlight that its closest competitor (no doubt *American Grocer* [8]) only published 12,266 copies – in other words, one third of its readership (1925, 07, 1 sq.).

Another essential component of the overall strategy lay in the establishment of a pricing policy that was just as "carefully reflected". We may note the price of $1 per year published on the covers but this cost, which in fact disappeared as of March 1923, probably only concerned the people who did not receive the publication directly. This is because *Progressive Grocer*'s real prices were located elsewhere: the magazine was based on the principle of a free press, which the end-of-the-century urban dailies thought they had invented; therefore it was supplied free to the "automatic subscribers" and on the other hand "sold" to the advertisers, who paid for the advertising space that guaranteed almost all of its revenue. In order to encourage more advertisers and retain them, rates decreased gradually: the $240 for a one-off, one-page spread fell to $200 for a monthly commitment over a year (1925, 07, 3). However, these prices were often presented euphemistically, expressed per reader: 5 cents a year per retailer for 12 pages a year (1922, 07, 2–3) or 10 cents for a two-page spread in colour (1922, 09, 3). They were also shown as a comparison, demonstrating that *Progressive Grocer* was aware of being on a market, and intended to highlight that it was a competitive and wise choice, if needed, using clever calculations. Therefore, the comparison was aimed equally at direct competitors ...

> It costs less per page per thousand to reach 50,000 of the best grocers and every grocery jobber in the United States through THE PROGRESSIVE GROCER than to reach less than one quarter that total through any other grocery publication.
>
> (1922, 11, 3)

... and indirect competitors:

> Contrary to custom [...] it costs no more to reach 50,000 consumers through the best general magazines.
>
> (1923, 09, 1)

Although the *Progressive Grocer* targeted grocers, its clients were actually the advertisers – in other words, all the companies that marketed supplies for shops, cash registers and other commercial equipment, but also all the magazine press (*Companion, Ladies' Home Journal, Life*) that advertised in *Progressive Grocer* in order to sell their own advertising space, and of course all food manufacturers, who were trying to persuade grocers to stock their products. *Progressive Grocer* was therefore "a business itself", trying to impose its own mediation between manufacturers and retailers.

From this point of view, this business was quite successful, if we look at the growth of its readership, the variety and number of its advertisers, its rise in turnover and its continuously increasing size, first in number of pages and then in terms of format. How do we know this? Just as earlier, regarding the "establishment" of the readership, we know this thanks to the magazine itself, which saves us the trouble of having to find out or count for ourselves and which, on the contrary, provides us with an explanation, formatting and staging the signs of its own efficacy. Here we have a very particular strategy, consisting in establishing recursive loops between utterances and their enactment, and thus establishing a kind of circular performativity, where the discourse becomes increasingly performative as it encompasses elements "attesting to" its past performance. From the outset, far from being simply recorded and published, these loops were also "provoked", in the sense given to this participle by Fabian Muniesa (2014) as an effect of a performative act.

One of the first particularly clever examples of this "provocation" lay in the organisation of competition which, beyond an apparent concern to entertain the readership, aimed more to measure its number and involvement.[9] Thus, in July 1922, the magazine announced it was holding a competition with \$100 in prizes, to be distributed to the readers providing the best captions to a picture showing a grocer preparing to violently slay a fly with a flyswatter … just above a crate filled with eggs (1922, 07, 24–25) – in other words, the cover of the issue concerned (1922, 07). In subsequent years the same caption competition for the cover was repeated, in 1923 for an image showing a young employee so engrossed in reading a magazine on the art of managing a grocer's store that he forgets he had come to draw off some molasses from a barrel, which is now overflowing (1923, 04, 20–21; see Figure 1.3, and Chapter 2, n. 2), in 1924 for a picture of a little girl in tears, who had gone food shopping on a very windy and rainy day, her dress being blown up, her umbrella turned inside out and her basket overturned (1924, 06, 20–21). Every year, not only were these competitions the subject of a preliminary advert, but also reminders aimed at maximising the number of participants (1922, 09, 22–23; 1923, 05, 20–21; 1923, 06, 1; 1923, 07, 58; 1924, 07, 20–21).

Who won these competitions? The question seems absurd given how obvious the answer is: the winners were the winners of course, for example, the winner of the first prize for the 1923 competition, an employee of a grocery shop in Kansas, whose caption for the picture of the young, distracted employee was a magnificent play on words: "storing the mind but not minding the store" (1923, 08, 20). However, as we shall see, one should beware riddles that are too easy; one winner could conceal another. The magazine was gambling on ensuring that the real winner of these competitions was most often not the receiver of the ten or so dollars for first prize but the organiser of the competition itself. How? By foreshadowing the technique of real-time competitions so dear to today's television channels. As we know, this method consists in promising a flat screen television, a holiday or a car to a happy winner, drawn by lots from all those who have called a premium rate number and given the correct answer to a bafflingly easy question. Thanks to the tens of thousands of small "phone bets" collected from all the participants, pleased that they know the answer and thus hoping, for a few tens of eurocents, to

Figure 1.3 How to run a retail store
Source: 1923, 04, cover

obtain an alluring prize, the channel manages to make a net profit of tens of thousands of euros. In the *Progressive Grocer* competitions, participation was free and the answers not as easy, but there was an economic gain, admittedly indirect, and one more "hoped for" than "achieved": the number of answers received was in fact a means of measuring the magazine's readership. Therefore every competition came with the simultaneous announcement of the number of participants. Five months after the 1922 competition, the magazine published a double-page spread of "self-publicity" entitled "Answering that question: 'DO GROCERS READ?'" The sales pitch that followed mentioned that more than 6,000 answers had been received in response to the recent competition as "proof", meant to dissipate the "common fallacy that grocers don't read" (1922, 12, 2–3). In 1923, the magazine reiterated the process as an advert, proudly proclaiming that "5,649 readers wrote The PROGRESSIVE GROCER in response to a recent contest". The advert itself emphasised that this figure represented "10% of its total circulation", adding that this would have been equivalent to a response from 200,000 readers had it been for a publication with a print run of 2 million copies – in other words, the coverage of a national magazine – and concluding on a triumphal question, whose (negative) answer is as easy to guess as the overpriced guessing games of today: "Did you ever hear such a response?" (1923, 08, 2–3).

The competition was therefore explicitly used as a very clever system for measuring readership, able to allay advertisers' suspicions, not only regarding the possible lack of appetite on the part of the grocers for reading, but more fundamentally, vis-à-vis the free press model, whose distribution did not in any way guarantee it was read, given that it was imposed rather than requested, and at the risk of the most common fate of all adverts, which was not to be read and thus ignored, even thrown away (Canu, 2007).

A second technique, intended to encourage the "consumption" of *Progressive Grocer* and its advertising space, consisted in bringing the latter into play, in the form of feedback. For example, one self-promotional advert, aimed at professionals, points out that jobbers requested 17,000 reprints of one of the magazine's articles on the sale of canned food in batches (1923, 01, 2–3). The magazine also published many personal testimonies taken from letters, recounting the positive experience of its readers: one designed a window display based on an example seen in the magazine; another prescribed reading *Progressive Grocer* in one of his Business Administration classes at the University of Nevada; a third wrote to the Panay Show Case Co. after seeing an advert in the magazine, and although in the end he did not go through with the purchase due to a lack of money, he assured the company that he had successfully advertised it to his colleagues (1923, 12, 2–3). The magazine repeatedly publicised its action to promote an annual canned food fair (see Chapter 3) thanks to reproducing readers' letters; one stated that he had "[t]he biggest week in 14 years"; another congratulated himself on selling 54 crates in the course of a week; a third went one better by posting a sale of more than 200 crates (1924,

02, 1 sq.). Most of the time these stories were not only reported but quoted verbatim, as demonstrated by the two examples below:

> I owe your little magazine a whole lot. In fact, it's my best friend as I carry one in my pocket most of the time and read it every chance I get. The ideas I got from it last year helped a whole lot to increase my sales from $38,000 in 1922 to $71,000 in 1923, in spite of chain store competition.
>
> (1924, 06, 1)

> What I get from the magazine is the fact that they tell the retailer something combined with a picture, which brings to his attention more forcibly the condition existing, than he could possibly get from any other magazine. For instance, I remember at least one dozen merchants commenting upon the picture showing the up to date grocery store, clean in comparison to the old-time, broken-package, filthy store.
>
> (1925, 04, 2–3)

Obviously, a perspicacious reader might perhaps have told himself that such messages seemed at worst to smell of pure invention, like some opinions published on e-commerce websites today, and at best to sound like solicited testimonies, given the extent to which they adopted the self-promotional sales pitch, hammered home by the magazine, such as its vocation to provide in pocket format (see below) the means of increasing sales, staying ahead of the competition from retail chains, of pragmatically illustrating its aims using photographs (see Chapter 3). Perhaps, in order to avoid counterfeit testimonies, or simply to make more of an impression, *Progressive Grocer* sometimes not only reproduced the text of some letters, but the photograph too, with the headed paper, corporate name and signature, implicitly operating as proof of authenticity and strengthening of argument. In one of the missives exhibited in this way, a company pointed out that it had received more letters following its advert in *Progressive Grocer* than in response to any other trade magazine throughout the previous year (1926, 05, 1). In another, a manufacturer who had placed an advert in *Progressive Grocer* for a garden spade, declared that he had received 1,309 information requests from grocers located all over the United States. The magazine rams the point home: "it demonstrates that grocers *do* read, that they *will* respond to the manufacturer who has an interesting message" (1927, 06, 2–3).

The magazine does not forget to mention the external advertising from which it benefits by noting it had been quoted in 160 press articles in May 1924, that other trade magazines had reproduced some of its articles, and that it received as many as 30,000 or even 40,000 individual requests for copies (1924, 08, 72). With all these techniques, from the competitions to the reproduction of personal testimonies, the idea was clearly not only to have a live audience, but more, to show this by inventing, before its time, the counting of clicks on "Google Analytics" that make up the good will of today's advertising market.

Lastly, a third circular technique encouraging the purchase of advertising space consisted in playing on the purchase itself, as if *Progressive Grocer* had understood that the readership going to the readers, there was nothing better than advertising the growth of advertising to obtain more advertising. This kind of effort is qualitative as much as quantitative. From the qualitative point of view, the magazine published a list of its main advertisers, specifying for each one the number and type of pages bought (less than one page, two-page inserts, two pages in black and white, in colour, etc.) (1924, 10, 1 sq.), in the hope, of course, of taking advantage of a reputation-based dynamic, as is very clearly demonstrated in an advert featuring a list of advertisers on a two-page spread with a simple boxed text providing a transparent reading key: "Advertisers in 'The Progressive Grocer' are in very good company – Look over this list from the January and February Issues [to judge for yourself]" (1926, 02, 2–3).

From the quantitative point of view, as from 1924 the magazine began publicly to demonstrate how delighted it was with the number of pages of advertising by posting the records achieved and immediately broken: 191 pages in 1922, 236 in 1923, 297 in 1924 (1924, 07, 2–3), then 328 in 1925, 483 in 1926 (1926, 09, 1), soon followed by the monitoring of progress on a monthly rather than annual basis (1926, 02, 1; 1926, 03, 1; 1926, 03, 2–3; 1926, 04, 2–3; 1926, 06, 2–3), whilst carefully not limiting itself to showing absolute figures, but rather giving these even more impact by calculating and posting impressive growth rates, such as a 45.9% increase in advertising volume during the first five months of 1926 (1926, 06, 2–3).

What should one make of such statistics? Must they be reduced to pure effects of language? Or should we not take their measurable nature into consideration, given that anyone could easily check the number of pages and advertisers referred to? Moreover, despite being measurable, were these figures related to the real economy, and how? In a two-page advert published in 1930 entitled "MORE MONEY EVERY YEAR", *Progressive Grocer* proudly showed a graph depicting the exponential growth of its advertising turnover between 1922 and 1929, together with following message:

> During each succeeding year, more and more money is spent in the advertising of food and grocery products. And every year a constantly growing share of this expenditure goes into advertising that reaches the grocer and his jobber through The Progressive Grocer. [...] this increase [...] is really far more than a prideful boast of growth. Its steady upward trend traces a great industry's realization of the value of promotion at the point of sale. It indicates, too, a mounting confidence in The Progressive Grocer as a medium for such promotion, a confidence supported by an advertising investment that has nearly tripled since the publication was founded in 1922.
>
> (1930, 01, 2–3)

Of course, this self-publicity was mostly based on text, in line with the literary technique of copy writing, characteristic of most adverts at the time (Strasser, 1989). However, the role played by images was no less important. A quick read through easily and assuredly associated the growth in dollars to the name of the magazine "PROGRESSIVE GROCER" and its distinctive logo of a booklet which, far from bringing together a group of abstract, boring and obscure concepts, appeared rather as a tool that every grocer could have in his pocket (see below). This first illustration reflects the way in which *Progressive Grocer* understood the specialised press: as it was aimed at professionals who were of a practical bent, the magazine prioritised a particular way of writing, where words were complemented by pictorial elements, where the arguments were extended by shows, demonstrations and visual representations, presented like so many windows on the world. We shall see this in detail in the next chapter.

This rhetoric shows how effective *Progressive Grocer* was, in terms of building and promoting the publication itself, and even more so, of connecting the magazine and the sales tools it was trying to market – see the comment, "[the] steady upward trend [in the chart] traces a great industry's realization of the value of promoting at the point of sale". *Progressive Grocer*'s success was presented to the advertisers and grocers as proof of the success of the new equipment they were selling and purchasing, respectively. In the following months, the magazine stressed

MORE MONEY EVERY YEAR

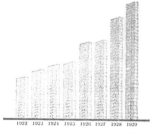

1922 1923 1924 1925 1926 1927 1928 1929

indicates, too, a mounting confidence in THE PROGRESSIVE GROCER as a medium for such promotion, a confidence supported by an advertising investment that has nearly tripled since the publication was founded in 1922.

DURING each succeeding year, more and more money is spent in the advertising of food and grocery products. And every year a constantly growing share of this expenditure goes into advertising that reaches the grocer and his jobber through THE PROGRESSIVE GROCER.

The chart on the opposite page depicts this increase in graphic form, but it is really far more than a prideful boast of growth. Its steady upward trend traces a great industry's realization of the value of promotion at the point of sale. It

The
PROGRESSIVE GROCER

The NATIONAL MAGAZINE
of the GROCERY TRADE

79 Madison Avenue · New York

Figure 1.4 More money every year
Source: 1930, 01, 2–3

its continuous growth again. In February 1930, only a few weeks after the previous message, it announced: "On the heels of the largest January issue ever published comes a record February issue. This issue shows of 19% increase in advertising volume over February of 1930. And the first two months of this year show a gain of 22% over the first two months of 1930" (1930, 02, 1). In 1930, this kind of self-celebration, already seen earlier, became recurrent: *Progressive Grocer* announced that it had broken its record number of pages and adverts in March, then April, then May and June 1930, etc. Every new step forwards came with comments such as: "Business is good among the upper group of retail grocers [...] business is good with The Progressive Grocer too; for it holds the enthusiastic interest of the 75,000 most important grocers and jobbers in the United States" (1930, 04, 2–3). Such comments clearly attempted to link the paper's own progress to that of the most progressive grocers ("the upper group of retail grocers") – that is to say (implicitly), those who applied *Progressive Grocer*'s solutions ... as opposed to those who lagged behind. In fact, what is striking, and what *Progressive Grocer* intended to emphasise strongly, was that the magazine was making progress at a time when the general economy, but more particularly its readers, were experiencing the Great Depression.

Of course, the economic crisis did not produce immediate effects, which the magazine was very careful not to underline, even if it did provide information making it possible to spot them: one statistic from 1951 showed that sales in grocery and general stores ("combination stores") fell from $9 billion to $8 billion between 1929 and 1931 alone.[10] Over the same period, independent grocers only lost 2% of their market to chain stores (68% to 66%). It was only in 1933 that the effects of the Great Depression severely affected them: sales fell to below $6 billion, with the greatest impact for independent grocers, whose share of the market fell to 63%. At the end of the 1930s, the grocery business had returned to its pre-crisis level. Business developed throughout the war and skyrocketed afterwards (from $9.5 billion in 1941 to $27 billion in 1950), the market share of independent grocers having remained surprisingly high and stable, equivalent to about two thirds of the industry's total turnover.

However, without waiting for the tangible effects of the crisis (and their possible impact on the magazine itself), *Progressive Grocer* used the difference between the general economic depression and its own success as an argument not to be ignored: on the very first page of its November 1930 issue, *Progressive Grocer* published a full-page advert proudly proclaiming, in thick, bold print: "In spite of well-advertised business depression, manufacturers have again invested more money in The Progressive Grocer in the first 11 months of 1930 than in any previous 11 months period" (1930, 11, 1). Once again the idea was to show that it was possible to win at a time when everyone else was losing (or rather feared that they would) ... as long as one read and applied *Progressive Grocer*'s solutions (and above all those of the advertising featured on its pages). This strategy, which was strangely similar to the rhetoric used by the founders of *Journal of Marketing* in 1934 (Cochoy, 1998), consisted in replacing one performance with another: the money invested by manufacturers in *Progressive Grocer* to advertise their "displays that sell" (1946, 08, 97) was presented as proof of these very displays' practical effectiveness.

Delving into, fuelling and fixing history

The difficulty in representing history is thus not mine alone; it is also that of *Progressive Grocer*. Every effort made by the magazine consisted in delving into the history of commerce but also fuelling and fixing it. Its mission consisted in connecting the rhetoric of its pages with business practice, either by using this performance as proof of its own power, or using the power of its words to promote business performance (or more precisely by playing upon both these elements in a circular fashion). The success of this enterprise was far from guaranteed.

It is here that we find the effects of visual distortion inherent in a medial focalisation. In fact, there is a structural discrepancy between what was shown by this press organ (which as a "window display of window displays" is very deserving of its name "*Progressive Grocer*"), and the general state of shops, which were far less "advanced" than those generally featured by the magazine. Although the magazine gives us the opportunity of understanding the chronology of innovations in a relatively accurate manner, by relaying the adverts responsible for promoting them, it is much less reliable in terms of giving us an idea of when and to what extent they were adopted and which methods were used in their adoption. Nevertheless and by chance, by taking into consideration some austere statistics, lost in the midst of modernising and promotional articles – the use of peripheral vision on the fringes of central vision – we see that the traditional form of counter services took rather a long time to give way to the modern arrangements of semi-self-service and self-service. In 1939, counter service was still the solution used by almost half of shops, with only 13% using self-service (the remaining 42% adopting the hybrid solution of semi-self-service); it was only in 1947 that pure self-service became the majority solution.

However, as from 1939 and despite the graph in Figure 1.5, sales at the counter had long disappeared from the pages of *Progressive Grocer* (with the exception of very rare cases dedicated to remembering the good old days – see Chapter 3). One might think that the supply logic inherent in free newspapers was responsible for creating such a gap between the representations available, given that sending an unsolicited publication in no way guaranteed how it would be received; consequently, a number of grocers remained impervious to the modernising innovations promoted by *Progressive Grocer*. However, I already pointed out that from 1930 the magazine claimed a distribution level reaching almost two thirds of independent American grocers. Even if it is very likely that a high percentage of addressees ignored the magazine or only looked at it distractedly, as with all advertising publications (Canu, 2009), it seems highly probable that there was a real significant impact on the world of grocers, as is in

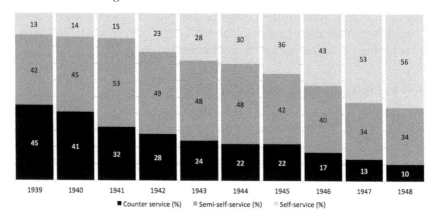

Figure 1.5 The development of sales methods
Source: According to 1949, 04, 59

fact shown by the magazine's growth, the continued trust demonstrated by advertisers and the gradual migration of the innovations presented in the sales areas photographed.

The reason for this discrepancy between what the magazine showed on a massive scale and other, more discreet interpretations of the state of trade, relayed nonetheless in its pages, must therefore be sought somewhere else, in its style and objectives. In order to modernise modern grocers, *Progressive Grocer* used a particular kind of rhetoric: the idea was to *make an impression* (on the pages and on the people reading them); it was a question of encouraging the progress of new merchandising techniques by showing the present as an image of time past (see the counter sales of the 1930s), by presenting some of the rare initiatives foreshadowing the desired future as being the present state of business (see the concept of "open display" throughout the same decade[11]), or by combining these two strategies and staging some spectacular developments using the dramatic figure of the "before/after", as in Figure 1.6.

Paradoxically, however, displaying such a difference does disqualify the magazine from representing the world about which it was talking. On the contrary, it highlights its aptitude in "re-presenting" this world effectively, in the Latourian sense of the verb (Latour, 1995): the magazine presents the world a second time, and differently, in such a way that the actors can recognise the world shown to them as being theirs, and can thus adjust their practices, in accordance with traditional performative logic in which discourse and actions are matched (Callon, 1998).

The re-presentation of the grocer economy operated by the magazine is even more effective since it is aimed at the grocer who rarely goes out and works a lot, and whose view is consequently as limited as Lippmann's (2008) public. Admittedly, our grocer belongs to a local community, reads the press, often owns a telephone, talks to his neighbours and customers, observes his

• Even a store only 14 ft. wide can be successfully modernized along open-display lines, as these pictures show. The store is P. John Conners', Lawrence, Mass. Sales jumped 50% after the cluttered, antiquated interior was transformed by new fixtures and light paint. Open shelves promote additional sales

Sales Jumped 50%

Photos Courtesy Lyon Metal Products

Figure 1.6 Between yesterday and today, sales jumped 50%
Source: 1936, 01, 19

immediate competitors and is sometimes a member of professional clubs or associations (Spellman, 2009). However, the view he obtains in this way is partial, limited, barely going beyond the confines of his family, street, town, club, association[12] or local newspaper, at a time when the unification of the American market was still far from complete (Tedlow, 1990). Therefore our grocer only sees the economic changes that constitute a threat or an opportunity from a distance,[13] or from his window display, whereas this brochure, which he receives regularly each month, by contrast provides him with an omniscient and miraculous view of the world of grocers in general – a view that he can only perceive as being an adequate image of the outside world. *Progressive Grocer* presents him with a multitude of experiences, equipment and discourse, which for him constitute just as many possible or even necessary practices and identifications. The medial focalisation inherent in *Progressive Grocer* thus leads our grocer to understand the avant-garde of distribution as the present state of business, and thus consequently his own state as the rear guard. Given that the poor man is worried about the competition and innovations presented in the magazine, he has no other choice, if he wants to stay in the race and remain worthy of his occupation, than to commit himself, his shop and his customers to this irresistible movement of modernisation that has apparently already swept most of his peers away. Our grocer is therefore driven to buying and putting in place the shop furniture, products and techniques presented to him as the means to allay his concerns, avoid bankruptcy and achieve his aims.[14]

This tension between what the magazine most often showed and other more systematic states of business it sometimes describes can perhaps be traced back to other important discrepancies that we observe, always as the dissonance between central and peripheral visions, between the articles and the many adverts and photos reproduced by the magazine. The adverts published in *Progressive Grocer* often precede the articles that later address the equipment they present. New practices and new equipment often appear as "pictorial externalities". For example, as we shall see later, whereas the journalists of *Progressive Grocer* neglected an innovation as decisive as supermarket trolleys, the same trolleys are nevertheless shown, right from their introduction, in photographs taken of shops to illustrate other subjects. The same is true for the use of trolleys for carrying children (1940, 02, 86; 1945, 10, 102). When we read *Progressive Grocer*, most of the time we are no more informed and sure of the state of business than the actors themselves. However, this uncertainty should not be viewed as a limitation of our knowledge, but rather as the comprehensive duplication of the state of business, as the intimate sharing of the grocer's point of view, in line with the logic of "medial focalisation".

As we can see, *Progressive Grocer* relied not only on words but also on money, economic events and adverts. Everything happens as if the magazine's concern was, insofar as possible, to avoid the gap between the conceptual and the material. Admittedly, the magazine's effort is no doubt sustained by its concern to promote and apply the market model, in terms of both supply and demand.

On the supply side, however, far from being expressed in long, elaborate submissions, this concern is picked up more in the very practical promotion of the figure of the small independent grocer (as opposed to chain stores, supported by the competing magazine *Chain Store Age*) and the money it is intended to make him earn. On the demand side, it is less the consumer's freedom of choice that is promoted (which would lead to service being abandoned) and more the very tangible improvements to the movement of people, goods and financial flows that this new form of sale allows. The magazine is careful to emphasise its "material" nature: from its earliest beginnings, it presented the adoption of the pocket format as a deliberate and thought-out choice given that this format meant it could be read in a practical context:

> It [the magazine] fits the pocket. That's one reason why it's read. The pocket size is the most practical development in the last ten years of business paper publishing.
>
> (1922, 06, 1)

Admittedly the magazine reminds us that it has not invented anything, as this format had already been used by *Printer's Ink*. However, it does highlight that this is an innovation in the grocer's trade. Nevertheless, a few months later, *Progressive Grocer* mentions, in support of its pocket format, another genealogy that is undoubtedly much more in line with the ideal of modernity and constitutes a practical tool allowing one to have immediate control over the present: in an advert from October 1922, *Progressive Grocer* claimed to be "[t]aking an idea from Kodak and applying it to the grocery business" (1922, 10, 1–3), by explaining the process using a spectacular visual parallel reinforced by the following argument:

> The popularity of the Kodak dates back to the day when it was made in a handy, convenient size that could be slipped in the pocket. *The Progressive Grocer* has always been pocket size and it has been steadily successful. Quality and pocket size made the Kodak. Quality, pocket size and *large circulation* made *The Progressive Grocer* an outstanding success in the grocery field [The magazine] differs from old time bulky trade magazines as the modern Kodak differs from the old box camera.
>
> (1922, 10, 2–3)

The following year, *Progressive Grocer* repeats this idea of a "pocket-tool" magazine in its front-page headline, using a superb mise en abyme of a man with the issue of the magazine in his pocket representing him, reproduced ad infinitum (1923, 01; see Figure 1.7). Lastly, a few years later, this figure would evolve to become the paper's logo, shown in the pocket of an anonymous reader. In this last version, the magazine is still under the reader's hand, ready to pull it out, but its pages are also dog-eared, as if to emphasise its recurrent use. *Progressive Grocer* thus shows its concern not to be reduced to a set of abstract,

Figure 1.7 Pocket size
Source: 1922, 10, 2; 1923, 01, cover; 1930, 05, 2

theoretical and "floating" messages, and its ambition to be used rather as a real, practical tool, always "located" and ready for action, like Roland Canu's (2009) "in use" advertising brochures and foldouts.

An archaeology of the present

Before examining the next chapter, tracking how the magazine functions as a practical business language, I would like to clarify further the method used to carry out this research. I started these pages by questioning the partial or non-partial nature of the source used. In fact, the assessment of the source's scope depends on where we stand. *Progressive Grocer* is a tiny source considering the immensity of other possible data for understanding the history of business. It is nonetheless a gigantic source from the point of view of the individual researcher, especially when he has limited time available.

Fortunately, the approach I adopted allowed me to overcome this second difficulty. When I arrived at Berkeley, with only three weeks in which to collect the data, I had already decided to study *Progressive Grocer*. I knew the library had the magazine but I had still never seen it and therefore had no idea what I would find or the time it would take to study it. Given my time constraints and what I discovered during my reading, I soon realised that it would be more logical, in terms of time and intellectually, to concentrate, at least initially, on the images rather than the text.[15] *Progressive Grocer* is a publication filled with photos, pictures and the adverts that go with them to illustrate and complete the articles on new ways to manage a grocery store. Prioritising the pictorial elements became a means for me to go through the paper more quickly and to adopt an historical approach that I see as an "archaeology of the present".

Usually, history is preferably based on handwritten or typewritten documents, which themselves prioritise events that are important from the actors' point of view – in other words, the categories of events that alone draw people's attention and thus are written about. However, these practices often omit the flow of daily life's more ordinary gestures, innovations and events, all the things that are done but not written about, at the risk of being forgotten or not included in a more complete work on "recollecting" the past.[16] Fortunately, *Progressive Grocer* brings precisely these two things closer together: the magazine has the great advantage of reconciling the writing of proper articles, on all sorts of topics, with the compilation of a whole series of illustrations, drawings, adverts, photographs, allowing us to understand, often tangentially, the objects and gestures involved in real business but about which we often find it difficult to find a written trace (I shall come back to this on the subject of trolleys).[17] Therefore, if I want to demonstrate what the magazine does, I must combine the methods of history and archaeology: I must be as attentive to the mute objects of the past as to the discourse of speakers and writers. Therefore, supplementing the historical approach with the archaeological position, completing the analysis of what is said with the examination of what is shown is the means to achieve the symmetry vital for dealing with objects and people (Callon, 1986).

The main difficulties faced by archaeology have always constituted its greatest potential: because by definition it does not have access to all written documents or eyewitness accounts, this discipline has long developed an extraordinary ability to listen to silent artefacts and to turn this exercise into a means of understanding the world it intends to study. The work of an archaeologist consists in "questioning" the mute material vestiges of the past as the substitutes for their absent owners or users (Gould, 1971). In archaeology, the concept of objects as the "missing masses" of society (Latour, 1992) is spectacularly reversed: for archaeologists, the "exclusive presence" of objects is the only means of reaching the "missing crowds" of people who have disappeared (even when they appear as "objectivised" forms, as bones, hair, teeth, mummies, etc.; Renfrew and Bahn, 1991). However, it could be that the easy access to the cultural and textual data from which historians and specialists in the social sciences benefit and thus enjoy is their downfall. Given that today's world and contemporary history are filled with texts and words, these disciplines are often content with a direct and privileged access to human stories, their representations and their arguments. Consequently, they often ignore the contribution material elements could make to understanding social action. Therefore, I believe that our analyses will be even more effective and efficient if they cross both traditions by joining the power of archaeological work (focused on non-human entities) and the traditional methods of introspection/interpretation (turned towards human beings). There are many situations in business, as we shall see in the case of supermarket trolleys, that are filled with objects and actions involved in the world's development, without actually leading to much discussion or introspective consideration. In order to deal with these situations, it seems wise to practise an archaeology of the present – in other words, a sociology of "market-things" (Cochoy, 2007b).

My decision to concentrate on pictorial elements would not have been feasible without a number of additional devices. The researcher and the grocer belong to the same world; they share the same constraints and the same resources. What they can do depends on the tools they have (or do not have). Just as grocers can earn more money with appropriate shelving, cash registers and shopping trolleys, a researcher can cover more data with ad hoc office equipment. In fact, intellectual work is as material as the world to which it refers, particularly when it is done in a library and when it is a matter of studying distribution: libraries and food shops share an astonishing number of elements, such as shelves, trolleys, counters and scanners.

In the top left-hand corner of Figure 1.8 we can make out three trolleys loaded with volumes of *Progressive Grocer*. These trolleys are carrying some of the thousands of pages I turned, one by one, during my three weeks of intensive research at the Northern Regional Library Facility (NRLF). By working in chronological order, page after page, I placed bookmarks in the volumes, corresponding to my research interests. After having marked one series of volumes, I put them in the area visible in the top right-hand corner of Figure 1.8. I placed them on the floor, in front of the chair in which I was sitting, and then leaned over, opening each volume at each bookmark, by keeping it open with my feet and by photographing the pages selected. The large bay windows and sunny climate of California helped me take the photos without a flash, and thus to take nice shots. Not only was it sunny, but the place was also very peaceful and empty, all the better for reducing my embarrassment: being barefoot turned out to be the most efficient way of keeping the volumes open! Thanks to the sun, the private nature of the location, the camera and my simian behaviour, I was able systematically to compile an archive of more than 2,500 photos.[18]

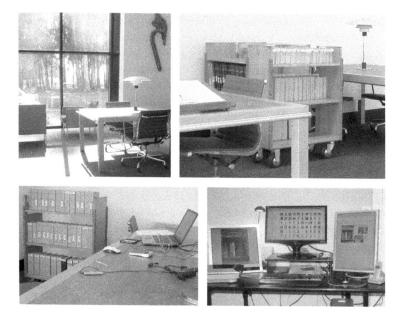

Figure 1.8 NRLF at Berkeley, United States, and the author's desk in Toulouse, France

The completion of my work also relied on a number of secondary yet vital devices that we can see at the bottom left-hand corner of Figure 1.8. The additional battery in the charger saved my project, given that my camera was incapable of running for a whole day. I used the PalmPilot that I had at the time to organise my schedule and take short notes, and the laptop to empty the camera's memory card, begin some initial "emerging" analyses, check the quality of the photos and organise them. A numeric keypad turned out to be useful for the latter activities, allowing me quickly to rename the thousands of photographs according to the volume number, month and page (the year, month, page format used in this book). Even the voice recorder, visible in the foreground, was salutary. Obviously I could not use it to interview anybody but the device worked perfectly as a jukebox, helping me overcome the work's fastidious nature. Lastly and above all, the most important and most useful tool was of course my dear camera, which unfortunately gave up the ghost shortly after this study, but which also allowed me to photograph this collection of research tools (which is why it is not in the picture!). A major advantage of digital photography, regardless of its ability to provide images of better quality than photocopies, is its ability to transform numerous data into files that can be easily taken with you for further study.

Back in France, technical devices once again played an important role in optimising my research abilities. By manipulating digital images rather than paper copies, I was able to copy the same elements into different folders, or even duplicate them, thus creating as many thematic collections as I wanted. In these folders, I classified the elements chronologically, in order to have speedy access to the longitudinal changes in which I was interested. Navigation software in the photographic files, compatible with my desktop computer, with three screens (bottom right-hand corner of Figure 1.8), proved extraordinarily useful for making sense of the data. Thanks to the "double screen" display option, I could navigate (see middle screen) through the list of images whilst simultaneously seeing them life-size (see left-hand screen). I was also able to modify each selected image with a single click, given that the same navigation software offers direct access to (well-known) software for photographic retouching. In this last case, I used a virtual, transparent marker to underline the elements that were of particular interest (namely the photographed texts). Thanks to this data access, and the use of the third screen in portrait mode dedicated to word processing, I was able simultaneously to analyse the image, develop my arguments, take notes, organise my ideas, and finally write my research report. The following chapters are the specific results of this method – one in which the practical tools and equipment of research cannot be separated from the analytical and intellectual contexts to which they contribute and which they transform.

Acknowledgements

This chapter includes elements taken from "Reconnecting Marketing to 'Market-things': How Grocery Equipment Drove Modern Consumption

(Progressive Grocer, 1929–1959)" by Franck Cochoy from "Reconnecting Marketing to Markets" edited by Araujo, Luis; Finch, John & Kjellberg, Hans (2010). Printed By permission of Oxford University Press.

Notes

1 On the notion of arranging and its interest for the social sciences, see Çalışkan and Callon, 2010.

2 The philosopher Michel Serres summed up the problem with a brilliant phrase: *"precise knowledge about a specific segment of the past would require the endless openness of the time to come.* As one needs an infinity of time to settle a limitless debt. History, like science, must be paid from the infinite remains of history as time. The ideal of exact, finite, closed, definitive knowledge, implies that the horizon must be pushed forward indefinitely to the future: strictly speaking, there is no difference between these two back-worlds. The knowledge of history costs the history of time" (Serres, 1977, p. 63, trans. by Jaciara Topley Lira).

3 For an illustration of the virtues of an historical tale in internal focalisation, see the excellent chronicle on the World Exhibition of 1937, written by Claire Leymonerie (2011). The author tells this story based on the archives of the French aluminium industry, allowing one not only to understand the dynamics of this kind of exhibition but especially its interest for a particular exhibitor, and even more so, the effect of such an idiosyncratic view: thus we see how the promoters of French aluminium are led to inventory and proudly display the uses for their cherished material to other exhibitors, including an aluminium grating on the glass door of the German pavilion, without being concerned about the implications of the decorative motif on the grating – the swastika of Hitler's Germany – on the eve of the tragedy that we know followed.

4 Just like photography, where creating a portrait reduces the depth of field and thus blurs the background, adopting medial focalisation produces a slightly short-sighted vision, from the historian's point of view: by giving priority to the clarity of details that draw the grocer's attention, there is less precision regarding the changes operating in the background.

5 According to http://butterick.mccall.com/butterick-history-pages-1007.php.

6 Sources: *The American Heritage Dictionary of the English Language*, fourth edition, Houghton Mifflin Company, 2000; online etymology dictionary, www.etymonline.com.

7 Susan Spellman highlights that mail order houses took away a substantial part of the turnover of independent retailers, even before chain stores became an additional threat to them (Spellman, 2009, p. 233).

8 *Progressive Grocer* was neither the first nor the only professional magazine aimed at grocers: other publications came with or preceded it, such as *American Grocer* (1869–), number one until *Progressive Grocer* appeared, but also other, more restricted publications such as *The Grocery World* (1867–), *New England Grocer* (1883–) and the *National Grocers Bulletin* (1912–) (Spellman, 2009).

9 For an economic sociology on contests as a strategy for the curious captivation of customers, see Cochoy, 2011a.

10 Estimate based on a graph (1951, 03, 43).

11 The concept of open display is presented in Chapter 2.

12 An association such as the National Retail Grocers Association is by definition committed to taking more of an interest in the general issues causing concern to its members than in defining particular solutions.

13 This is when he is aware of it. One very revealing indicator of the lack of information that independent retailers had regarding their own activity is given in an

opinion poll involving 1,700 of them in 1939, three years after the adoption of the Robinson-Patman Act meant to protect them: we discover that the professionals know very little about this law (13% admitting they had never heard of it, and 35% declaring themselves incapable of saying how it could benefit them), despite the considerable coverage it was given in the trade and local press (Bader, 1939, quoted in Spellman, 2009, p. 298).

14 In order to present a more complete picture, it should be noted that *Progressive Grocer* controlled not only the grocers but also the advertisers who followed and funded the magazine, even though the efficacy of the messages placed by the latter was by no means guaranteed.

15 The material constraints that weighed on my research should not be ignored: just like archaeologists, who have limited time and space for excavating on land intended to be built on, I had to carry out my research in two sessions, on two clearly defined subjects. Firstly I worked based on one of the most complete collections of *Progressive Grocer* in the United States, a collection that is nonetheless missing the first seven years of publication. Considering these limitations, I decided to study the magazine from the first available year (1929) and stop in 1959, not only because I lacked the time to go further, but above all because as from 1957 it lost its identity as a grocery trade magazine, becoming instead a merchandising magazine aimed at all types of shops (see below, p. 140). As I was very eager to complete my research and since it seemed impossible to tell the story of commerce from the point of view of a magazine whose beginnings I barely knew, on the last day of my trip to Berkeley, I asked a librarian to help me identify another place to dig, that is to say a collection of the first issues. The only one we were able to find, for all of the United States, was located at the Center for Research Libraries of Chicago, which held a collection covering the period 1922 to 1927 and I had to wait seven long years before I was finally about to find the resources and especially the time to go there in January 2013. Nonetheless there are still some gaps, given that the first four issues of 1922 and all of 1928 are missing, whereas only the issues from February, June and August of 1927 are available. These gaps are very frustrating as I was not able to investigate the first issue or most of the material from 1927, which was nevertheless an important year for the magazine given that this was when it launched a campaign to promote the concept of open display. These constraints thus affect the validity of my work to a certain degree but to no greater or lesser extent than what is very often missing or disappears during archaeological work, and with which archaeologists have long been able to cope.

16 A recent issue of the magazine *Vingtième siècle*, dedicated to the recent history of advertising, clearly observed the paradox of a period when the proliferation of images clashes with the habits of historians of the present, who are less attentive to this type of material than medievalists (Bertrand-Dorléac et al., 2001).

17 See the history of the supermarket trolley: although Catherine Grandclément (2006) clearly retraced the industrial history of this device, its ordinary use is harder to grasp, unless we are willing to use sources other than texts, for example photographs, where it is possible to see them in action (see Chapter 5).

18 A few years later in Chicago, thanks to a more modern and better camera, powerful lighting and especially to the fortuitous availability of unbound issues, I was able to work comfortably and quickly, avoiding the painful contortions that had marked my first mission.

2 Making people do business with words-things

In this chapter I aim to familiarise the reader with *Progressive Grocer*'s very particular and skilful use of language by demonstrating how the magazine's specialist journalists intertwined words and practice, or to put it in linguistic terms, played on the performativity of language – on the ability of certain types of statements to "do things" (Austin, 1961).[1] It should be remembered that the linguist J.L. Austin distinguished between "constative" utterances, whose true or false nature can be established by referring to the external reality they describe (for example, "the cat is on the mat"), and "performative" utterances, which are neither true nor false, but which bring into effect the world to which they refer (for example, "I now pronounce you husband and wife"). It is precisely the ability of the utterances in *Progressive Grocer* to be more performative than constative that I intend to examine.

More precisely, we shall see that in the case of *Progressive Grocer*, performativity concerns particular situations in which words and things, instead of being the origin and result of the action, as in Austin's theory, are deliberately combined to produce different words and different worlds. In a way, this type of combination represents nothing new, either from the point of view of the philosophy of language, which has long admitted the lack of distinction between words and things in their ability to refer to something (Pierce, 1934), or from that of the anthropology of sciences and techniques, which has consistently recorded the ubiquitous nature of such hybridisation (Latour, 1991a). However, for working grocers, the emergence of writing in their primarily manual practice posed a problem, and providing a language capable of "speaking their acts", of displaying the "things" being referred to as photographs, pictures and illustrations, or even, as we shall see, of "showing their words", was a means of overcoming this difficulty.

In order to explore the pragmatics devices of *Progressive Grocer*'s "words-things", I shall begin by analysing a cartoon aimed at examining "how to build displays that sell". Analysing this picture and taking its implications into account will help us later to explore the particular techniques and rhetoric that *Progressive Grocer* used and combined to promote successfully the building of these "displays that sell".

"How to build displays that sell"

To my knowledge, there is no better illustration[2] of the fundamental problem of performativity than this cartoon in Figure 2.1, published in 1946.

As we can see, this picture depicts an employee sitting on a box of soap, engrossed in a book called "How to build displays that sell". The employee is fascinated by the promise of new self-service "tricks" that will allow him to act without doing anything, to sell without being the salesman (Grandclément, 2008). However, his boss interrupts to show him, with a broad gesture, the near-empty shelves we can see around him. He thus informs him that all the "performative equipment" probably included in the book may not be enough to perform anything. The drawing reminds us that sometimes performative utterances such as "I promise you displays that sell" do not work, and worse still, that they distract people's attention away from the action.[3]

At first glance, the merchandising handbook is to a grocer what a magic book is to a wizard:[4] it is a genuine book of "magic sales", proposing that people build things that are able to act by themselves, as if by magic (Latour, 1999). Thanks to specific devices, such as self-service, open displays and wide shelves, the task of selling and merchandising expertise is "delegated" to material artefacts. Just as a barrier can contain a flock whilst the shepherd is sleeping (Latour, 1996a), the new displays can sell goods whilst the grocer is absent. Commercial magic thus operates in the same way as the wizard of Oz – in other words, behind the scenes (Canu, 2010).

However, most of the time the grocer's original script is not performed to the letter but transformed – or rather interpreted (Callon, 1986) – by the device entrusted with it. As Bruno Latour (1991b) demonstrated, the heavy, cast iron keys of a hotel do not have exactly the same meaning that the hotelier thought he had given them: instead they convert an appeal to altruism ("thank

Figure 2.1 How to build displays that sell
Source: 1946, 08, 97

you for sharing the hotel's point of view and leaving the key at the front desk")
into a selfish concern ("I do not want my pockets to be misshapen"). Similarly,
the displays can sell but when they do, they are not proceeding exactly as the
grocer would have done: self-service devices can sell continuously and more
than human employees, given that they are always there; however, they cannot
answer questions or adapt information and commercial offers selectively to each
customer. On the contrary, they promote brand names, fixed prices, detailed
information, etc. to everyone and thus change both the retail trade and consumer behaviour (Strasser, 1989; Grandclément, 2008). In other words, the
performativity of the "book of magic sales" teaches us two lessons for studying
the more or less performative nature of economic utterances. First, this book
shows that performative effects are often indirect and driven by mediation
(Callon et al., 2007). Second, because it is delegated and thanks to the "inter-
pretative" power of all mediation, what is performed does not correspond
exactly to the message initially delivered.

However, performing the world indirectly and/or differently is not the most
serious problem the "book of magic sales" must face. More fundamentally, this
book must perform something, and performing something does not depend on
the power of the printed words alone. The boss who questions his employee or
the people who wrote the book are well aware that no magic will be possible
without the help of a magician (Canu, 2010); they know that words can do
nothing by themselves, that theories are implemented insofar as their action
gives them sense, direction and meaning. Now, the title "how to build displays
that sell" refers felicitously to the particular alchemy of "making people/things do
things" identified by Bruno Latour (1999). Latour studied the situations where the
ability to act is neither that of humans nor technical devices but is split between
them. The author gives the example of cigarettes: the smoker cannot say he
controls his smoking given that he finds it hard to stop; however, nor can he
say that the cigarette is smoking him, given that obviously the cigarette can do
nothing without him. In fact, the cigarette "makes him smoke". Merchandising
theories and equipment operate according to this pattern: building displays that
sell is clearly aimed at creating things that do things "for", "with" and "to" us.
Using merchandising know-how and techniques, using devices such as open
display fixtures rather than enclosed counters, the "act of selling" is shared
between the grocer who installs the displays, the displays' selling "affordance",
and the knowledge linking the grocer to his furniture.

In the performative utterance "I promise displays that sell", the "I" is
immediately shared between three entities: the employee building the displays,
the displays doing the selling, and of course the handbook providing them each
with the necessary ideas and techniques. However, if one of these entities fails,
it is highly probable that nothing will be performed at all. This pattern reminds
us that, according to Austin's own point of view, pure "performative utterances" do not exist: the success or failure of such utterances is linked to
favourable felicity conditions. When the handbook says "I promise displays that
sell", there is no guarantee that the shopkeeper or consumer will take this

proposal into consideration and will begin to act "as appropriate". Performing the manual could, for example, depend on the fortuitous presence of the boss, who wisely suggests establishing a link between theory and action. Without him, it is very possible that nothing will happen (the employee might not be able to read or act; the consumer could refuse self-service or go to the competitors instead, etc.). The performative property is not a property of words, but is rather a potential registered between words and action. This difficulty can be presented as the "aporia of performativity": performativity is a linguistic theory whose success is left up to risky extra-linguistic circumstances (hence Austin's doubts about his own theory (Denis, 2006) and its incessant re-evaluation by his successor; Loxley, 2006). However, what can be a problem from the linguist is a blessing for philosophers and sociologists – and for ordinary actors. Words create opportunities that must be seized and reworked, and creating and managing these opportunities is precisely what the "book of magic sales", in other words *Progressive Grocer*, attempts to do successfully.

It is important to emphasise that the drawing I started with appeared in *Progressive Grocer*, a magazine that itself is specifically dedicated to doing things with words, to building displays that sell. In my example, *Progressive Grocer* is both around and inside the picture. The magazine is inside, given that "How to make displays that sell" is just a generic way of mentioning what *Progressive Grocer*, the "National Magazine of the Grocery Trade", does and the monographs it has published – *Better Grocery Stores, Getting Down to Real Facts in the Grocery Business, The Modern Grocery Store*, etc. *Progressive Grocer* is filled with titles of an almost performative nature, such as "Cutting down the handicaps is one way to beat the chain store" (1922, 09, 5), "Put on a sale of canned goods in dozen lots this month" (1922, 10, 5), and "Sell the old stock first or you drive away trade" (1923, 03, 5). However, *Progressive Grocer* is also and above all "around" the picture, in the sense that it is published in the same magazine that it features. Therefore, the picture and magazine question but also shift and enrich the context of performativity.

First, they playfully call into question performative logic by widening the gap between language and action. Whereas on the one hand the language is extremely concise on the book's cover, and to some extent trapped in the whirlwind of its self-referential content, the material layout and real action are in some way suspended on the other side. The dualistic nature of the staging of the picture underlines magnificently that managerial and economic forms of knowledge are always only half performative: they introduce a break, a suspension, an "economic action detour". Things are said and then done, rather than said-done as implied by the pure theory of language acts. Instead of ignoring this problem, it would be better to take it into account and deal with it, given that it plays a vital role in suspending market fluidity and performative logic.

However, the drawing and the magazine also extend the performative logic they suspend. They do this by neutralising, paradoxically, its central discursive device. Significantly, there is no utterance in this picture, with the exception of the book's silent title. No word is said, no one speaks, no caption is written. As in a silent film, only the gestures tell us the story: the very simple acts of reading and pointing to something that must be done are pitted against the absent gestures of work and speech.

We might have thought that in the absence of any discourse, words would have been replaced by things, meaning by violence, right by might (Latour, 1997), given that in sociology "understanding" is often opposed to "objective causes". However, what the picture shows us is very different. What is achieved is physical but not violent; objective but also very delicate and subjective: the boss' interference is not authoritarian and coercive but questioning and meaningful. This intervention connects two very light gestures: the first is the boss very gently pressing his finger against the employee's back to gain his attention; the second is the broad gesture of the other hand, meant to show where the employee's attention should be focused. The combination of both gestures forms a genuine language, filling the gap between theory and practice, but also promotes practice as the main (and perhaps exclusive) theory. This language suggests that talking too much and/or exclusively, like the book, sometimes leads to doing nothing; conversely, it suggests that in order to do something it is sometimes better to refrain from talking or reading; it teaches us "how to do things without words". Thus we understand that in the drawing, language and meaning have not been erased but moved. By removing almost all the attributes of traditional speech from the scenario, the picture highlights another form of language, in which human behaviour and the material entities – such as the box of soap, the tins and shelves – can be correctly combined, like verbs, nouns, adjectives, etc., to develop both a meaningful sequence and appropriate action. In a way, the picture offers to extend acts of language to the language of acts.

Lastly, the picture and *Progressive Grocer* are brilliantly introspective. By accepting being represented in this drawing, the magazine *Progressive Grocer* looks at itself in the mirror and presents the central problem facing it: that of a publication designed to sell "how to build displays that sell", with no assurance that it will succeed in such an enterprise. Nonetheless, by showing the problem in this way (using a picture), *Progressive Grocer* finds the means to resolve it. In fact, and as we have just seen, doubting purely language-based performativity is a way of finding a broader and more effective language. Not only is *Progressive Grocer* a magazine gathering words, theories and ideas, but one that deals with real action, with "living" testimonies, tangible equipment and cold, hard cash. The paper is not only a set of formal performative utterances aimed at an external and material world; it is also a collection of more or less connected proposals, displays, ideas, photographs, concepts, adverts, pictures. *Progressive Grocer* gathers, hybridises and articulates all these resources in a complex and multidimensional language, which appears to be made to "perform performativity". In the following sections I intend to explore the know-how that manages performativity hinted at in the picture, but which takes on different and sophisticated forms in the rest of the magazine.

Models: building business

As suggested in Figure 2.1, modernising the grocery industry consists in resolving the following dilemma: we must find a way of activating a symbolic language given that for a magazine this kind of language is the only way to describe and perform new merchandising solutions (that do not necessarily exist), but at the same time we must avoid relying on words alone because even if they are capable of transporting the world from a distance, there is a large chance that the readers, who are not very-literate, will accuse them of being too abstract, rhetorical and theoretical, too far from the issues at hand, from the real practices and material arrangements that are of the utmost importance to the day-to-day life of business.

In its first years, *Progressive Grocer* considered that one of the best solutions for resolving this dilemma consisted in using the model of an ideal shop as a demonstration. We know how much this kind of device supports action (Jeantet, 1998; Vinck, 1999), and *Progressive Grocer*'s models were no exception to the rule. The first device of this kind was the work of the editor-in-chief, Carl Dipman, who developed a small-scale model of the ideal shop in 1927 and used it for demonstration purposes from coast to coast in the United States, during meetings with tens of thousands of grocers (1954, 09, 37), in order to promote the idea of an "open display", a new merchandising concept that we shall present later on in detail (see Chapter 3). Suffice to say, at this stage, that the open display was meant to help independent grocers modernise, in light of the competition from chain stores, but also preserve their owners' strong commitment to service, by giving customers the best visual access to the products so as to arouse new ideas in their minds and get them to buy more than they had intended. Far from being simply a concept, the open display was also a genuine technology. In fact, in order to implement it, the long counter of old shops needed to be replaced by a smaller piece of furniture so that consumers could move around the shop; new equipment had to be introduced, such as glass showcases in the shape of "islands" (in other words, isolated furniture around which consumers could navigate). This furniture, completely covered in glass, allowed customers to see more whilst preventing them from touching the products. In order to put this concept-arrangement into practice, Carl Dipman and *Progressive Grocer* felt it was better to show rather than just talk about it: the magazine's team photographed the model and distributed millions of copies of it to professionals in the retail trade (1930, 06, 24).

With the model, "the display that sells" is not, as in our drawing, "around" the book of magic sales but directly at the heart of it (when reproduced in *Progressive Grocer*) or like an extension of it (when disseminated separately). Moreover, these are not just any old displays, like those photographed in many illustrations. In fact, there is a considerable difference between the photograph of a shop and a model. A photograph has the great advantage of being a lot more "realistic" than a model, but it also has the drawback of referring to a specific shop. What is specific, in terms of size, equipment, organisation, etc., is

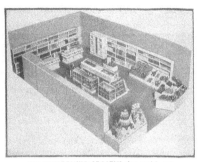

THE PROGRESSIVE GROCER'S *first model store—a
miniature built three years ago of which millions of
pictures have been reproduced and distributed throughout the grocery and allied trades*

Steiden Stores, Louisville, Ky., 3-column ad.

How well do you know
your own business?

Figure 2.2 Models
Source: From top to bottom: 1930, 06, 24; 1941, 07, 67; 1945, 02, 36

not at all flexible. It is easy to show grocers wonderful, modern shops (as *Progressive Grocer* often does), but grocers might object that the shop shown is clearly not theirs, and that it is almost impossible for them to turn one into the other. Conversely, the model has the drawback of being far more abstract than real shops, but this defect is actually its main advantage. The model helps move from this rigid "individual case" to a "generic type" of shop that is a lot more flexible. Models are simultaneously material and symbolic, theoretical and practical. They are "personified theories", concepts turned into an object, words into things, but also meaningful materials, "displays that speak". Like the business plans of today that stimulate future business (Giraudeau, 2007), models appear as a kind of possible business plan, operating in the manner of previously performed performative proposals. By looking at a model we understand it is presenting elements that can be redistributed and adapted, rather than a fixed solution.

Moreover and by doing this, models suggest that a shop can be considered from afar, introspectively, and that any grocer can play with its components to improve his business. With a model, we move from poor Baudu's "my shop as it was, as it is, as it will always be", in *The Ladies' Paradise* by Zola (see the Introduction), to "my flexible business that I can constantly modernise". With the model, every shop suddenly appears as an organisational set-up made up of mobile elements that professionals can separate, throw away, replace, supplement or rearrange as they see fit, in order to improve their results. The model allows the grocer to move from his routine equipment and stable identity as a traditional retailer, to the new position of experimenter, working on a shop that can be reshaped at will. As a result of its smaller scale, commercial equipment seems a lot more mobile than before; models convey the idea that displays can be played with, like a small child with a doll's house, or rather like scientists with their rats. Models do not simply provide examples of possible shops but rather a real lesson in modernisation, suggesting new ways of thinking and acting. It is therefore not surprising, in light of the properties of models, that companies selling new commercial equipment or management solutions adopted *Progressive Grocer*'s technique to promote their own businesses, as the Steiden (an equipment manufacturer) and National Cash Register (NCR) (see Figure 2.2) adverts show. The grocer's status changes from one advert to the next as the scale is reduced: in the Steiden advertisement, a first reduction helps to turn traditional grocers into expert grocers, working with their shops like scientists with their laboratory experiments. In the NCR commercial, a second reduction of a larger shop contributes to changing laboratory grocers, with their white coats, into a type of scientist who is more remote and abstract: seated, in suit and glasses, chin on fist, this man is clearly studying far more than taking action, examining his company in order to answer the delicate question: "How well do you know your own business?"[5] As the grocery store is modernised, so is the grocer; thanks to models, we go from displays that sell to grocers who think … about building displays that sell more. The circle is complete: with models there is no longer a gap between theory and practice; thoughts and things merge into one and the same entity.

Testimonies: making grocers talk

However, it would be a mistake to think that models totally disqualify ordinary words as a means of performing new ways to sell products. As a press organ, the magazine naturally resorted to traditional language, given that its core business consisted in writing articles and promoting ideas. Nonetheless, the magazine also used language because it knew perfectly well that words could also para-doxically be made as "hard" as real things. This is what is demonstrated by the very widespread use of reports, accounts and quotations. Some of *Progressive Grocer's* articles are nothing but a collection of (allegedly) true experiences resembling readers' letters. One of the best examples of this kind of article is a text from 1943 entitled: "12 Food Merchants Say: 'Self-Service Solves Many of Our Wartime Problems'." In this article, we find points of view such as this one:

> "Since I changed to semi-self-service we don't need a lot of help. Custo-mers are their own clerks. Sales the last week of 1942 were more than double the sales of the last week in 1941. All information I received from THE PROGRESSIVE GROCER and your book, 'Self-Service and Semi-Self-Service Food Stores'."
>
> (*T.W. Smith, Tom Smith Grocery, Miami, Fla.*: 1943, 05, 58)

At first glance, this kind of information is made up of nothing more than words, meaning, ideas and opinions. However, upon closer inspection we see there is actually a lot more to it. The inverted commas and the signature introduce a huge difference. The situation is composed of words but these words come from outside and from real grocers. In her ethnography of supermarkets as "paper jungles", Catherine Grandclément (2008) shows that prices are not only sym-bols and abstract economic variables, but also and above all colourful and material artefacts, with their own attractiveness and affordance. Similarly, per-sonal testimonies such as the one I have just quoted are not only words, but genuine samples of the real world of grocers. They are materialised and circulating statements. Now, if we look more closely at this type of uttered statement, we discover that everything happens as if the readers were themselves filling in the book of magic sales they were supposed to read. The story quoted refers to a powerful formula – "customers are their own clerks" – giving substance to and expanding on the ideas of "building displays that sell", and of self-service. It is not a magic but rather a financial formula, as can be seen with the weekly increase in sales that "more than double[d]" from one year to the next. Lastly, the personal testimony recognises the selling power of the book of magic sales he received, by once again completing the circle that starts with the reader writing to *Progressive Grocer* ("All information I received from THE PROGRESSIVE GROCER and your book"). *Progressive Grocer* and the testimonies carefully chosen by the magazine operate as a two-way mirror: on the one hand, the magazine is reflected in what is said by the readers and vice versa; on the other and thanks to this first mirror, the readers can see and recognise themselves, both as a group and as a new possible professional identification. In the end, each mirror is reflected in the other making it impossible to establish the origin of what is said and done, the opinions and facts, what is performative and performed.

Photo stories: objectifying the actors, bringing the objects to life

Although words can be turned into things with quotations, inverted commas and signatures in italics, they can also be reinforced with images. This is true for the accounts I have just mentioned, supported by "before/after" pictures and photos illustrating the changes about which the witnesses were writing. However, this is particularly true for some articles which, instead of "illustrating" words using images in the traditional way – words on one side and pictures on the other – mix and combine them, as if these two elements belong to a single "extended" language, in which real things can be linked to symbolic meanings:

These extracts from two articles – one called "CHECKERS are important people" and the other "How to Lose Customers [Without Speaking]" – wonderfully hybridise what is real and artificial, human and non-human, discursive and objective. These articles appear as genuine "photonovelas". They depict a set of display shelves, words in capitals and lowercase, cashiers, many questions, two shops, lots of suggestions, a female consumer, packaging with a smile, a paper bag, four captions, many different products, four photographs, a shopping trolley, comic book speech bubbles, etc. These elements are both

Figure 2.3 Photonovelas
Source: 1946, 09, 78; 1946, 02, 72

natural and arranged. The setting of the grocer's store is real but the characters are extras: the three women and props play the roles of smiling cashiers, upset customer and defective artefacts to illustrate the relevance of a commercial technique and the importance of a technical detail (respectively). By "staging reality", *Progressive Grocer* combines the power of performativity with that of performance: as in theatre pieces, the words pronounced are directly put into action – here occurring through the use of speech bubbles – so that there is no longer a time lag between "how to build" and the "displays that sell" (or do not!).

Actions and words are no longer performed one after the other but together, simultaneously, and in the same universe. The power of discourse is reinforced by the strength of "living examples". The generic performative sentence, summarising the four scenes – "I declare that the shop now uses self-service" – is matched by the corresponding generic performance: "I will show you what a real self-service shop should (or should not) look like." In fact, in our photo stories we can see two different ways to construct the appropriate discourse and action: one proposes what to do (suggesting additional purchases); the other does the same thing using an antiphrasis – it suggests doing things that prevent people from doing their shopping (placing detritus in the aisles, putting products at ground level, etc.). Adding erroneous actions to the spectacle of correct ones – reinforcing performativity by anticipating its possible "failures" (Butler, 2010; Callon, 2010) – is used as a way of channelling grocers' practices, in the same way that in utilitarian tradition, the hope of rewards and fear of sanctions are meant to lead to appropriate kinds of behaviour (Andreoni et al., 2003).

Lastly, these pictures finish by generalising performative logic. Instead of reproducing the division between words and things, the photo stories extend the ability to think and speak to mute things and, conversely, give objective properties to human actors: whereas the detritus and shelves strongly harangue the female consumer with sarcasm, the cashiers are meant to offer the customers their professional smiles and scripted words in a repetitive and mechanical fashion. This hybridisation of words and things helps us understand the socio-technical nature of self-service.

Max Weber explained that a collision between two cyclists was not a "social activity" but a simple, natural event, until a meaning is given to the scene and reciprocal exchanges occur between the cyclists (fighting each other, arguing, reaching an agreement).[6] This famous definition of social activity served as the basis for a tradition according to which culture and nature are considered two distinct spheres, sealed off from one another, one governed by human meaning, the other by natural causes. However, closer scrutiny of Weber's argument shows that nothing prevents us from extending his restrictive definition of a social activity to objects. In order to better understand how and why, we simply need to change the vehicle: we must get off the bicycle to push a shopping trolley.

In a self-service context and by definition, consumers are often deprived of any human partners. Most of the time they do their shopping alone, only encountering displays and products. However, the *Progressive Grocer* photo-novelas show that even in these situations, interactions and meaningful reciprocal exchanges still occur, even if they appear in the hybrid form of what Latour calls "interobjectivity" – in other words, a situation in which humans interact with technical objects (Latour, 1996a; Cochoy, 2007b, 2008b). With these photo stories we understand that the interobjectivity in self-service has two essential characteristics. First, we realise that despite being mute, the objects in the commercial stage, far from lacking the ability to communicate, instead speak their own sign language (interpreted as speech bubbles in the photo story). Second, we discover that, contrary to what we might have thought, we are perfectly capable of understanding and even speaking this language: we negotiate no differently with things than we would with our own human brothers and sisters; we attempt to find a more or less acceptable agreement between us and them.

Humour: the funny war of the grocer's newspaper

After having examined a few concepts that became reality thanks to models, a few abstract words transformed into hard facts thanks to testimonies, and some images made to talk using photo stories, I would like to end this overview of *Progressive Grocer*'s discursive methods by mentioning a few images of fiction and the words associated with them. It is, more specifically, a question of considering the role of humour which, taking cognisance of the crisis, whether as something negative because of the labour shortage during the Second World War, or positive because of the introduction of self-service (an innovation that brought productivity gains), invented a language that was able to control the separation between utterances and reinvent the paths that were likely to re-establish (but also thoroughly reorganise) the link between words and things.

One of the magazine's characteristics is in fact its recurrent use of cartoons. A cartoon can be described as a kind of performative device: as we shall see, pure fiction is paradoxically a way of making reality more "real" than itself, and thus of creating a definitive solidarity between words and things. Humour is continuously used in *Progressive Grocer* in times of crisis as in times of prosperity, but as we shall demonstrate, it takes on particular importance in crisis situations, whether positive or negative. In *Progressive Grocer* the positive crisis is the advent of self-service, which destabilises the actors' points of reference (see Figure 2.4).

The negative crisis is the war, with men leaving for the front to fighting and rationing, which disturbed work and eating habits (see Figure 2.5).

To my knowledge, the role of humour in society has not received enough attention from the very (too?) serious social sciences, at the risk of important aspects of the objects they claim to study being overlooked. Humour is entirely aimed at knowing "how to do things with a smile". In this particular variant of the performativity pattern, the word "smile" must be understood literally and figuratively: a smile is a question of both mind and matter; smiling gives a twist to a person's intelligence and face. More specifically, humour triggers the sharing and understanding of a situation between two people: the person telling the story and the person who must understand its meaning and respond with a

"How did they know
we were coming along?"

Figure 2.4 "How did they know we were coming along?"
Source: 1939, 10, 195

smile in return. In this way, funny stories are always small self-service devices: their own significance is to mean nothing by themselves. In fact, they need the receiver's cooperation and creativity to express fully what they are referring to. Let us examine Figure 2.6.

Placing a cow in a grocery store and asking customers to milk it makes no sense in itself.[7] Or rather, it makes no sense until the reader reframes what he sees, expands the narration and makes his own interpretation. More than any other kind of language, humour consequently stages a kind of "joint

Figure 2.5 "I understand their clean-up man has been drafted"; "Isn't rationing wonderful? Think what it's doing for our figures!"
Source: 1944, 03, 211

Figure 2.6 "I think this store is carrying self-service a little too far"
Source: 1942, 03, 186

performativity": what is implied is simultaneously produced by the narrator and the reader. All the pleasure in humour comes from this addition, from this game consisting in "guessing" the secondary/additional meaning, in personally producing the story's true message. If the message is explained by someone other than the reader, humour disappears: we all know that a good joke is not explained.

The distinct nature of the joint performativity of funny speech has strong and serious social implications, to the extent that humour is used as a way of enlisting the audience in producing (and accepting) the meaning not only of a story, but even more so, of the tangible world to which the story refers (Parasie, 2010). Showing self-service shops where customers must do their own milking consists in giving the reader the full experience of the uncertainty surrounding the development of the grocery sector and the extension of the movement towards self-service. By acting this way, the pictures shape and channel real concerns in a cathartic manner; even more, they establish a collective test on what self-service is and what it might be. The representation of extravagant kinds of self-service is a way of both indirectly reminding us of its real contemporary forms, and of exploring the limits of its acceptable future. The drawing plays particularly on the second method as it invites readers to be worried about the development of self-service. However, acting like this, in a humorous way, is also a means of reassuring them. Implicitly, the drawing suggests that the development has already taken place and that we should therefore accept it rather than resist it. By exaggerating the future, the picture plays down the present. What is "un-performable" operates as a prop for what can really be performed, according to the logic where things could after all be worse, and it is thus preferable to accept the situation.

However, it is vital to stress the importance of the first method: although the pictures are fiction, these fictions are paradoxically closely connected to the world. This is what is wonderfully demonstrated by drawing a parallel between a variation of the previous drawing and a genuine poster from 1944 (Figure 2.7). Both aim to link closely positive crisis (introduction of self-service) and negative crisis (context of war).

There are two ways of interpreting this parallel, which help us understanding the final and perhaps most important figure in *Progressive Grocer*'s policies of performativity. On the one hand, the picture refers to the same real problem as the poster – which itself is simply a photograph of a genuine shop window in a country that was, without a shadow of a doubt, at war. What is said in both representations does nothing more than confirm a fact that is as simple as it is meaningful: the war played a significant role in converting American grocers to self-service. Because of the war, many men had to leave the labour market, thus leading to a labour shortage. Although this problem is merely alluded to in the picture ("Due to labor shortage"), it is clearly pointed out in the poster ("We have lost some of our clerks to the service"). Both images simply present, in their own way, what they consider to be the necessary solution to the labour shortage: the number of services that grocers could no longer provide had to be

Will it come to this?

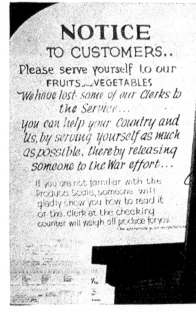

SELF-SERVICE IN PRODUCE
dept. is encouraged by above sign.
All items possible are pre-priced.

Figure 2.7 Will it come to this?; Notice to customers
Source: Respectively: 1943, 10, 215; 1944, 12, 54

provided by customers themselves (in the drawing sweeping the floor, turning the lights out; in the poster serving and weighing your own fruit and vegetables). Far from being limited to drawings and the poster, the endeavour, aimed at recognising/making a connection between the labour shortage and self-service, was a recurrent theme in many articles published by *Progressive Grocer* throughout the war.[8]

From this point of view, we can identify two sub-periods. At the beginning of the war problems were anticipated rather than dealt with, and self-service was presented as a theoretical, possible solution: an article from 1942 entitled "How War Affects the Food Trade", predicted that "[w]ith gas rationing and a tire shortage service stores will adopt more supermarket techniques, more self-service features, perhaps greater inducements to cash-and-carry buyers" (1942, 04, 136). In August of the same year, one article titled, "Employing More Women? Here are Suggestions", noted that "one of the most important changes war is bringing to food merchants is the change in personnel". This statement led the author to draw conclusions about the current "necessity of employing women". At first glance, employing women seemed to be an alternative to self-service in an effort to compensate for the departure of male employees, but actually, *Progressive Grocer* was making a strong connection between female employment and the idea of self-service. Indeed, the paper argued that woman could not entirely replace men, or rather that they could through technical adjustments … such as the help of self-service devices:

> A woman can, of course, be taught and adapted to food store work to an extent, but her physical limitations require that the merchant employing her must also learn and must change some of his methods of operation to get the most of his new employee […] Much unnecessary carrying can be avoided, however, by permitting the women to use gliders or supplying them with some sort of flat rolling truck for moving case goods.
>
> (1942, 08, 46–47)

In 1943, things became somewhat different: what a year before had been considered a possible yet abstract solution, was presented as a common and tangible practice. In January, an article entitled "Woman can replace men in most jobs, grocers find" (1943, 01, 28) used a questionnaire to demonstrate the feminisation of labour: "the number of women employees in the large-volume food stores has about doubled in the past year, jumping from an estimated 75,000 to 150,000." In May, an article appeared with the following title: "12 food merchants confirm: 'self-service solves many of our wartime problems'" (1943, 05, 58–61).[9] All the testimonies collected supported this idea, using hundreds of personal experiences similar to this one:

> when the present labor shortage came along, we soon learned that it was impossible to handle our business in a counter-service store with the limited help available. The self-service arrangement enables us to do half again as much business with actually less help than we had in the counter-service store.
>
> (1943, 05, 58)

On the one hand, the drawing, poster and many other articles used the war as a "necessary" force accelerating the changeover to self-service. The labour shortage, in particular, was meant to "push" grocers to employ more women and self-service devices, both being linked, thanks to the use of shopping trolleys and cashiers, as different ways of offsetting the apparent physical differences between men and women. However, on the other hand, self-service did not begin with the war and its development did not cease with the end of the conflict, as shown by the statistics I mentioned earlier, and more generally by everything published by the magazine. Similarly, *Progressive Grocer* did not wait for the war to promote self-service, and did not, of course, stop supporting it once the conflict had ended. During the war, the labour shortage was simply used as an additional argument, amongst many others, for the development of self-service.[10] This way of working was best expressed in the very cynical caption accompanying the poster. The caption implicitly suggests the wording on the poster – that is, playing on the patriotic sentiments in times of war in order to do more business and make more money: "self-service in produce dept. is encouraged by above sign" … which you should therefore use as a source of inspiration for your own shop.

Bringing both of these elements together – factual and rhetorical, drawing and poster, poster and caption, war and articles dealing with it, etc. – helps to reveal what is probably performativity's greatest trick. Effective performativity is that which promotes things that were going to occur anyway. We can find an admirable representation of this in Romain Rolland's *Jean-Christophe*:

> [Jean-Christophe] was also a magician. He walked with great strides through the fields, looking at the sky and waving his arms. He commanded the clouds. He wished them to go to the right, but they went to the left. Then he would abuse them, and repeat his command. He would watch them out of the corner of his eye, and his heart would beat as he looked to see if there were not at least a little one which would obey him. But they went on calmly moving to the left. Then he would stamp his foot, and threaten them with his stick, and angrily order them to go to the left; and this time, in truth, they obeyed him. He was happy and proud of his power.
>
> (Rolland, 1911, n.p.)

Saying, "I declare that the time for self-service has come", as *Progressive Grocer*, our book of magic sales tirelessly repeats, is like ordering the clouds to go left when the wind is blowing from the right. In order to perform performativity, it is better to pronounce performative sentences with "reasonable" ambitions; better to talk about things that were on the verge of developing almost "of their own accord". For all that, does this somewhat discouraging definition of performativity mean that no word is ever performed, that what is said bears no influence, that the correspondence between words and things is purely coincidental? Not at all. When we say things that were going to happen anyway, we add two decisive elements to the scenario: first, we gather together the things that are happening and make them significant; we "express" them, according to the beautiful expression used by Emmanuel Didier (2007); then we gain the position of the author of what is expressed/what we are expressing. In fact, when we say something and whilst at that same time what we are saying is happening, there is every chance that we will be recognised as the source of the event. In *Progressive Grocer*, everything happens as if Jean-Christophe's clouds were listening to their master and moving further left the more they recognised this order as effective and almost irresistible.

Words, objects and images thus contribute strongly to organising the flow of business. Admittedly, a problem of causal imputation arises here: it is one thing to point out the language-based action of *Progressive Grocer* and how it is referenced in practice, and another to attribute to it the set of changes identified. However, this problem is resolved if we conceive of *Progressive Grocer*'s action as aiming to rearrange a flow: organising commercial innovations throughout the twentieth century was similar to trying to make logs of wood go downriver. On the one hand, *Progressive Grocer*'s discourse would not change the direction of the current nor prevent it from flowing. On the other, its action could weigh on the faster or slower delivery and relevance of what it carried: like log transporters on large rivers, the magazine's work consisted in aligning things as appropriate, in the right order and direction so as to avoid a bad arrangement hindering the flow of the convoy. In this task, humour plays a vital role: it allows us to deal with the muddles and untangle them, by inviting us each to make a contribution to give a positive, collective and convergent meaning to the developments underway.

However, the empirical examination of performativity techniques in *Progressive Grocer* shows that the actors could be even more pragmatic than pragmatists themselves. We should not forget that *Progressive Grocer* was just one particular occurrence in a more general category of marketing devices to which the magazine belonged: the trade press (Laïb, 1955). As we saw, trade magazines were wary of using only words and discourse, given that they were often too abstract and too far removed from the real action and actors they were seeking to influence. In other words, the trade press faced a very serious dilemma: whereas its mission was to introduce new ways of thinking, behaving and objects into the real world, in order to achieve this goal it had no other choice than to resort to the very distant medium of paper.

Progressive Grocer demonstrates how such a dilemma could be overcome. The magazine accomplishes almost everything that can be done with the simple medium of paper. Instead of merely placing words on its pages, *Progressive Grocer* relies on a type of language that is different from economic theories and management handbooks, and in which it is often very difficult to distinguish between what is said and what is shown, ranging from signs to artefacts, and so on. Many elements employed by *Progressive Grocer* are neither words nor objects but rather a hybrid of the two, which we could call "wordjects" and which are best illustrated, as we saw, in the photonovelas, readers' testimonies, models and cartoons.

In fact, words, things and people work together, just as what occurs with PowerPoint software (Yates and Orlikowski, 2007). From this point of view, the idea of "felicity conditions" is both excellent and subject to caution. It is excellent because it indicates that words are always "indexed" to real situations; what words mean and do is deeply rooted in their objective counterpart (Latour, 1996b). However, the idea of felicity conditions is questionable, to the extent that this expression suggests a "given" situation, distinct from the words that refer to it (Denis and Pontille, 2010). *Progressive Grocer* shows instead that such conditions can be created, transformed, "uttered", articulated in the language itself – see the personal testimonies and photographs. Words and things do not belong to two separate universes – language on one side, the world on the other – even if they were folded back on one another by virtue of performative utterances. Some actors are smart enough to mix and link them within a broader language, using an uninterrupted circularity: things build words that build things that build "wordjects". In *Progressive Grocer*, what is performed comes both before and after the words. Reality is as much the starting point as it is the horizon of *Progressive Grocer*'s rhetoric, and vice versa.

As soon as language is extended to the world itself, signs are consigned to their total materiality, as soon as we emphasise the grammar linking words and things, as soon as we take what is cultural and economic as two interconnected sets of vocabularies and artefacts (McFall, 2008), performativity is performed. This is *Progressive Grocer*'s great lesson. What is involved in the "book of magic sales", drawings and text, is re-establishing the link between knowledge and practice, and re-establishing this link involves language as much as objects; it is a matter of signs and meaning, but also tools and gestures. This re-establishment relies on socio-technical "agencements" (Callon, 2005; Çalışkan and Callon, 2010). Words are not given priority. We can say or read words that do things (or do nothing – see the employee in the drawing), but we can also show things (or bodies) that operate as words (see the boss). Instead of renouncing performativity like Austin (Denis, 2006), we should instead recognise the existence of a certain type of "radical performativity" – in other words, a performativity in which signs and things, although completely different and discernible, are combined in the same universal language/society.

Acknowledgements

This chapter includes elements taken from "How to Build Displays that Sell" Franck Cochoy, *Journal of Cultural Economy*, Vol. 3, Issue 2, pp. 299–315, Taylor and Francis Ltd., reprinted by permission of the publisher.

This chapter also includes elements taken from McLean, C., Puyou, F.-R., Quattrone, P. and Thrift, N. (eds.), *Imagining Organizations*, Chapter 8, London and New York, Routledge, pp. 173–188, reprinted by permission of the publisher.

Notes

1 Under the impetus of Michel Callon (1998, 2007), this notion of performativity was of great interest to social studies on economics (MacKenzie and Millo, 2003; MacKenzie et al., 2007), which saw it as a means of moving beyond the traditional opposition between economic facts and social constructs: armed with the theory of performativity, the sociology of markets no longer tries to decide whether economic theories are true or false, real or constructed, but attempts instead to show how and under what circumstances these utterances themselves eventually shape market practices. If the notion of performativity has been so successful when applied to economic issues, it is certainly because (*inter alia*) the economic world is one of the best examples that can be given of a clear relationship between a set of words and a set of things that must be understood and transformed.

2 Nonetheless, there is one that is (almost) as good, and with good reason: the cover of the April 1923 issue of *Progressive Grocer*, which is featured in 1946 as a wonderful commemoration and as brilliant plagiarism. The original cover (see Figure 1.3)

shows a young employee in a grocer's store, so engrossed in reading a booklet entitled "how to run a retail store", that he forgets he had come to fill a pitcher of molasses (see opposite). We can measure the progress made from one illustration to the other, from the time of barrels of outdated products and the original personal service, to the time of open display and self-service of the following decades, from the time when *Progressive Grocer* was mainly interested in the way to "run a retail store", to when it is promoting, above all, the art of putting in place "displays that sell". The reflective importance of this illustration for *Progressive Grocer* is substantiated by its selection as the basis for the second caption competition organised by the magazine (see Chapter 1).

3 To put it in technical terms, illocution (the use of a word that is open to action) offers no guarantee that perlocution (the execution of an action) will occur.

4 For an argument regarding the relevance of the witchcraft metaphor to a better understanding of grocery practices, see Cochoy, 2008a.

5 This illustration was taken from a more complete advert in which the NCR asked grocers to fill in a questionnaire aimed at giving them some specific advice, with the following argument: "Alert grocers today are 'putting the question mark' upon every phase of their operation [...] asking themselves if their present methods are the best both for now and in the future. [...] The size of your store makes no difference. Without obligation to you, a National representative, experienced in the grocery field, will be glad to analyze your method of controlling the turnover of your stock, the efficiency of your clerks, and the cost of giving better service to each customer" (1945, 02, 36).

6 "Not every type of contact of human beings has a social character; this is rather confined to cases where the actor's behaviour is meaningfully oriented to that of others. For example, a mere collision of two cyclists may be compared to a natural event. On the other hand, their attempt to avoid hitting each other, or whatever insults, blows, or friendly discussion might follow the collision, would constitute 'social action'" (Weber, 1978, p. 23).

7 Although modern-day situations could demonstrate the contrary. See Cochoy (2007b) for the presence in supermarkets, and Dujarier (2014) and Koch (2012) for the extreme generalisation regarding consumers' hard labour.

8 The First World War and its effect on the American labour force had already been the subject of a similar leaflet in favour of promoting cash and carry sales, see Chapter 3.

9 It is highly significant that the rhetoric of the personal testimonies and quotations appears as from the title.

10 For excellent monographs on the introduction of self-service, see Du Gay, 2004; Kjellberg and Helgesson, 2007; Grandclément, 2008.

3 The beginnings of *Progressive Grocer*

Improving commerce before transforming it

We now know the way *Progressive Grocer* uses words, the precautions needed to read it, but also its means of representation and way of "producing" effects: showing them (producing in the theatrical sense) to perform them (producing in the industrial sense). Given that they are inseparable, we are now able to explore the methods by which commerce was mentally and physically modernised – in other words, to recreate the story of everything the magazine and its advertisers featured: everything they showcased but also promoted.

Since its inception, *Progressive Grocer* intended to *fully* deserve its name. In fact, the magazine not only made an effort to do justice to the adjective "Progressive", marking its explicit and resolute support of the unbridled dynamic of modernisation that had been sweeping America along since the beginning of the century ("Progressive Era"), but it also strived to justify its loyal commitment to the interests of the noun "Grocer", demonstrating its dual attachment to the small, independent grocer on the one hand, a fundamentally human mediation, and on the other to the central idea of "service" implicit in the former, contrary to the technological "sales without salespeople" of self-service that would come later (Grandclément, 2008) … but not necessarily from elsewhere (see below).

Progress was rightly associated with the image of an "arrow of time", meant to break from the world of multiple and contradictory ontologies from the pre-modern era, in order to make it converge, thanks to the unequivocal procedures of scientific reasoning, in a single endeavour to modernise (Latour, 1993). However, the person who aspires to pull things towards the future, even armed with a single arrow, often faces not one target but a horizon that is as blurred as it is broad, so that he has the choice of directions in which to shoot, rationally, in order to "progress". When the shooter finally releases his bow, the person observing must therefore be careful not to assume that the direction chosen was the only one possible and in line with the objective of progress (or conversely, to think that he refused to progress by choosing the wrong direction). Thus we shall see that the modernist grocery sector did, in fact, move forward, in the sense that its actors did not remain immobile, but that, on the contrary, they used every possible means to modernise their conditions. However, in order to look to the future, they did not actually choose the supposedly single path that a modernist vision of history would have imposed on them. Even para-doxically, we shall discover that from its first year, *Progressive Grocer* tried hard to find the means of moving forward by consolidating its rear: the magazine attempted to defend and promote a modern grocery sector by reinforcing its dual identity as human grocer and market service, which are the distinctive traits of its past.

More specifically, we shall see that *Progressive Grocer*'s development reveals and illustrates two peculiar meanings of the process of modernisation. Moder-nising does not necessarily mean *transforming* the world; it also means *improving* what exists. In other words, improving and transforming are two distinct and complementary aspects of any process of modernisation. In the case of the grocery sector, the first modernisation was synonymous with improvement to service, before a second, more radical movement of transformation, con-siderably influenced by the first, and which even began simultaneously, but of which it was generally unaware, came to complete it and then overtake it.

Far from being reactionary or suicidal, the service improvement approach appears, after analysis, on the contrary, as a clever way of dynamically resisting competition, in particular from chain stores, by promoting the advantages of independent commerce, rooted in a local social relationship, based on differ-entiation through quality and personal ties to the customer rather than as an anonymous price war (because of the horizontal and vertical integration stra-tegies of business adopted by the chains). This modernisation-improvement was deployed using four complementary methods. The first concerned the service itself, given the importance of good customer relationships. The second relied on the hygiene needed to accomplish the former: given that the products being sold were loose and generic, and that customers were being physically served, tackling product deterioration was a *sine qua non* condition for preserving ser-vice. The third method consisted in introducing a Taylor's logic of work rationalisation, by developing rational staff management and acquiring equip-ment such as scales, meat-cutting machines, etc. which, far from replacing the grocer, would on the contrary make him more mobile and increase his pro-ductivity. The final method involved modernising the grocery store not by removing service but by radicalising it, with the help of telephone sales and motorised deliveries.

Improving service

We have too often read the history of commerce in light of its recent devel-opment and in doing so, we have too often been the victims of what psy-chologists and economists refer to as "hindsight bias" (Fischhoff, 1975). This term refers to the illusion leading those who are its victims to consider events that actually occurred as being more likely than other courses of action avail-able to them when they took place. Today's historian has seen progress of chain stores, then the advent of self-service and found it reasonable to conclude that the weakening of service was a quasi-necessary effect of the new methods advocated by the chains, that the evolution towards sales without salespeople was inevitable, the replacement of human service by a technical medium had to take place, there was no possible or credible "rational" alternative able to resist the course of history. However, more caution might be enlightening. Admittedly, the spectacular development towards – and if not the hegemonic reign then at least the ubiquitous use of – self-service did indeed take place. However, traditional grocers had good reasons and excellent strategies for modernisation in which they believed, whilst protecting, even reinforcing, the service that was later (but is not necessarily today) considered a mark of the past. The magazine did not, therefore, stake its bet initially on modernising independent grocers by removing service but, on the contrary, on modernising service to protect independent grocers.

The choice of this paradoxical, backwards modernisation is of course a matter of expertise, materiality and above all ideas and values (Shove et al., 2012). Grocers were not only attached to their counter, foodstuffs and know-how, but in particular to the service defining their professionalism and even more so their very existence: "courtesy, service and dependable goods are absolutely necessary for the success of the small town merchant" (1922, 05, 32). Far from being only cultural, the attachment to service was linked to the gro-cer's well-understood interest, given that it strengthened community ties between the shopkeeper and his "community" (Spellman, 2009), attached customers to shops in a circle of exclusive relationships, allowed one to have an in-depth knowledge of one's customers, through credit books and delivery notebooks, which to the grocers of the time were what customer files with loyalty cards are to business today (I shall come back to this).

For all that, was the commitment to service synonymous with immobility? No, given that service could be subject to continuous improvement. This could be very simply done, for example, by applying the good advice given by Pop Keener, a retired grocer, who recommended "think[ing] about your cus-tomers, not of yourself", and remembering four important things every time a customer entered the shop: "don't be nosey, don't monopolize the conversa-tion, don't gossip – and beware the high hat" (1926, 12, 21 sq.). Service could also be improved by introducing more recent and sophisticated innovations, such as the customer satisfaction survey, as advised by an article called "Grocers Pay to Learn the Worst About Themselves", by retelling the story of a shop-keeper who decided to give a best quality ham as a prize for the best suggestion received, using a coupon system for collecting customers' complaints and other ideas (1922, 05, 27).

However, this attachment to service, in its simplest and most traditional form, does not mean that the magazine was blind to the development of the market environment and to alternative selling methods. On the contrary, *Pro-gressive Grocer* shows it paid close attention to the changes affecting the organi-sation of the commercial relationship, as demonstrated in a very detailed article published in the January issue of 1925 and dedicated to one of the almost Shakespearean issues perplexing grocers at the time: "Shall I change to cash and carry or stick to credit and delivery?" (1925, 01, 21 sq.). The cash and carry system, mainly used by chain stores and mentioned by all historians of the sector, was in fact one of the main innovations to upset the balance of the retail trade at the turn of the twentieth century. Admittedly, it was not yet the organisation of sales as self-service, given that cash and carry only concerned the method of paying and carrying merchandise once purchases had been completed, without necessarily affecting the way they were chosen and collected in the shop, and thus without questioning the retention of the systematic mediation of the human salesperson. Cash and carry nonetheless destabilised the previous arrangement of the commercial relationship, given that it ran counter to its two traditional pillars: credit (replaced by "cash" payments), and delivery (displaced by takeaway sales). The article's title clearly highlights the underlying dilemma of the alternative offered, between the hope of an appealing prospect (leading to a reduction in costs, a competitive price advantage and increased profits) and the fear of a worrying rupture of the very strong ties with the clientele (resulting from a loss of the human element and above all control, given how much credit, service and delivery created if not an exclusive relationship at least a very strong one between the grocer and his customers – one that was admittedly detrimental to the latter, who were prisoners of the salesman's social and commercial control; Deutsch, 2001; Grandclément, 2011).

As I have already suggested, knowledge of the future can often paradoxically obscure the analysis of the past. We know that chain stores were largely based on the cash and carry model and that they proliferated at the expense of small business, attached to the opposite model of credit and delivery, significantly called "service stores" (Deutsch, 2001). It is very tempting, then, to see cash and carry as one of the reasons behind the relegation of independent retailers, who were unable or did not want to adapt to the times. However, to reason in this way is to make an error of causal attribution: the actors at the time remind us that the weakening of service was less the effect of chains, of which there were infinitely fewer at the beginning of the century, than there were small, independent grocers,[1] and which were therefore themselves incapable, at the time, of producing alone the changes attributed to them,[2] and more a specific effect of the First World War which created a shortage of labour and consequently led the American State, rather than chain stores, to promote a form of sale to all those in commerce that was able to offset the consequence of the temporary lack of service:

> There is no question that the war has promoted the cash and carry business. When the Government preached "carry your bundles, pay cash and make a saving", many people were for the first time taught to pay cash and carry their purchases home.
>
> (1925, 01, 74)

Depending on whether we present cash and carry as a business technique imposed by store chains or as a temporary governmental response to the difficulties of war, our appraisal of the mechanisms involved and the directions to take changes completely. In the first case, we might tend to see the signs of a fundamental economic movement that is perhaps hard to resist, especially given the pressure on prices permitted by the cost reductions inherent in the weakening of service; in the second, however, we are confronted with a temporary political solution to a short-term problem, and the idea of a structural movement might be reversed: once the peace had been re-established, once the men had come back from the front, was it not most likely that things would return to "normality", even if this happened slowly? In other words, are there not good reasons to think that the modern development of business would move in the direction of increased service rather than it disappearing?

In any case, it was this theory, of a societal trend towards the intensification of service, which was supported, even almost ten years after the armistice, by a text entitled "Woman's New Freedom and the Service Grocer" (1927, 06, 22 sq.). The author does not present service as a vestige of the past but as an expression of modernity, like an extension of the socio-technical changes underway affecting other aspects of society, and more particularly as a response adapted to the increasing emancipation of women (at least in terms of carrying out daily chores), or even as an appropriate tool for supporting this new freedom:

> Housewives will keep on demanding more service and more personal leisure. Do you imagine they'll buy service of every other kind and then make an exception in buying food supplies? They're hardly so inconsistent. They get light over wires, and gas and water through pipes – delivered to the house and paid for by the month, thank you. And they have the ice man, the laundry man, the newspaper boy. There I've named you six forms of service as staple as sugar. And the forms are multiplying. Don't make me laugh by saying that the housewives of the future won't want credit service and delivery service for groceries. They will *demand* those services. [... T]he grocer of the future will give service with backbone in it: deliveries on exact schedule, as trains run; credit payments, as exact to agreement as spot cash is.
>
> (1927, 06, 25)

Another article, published two years previously, espoused the same view, believing it could detect a decline in "carry" sales, and by highlighting how much the new telephone technology[3] favoured the development of service. The article on the cash and carry dilemma (1925, 01, 21 sq.) took a similar view, believing it could discern a trend towards the return to credit, not only because this practice was rooted in people's habits but above all because it was used in large shops:[4] one could therefore, according to the author, expect a tendency on the part of consumers to demand that they be offered the same service for food provisions as provided by these more prestigious shops for other products.

More fundamentally, the article aimed to support the modernity of service based on a very pragmatic, systematic and measured examination of the situation. It did this first by attempting to dispel the false hope of a 10% to 15% fall in price. To support its views, it quoted a recent study by the Harvard Bureau of Business Research. This procedure was in itself a two-fold sign of modernity: on the one hand, the argument uses a modern method of calculation and scientific expertise, meant to establish a truth that is generally applicable; on the other, the Harvard Bureau of Business Research, created barely ten years before, was at the time the very first scientific laboratory in the history of American management sciences (Cochoy, 1998).

The study referred to was carried out by the National Association of Retail Grocers. It shows that operating costs rose to 14.7% for forty cash and carry shops, and 19.7% for traditional shops giving credit. The gains, in terms of costs, brought by the new method of sales were thus barely 4%, whereas average profit was 1.8% for all shops. This small difference might seem unexpected, given the savings on delivery rates and interest rates allowed by reducing service, but it can be explained by the increased spending on advertising that cash and carry stores were obliged to do in order to capture a more volatile clientele. The author also points out that the most profitable type of sale in the end depends on the additional turnover that can be generated by selling merchandise 4% more cheaply. Instead of attempting to make a very general judgement, concluding with the advisability or not of cash and carry sales, it relates this calculation to specific local situations that are likely to support one of the alternatives: either service and delivery or cash and carry sales.

The author scrutinises all social, geographical, technological and even meteorological circumstances that are likely to weigh in the balance, for the one or the other. Therefore, cash and carry works when addressing working-class customers, for example, near a railway centre where employees receive their pay on a fixed date, when dealing with farmers with steady incomes, in particular in the dairy sector, or if one were considering the "penny-saving class" and other "bargain hunters". In New York, where there were 1,100 families per block, the corner grocery store got most of its sales without having to deal with a high demand for service. Conversely, in low-density areas with dispersed individual housing, customers are on average much further from the closest shop, meaning that in such an environment a cash and carry barely has a chance of making headway. The author, an excellent analyst, observes that the car "is a factor", given that its generalisation favours takeaway sales. Lastly, the weather plays a contrary role, given that an unfavourable climate leads families, above all the wealthy, to prefer delivery. The article concludes this synoptic examination, clearly illustrated using eloquent thumbnails (see Figure 3.1) by giving no definitive answer to the initial question: there will always be two groups of customers, those who are interested in price and those looking for service and quality, and therefore there will always be two types of shop to meet the needs of both types of customer. All in all, the article uses a modern

If you are located where the conditions and types of people shown above prevail, a cash and carry type of business will flourish

If your customers live under the above conditions, then it might be well to stick to the service and credit method of doing business

Figure 3.1 Credit and delivery, or cash and carry?
Source: 1925, 01, 22; and 1925, 01, 23

way of envisaging modernisation, not as a belief, value or ideology, but as a rational adaptation to the local conditions of the grocery trade.

The belief in the modernity of service, stated either forcefully or in a more measured tone, is supported elsewhere in the magazine with some remarkable examples, based either on an individual or a more collective logic.

The individual logic is the roll of honour, the "best practices", the example of the grocers who succeed thanks to the further development of service. This is the case of a shop near Greenwich Village in New York, which by thinking ahead, managed to disprove the general argument developed above regarding that city. Admittedly, this retailer did face a competitor practising aggressive pricing but instead of following him down this suicidal path, for which three other neighbourhood colleagues had suffered the consequences, he chose to focus resolutely on service in his grocery store, in particular through differentiation by supplying a small amount of fruit and vegetables (1923, 08, 14 sq.). The individual logic is also that of innovation, like that of this grocer, who proudly recounts: "We meet cash and carry prices, yet give credit and delivery" (1925, 02, 9 sq.). In order to perform this tour de force, the grocer developed a "four-way system", a genuine compromise between the different sales methods: the solution consisted in distinguishing between cash and credit payments on the one hand, and takeaway (carry) sales and delivery on the other. Service was only paid for by those who benefited from it. All stock prices were shown on a basis of cash and carry sales, but sale on credit was granted to several hundred customers for an additional 3% (for a maximum of 30 days). For all deliveries on orders of less than $4, 10 cents was added. Therefore, "everyone [gets] just what she paid for".[5]

The group logic behind promoting service consists, for independent grocers, in joining forces to defend their sales model. The magazine thus mentions the initiative of a group of shopkeepers from Dallas, Texas, who pooled their efforts to teach consumers about the appropriate use of service (1926, 01, 32). More specifically, this city's Service Grocers' Association, which at the time had grown from 25 to 150 members, carried out a cooperative advertising campaign listing the ten advantages of the service-based grocery sector: time saved for the housewife; less physical effort; the offer of a full delivery service, whatever the conditions; saving on the drudgery of parking and food shopping; the offer of a suitable phone service; the offer of service at no additional cost; the guarantee that merchandise will be provided; benefits in terms of cost reductions from telephone orders;[6] the offer of a full range of stock and thus a vast choice; and the offer of personalised service.

A group of retailers from Cleveland embarked on a similar mission, aimed at selling the idea of service to their customers, by claiming, for example, that "the individual grocer is more than just a grocer; he is your friend and neighbor", and by asking customers "Why burden yourself by carrying your packages home when the individual grocer will give you service?" The corresponding campaign was supported by an emblem guaranteeing "quality, courtesy, honest weight, personal attention and service" (1926, 07, 56).

We therefore understand how looking at the development of commerce through the eyes of today, considering self-service as an expression of modernity, and thus interpreting the defence of traditional service as at best an ultra-conservative and at worst a reactionary attitude, is completely anachronistic and even devoid of meaning. At the beginning of the twentieth century, the paths to follow for modernisation were not yet fixed. The promotion of service, far from conservative or a simple defensive strategy, came with a series of advances and innovations, able, on the contrary, to make it one of the distinctive traits of the modern economy. That economy was concerned, as we shall see, with expanding the benefits of the technical assistance at work to shop staff and customers, to the extent that improving service might even seem a lot more modern than doing away with it. In order to understand the history of commerce, it is in fact very important to bear in mind that all stakeholders – chains as well as small, independent grocers, or in any event their spokespeople and spearheads such as the promoters of the progressive grocery sector – were involved in a vast programme of modernisation, following a very Tourainian logic of "movement against movement". Of course, chains used management principles specific to them (standardisation, centralised purchases and management) that independent retailers by definition refused, even if they did not hesitate to group together in order to defend their interests, carry out joint campaigns or undertake group purchasing to benefit from better prices (Spellman, 2009). However, chains and independent retailers used the same tool box, bought the same equipment from the same suppliers, adopted the same solutions, and could thus implement innovations allowing them to develop the same kind of sale or, on the contrary, find a way to promote their distinctive advantages.

Getting rid of vermin

Nonetheless, the corollary of preserving service was the perpetuation of a unique kind of sale, where the supply of bulk products, weighed and packaged on site, by hand, if non-exclusive, was a question of choice. Yet, safeguarding this method of sale posed serious challenges, not only in terms of time, cost and labour, but above all in terms of hygiene. In other words, maintaining the sale of foodstuffs through the intervention of a grocer required a serious improvement in food safety.

At the beginning of the 1920s, *Progressive Grocer* initially focused on ensuring its readership understood the problem and to this end did not hesitate to resort to the most spectacular dramatisation.

In a series of articles that appeared on the topic, we thus learn that insects cause considerable damage, not only in financial terms, with estimated annual losses of no less than $200 million, but also in terms of ruined reputations – an effect with incalculable consequences but perhaps a matter of even greater concern (1923, 06, 12 sq.). The magazine was careful not to give into the temptation to see this as unavoidable or to deny the responsibility of the grocers concerned, by refusing to believe that the vermin were inside the merchandise. Admittedly, the problem might have originated higher up the distribution chain but, as unfair as it might seem, the last person involved would always be held responsible. The magazine therefore exacerbates the grocers' level of concern by making it clear that for them this is a matter of fighting against an almost invisible enemy, especially in the form of microscopic eggs such as those of the American flour beetle which lodges itself in the cracks of barrels, thus leading to a risk of the infestation spreading quickly in the

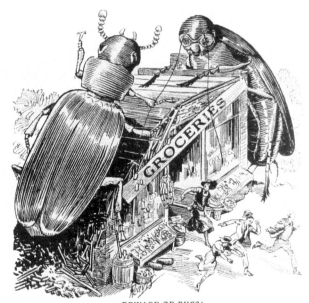

BEWARE OF BUGS!

Millions of these bugs are eating away the grocer's reputation and trade. They get into even the cleanest groceries, and once in, it is difficult and costly to get them out. They thrive on tiny crumbs and scraps which are overlooked in cleaning Keep them out and you save your share of the $200,000,000 damage which they cause every year. Let them in and you must pay for their upkeep

Figure 3.2 Beware of bugs
Source: 1923, 07, 51

summer months in shops lacking modern methods for regulating heat and humidity which, by contrast, large warehouses had (1923, 07, 49).

These dangers and their possible disastrous consequences were identified in the editorial section of a magazine which, moreover, published during the same period many adverts for insecticides or rat poisons. These adverts proliferated like the vermin they were intended to combat, rather like the antivirus software contaminating today's IT world: the adverts for the leading insecticide, "Fly-Tox" (1924, 02, 94–95), faced competition from its competitors "Tanglefoot" (1924, 06, 97), "Flit" (a product by the chemical product division of the Standard Oil Co., 1924, 01, 84b–84c) or Lowell (1925, 08, 98), not to mention the solutions aimed at other pests, such as "Rat-Tox" (1926, 02, 121), mousetraps (1927, 06, 124) or fly swatters (1927, 06, 136), or even "Giant-Lye", a miracle product that came from a long line of almost magical elixirs to which ancient America held the secret, meant to kill flies, like the Brave Little Tailor, capable of "kill[ing] seven at one blow",[7] as well as stripping paint and plumbing, slaying rats, disinfecting, cleaning, sterilising and deodorising.[8]

Nevertheless, and contrary to all expectations, we notice that there is a rather remarkable disassociation between these curative products and the line adopted in the magazine, which takes the very reasonable, independent and virtuous

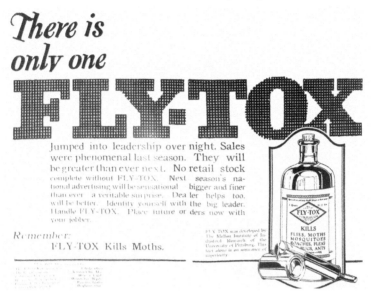

Figure 3.3 There is only one Fly-Tox
Source: 1924, 12, 54–55

decision to adopt an exclusively preventative approach, perhaps to build readership trust in the reliability and importance of the new medium, but also to establish its authority and usefulness by offering advice. In fact, it is due to the lack of any alternative for getting rid of a possible infestation, other than "thorough and costly fumigation" that one should do everything to avoid such extremes by implementing appropriate preventative strategies, in line with the sound principle that "It's easier [...] to prevent a disease than to cure it" (1923, 07, 49).

A first step, of course, consists of intervening as early as possible: thus the magazine recommends close inspection of merchandise upon receipt, particularly grain. Although the eggs are not visible to the naked eye, there are several tell-tale signs of infestation, such as fine, silky filaments between the grains, or seeing movements or small holes on the grain's surface appearing overnight. Although packaged products, in particular cereals, are healthy at the point of production, because they are heated sufficiently to destroy the eggs, they should nonetheless be checked to ensure they are not damaged, that there are no spiders' webs, little holes or stains which are likely to indicate the presence of vermin.

However, the main steps concern the shop's daily life and come down to implementing three very clearly stipulated rules: "(1) sell the old stock first; (2) buy in small quantities and as often as needed; (3) keep the store thoroughly perfectly clean at all times" (1923, 07, 50). By systematically sliding the packages at the back of the shelves to the front, one can ensure that any merchandise that might contain insect eggs is sold before they hatch or reproduce (at the risk, which the magazine fails to mention, of passing the problem onto the customers) (1923, 06, 16). Purchasing in small quantities would not only be "a method of protecting yourself against food-destroying pests", but a means of "increasing your turnover", as well as "giving your trade fresher and better food and thus building your reputation and your profits" (1923, 06, 16).

As regards regularly cleaning the shop, which is done simply using soap and hot water, not to mention ensuring staff do not leave out nooks that are difficult to reach, this action "makes it unnecessary to use any [other] disinfectants" (1923, 07, 71).[9] In the event of contamination, the magazine prescribes inspecting every item of stock individually, in order to find the slightest sign of infection. Therefore, it is only as a last resort, in case prevention has failed, that the magazine mentions modern methods of disinfection, such as gasoline, kerosene, or even carbon tetrachloride, carbon disulphide or sulphur dioxide – poisons that the magazine is careful to warn are dangerous if inhaled, mentioning also the risks of explosion with carbon disulphide, without of course knowing the extent to which its caution was premonitory, as most of these products were subsequently banned for non-industrial use.

Taking care of staff and optimising equipment: a Taylorian improvement

Amongst the elements that contributed to ensuring shop hygiene, at least in terms of appearance, I could also have mentioned a small article presenting a clever device allowing a grocer to keep his apron looking clean, thanks to a flap of cloth he could use when touching or carrying dirty objects, and then turn inside out when he intended to present himself immaculately and handle non-soiling objects (1923, 08, 30). Despite its probably anecdotal, short-lived nature, this little innovation had the advantage of pointing out another dimension to the modernisation of service – that is, the care put into improving the work of employees in a physical way.

Once again, we are confronted with an endeavour which, far from focusing on doing away with human service, aimed on the contrary to improve and assist it, and make it progress. As is highlighted by an academic in the magazine's pages, "Employees are important – they can make or break your store" (1926, 06, 35 sq.). Therefore, fighting the competition, joining the progressive grocers' movement, did not (yet) mean cutting staff; it was rather a matter of improving their performance.

This concern was not only applicable to the grocer's stomach, as our reversible apron has just shown, but extended from head to toe, in the literal sense, via the hands. In 1927, the magazine published a long article aimed at raising grocers' awareness: "Care of the Feet for Employees Who Stand Up All Day" (1927, 02, 16 sq.). The year before it presented a device for helping grocers' heads, brilliantly anticipating the cognitive artefacts dear to contemporary specialists of equipped cognition (Norman, 1991; Lave et al., 1984). George

Reuter, a grocer from Rochester in New York state, thus displays a voucher system with a to-do list for the shop, such as items to clean, objects to repair, etc. Every time, a ticket specifying the nature of the task and name of the employee responsible is filled out so that nothing is forgotten and everything is perfectly monitored (1926, 11, 43 sq.). Apart from these articles, we cannot leave out all the adverts showing, throughout the pages, work gloves by Coshocton Glove Co. (1922, 07, 92), Indianapolis gloves (1925, 10, 104) or Twin-seam Leather Palm Work Gloves (1925, 11, 111), claiming to take the greatest care of grocers' hands. By embodying the opposing dimensions of the body and mind, jointly involved in the sales activity, the head-to-toe approach makes it possible to order, quite effectively, the areas where the effort to modernise grocery work can be made, between training staff operations and the acquisition of equipment that would help them physically.

Edward S. Johns (with a PhD from the University of Buffalo) wrote an article that drew attention to the importance of the human factor in the grocery sector (1926, 06, 35). It focused less on the work itself and more on issues to be taken into consideration when recruiting. Notwithstanding, it emphasised the importance of identifying the employees' teachable nature, of taking their ambition into account as a sign of their subsequent professional abilities. Elsewhere in the magazine, the actual improvement of a grocer's work as such is not, for all that, ignored. Thus, a text entitled "Some things worth knowing about wrapping and tying packages" was intended to make shop owners aware of the art of and way to wrap merchandise, choose quality paper, cut it, fold it, place and tie the string, and hand everything over to the customer, with the help of instructive drawings (1923, 08, 46 sq.; see Figure 3.4).

As earlier, with the issue of hygiene, concern in connection with human work is closely linked to selling loose products, which was not yet being radically called into question, in favour of cans and pre-packaged products (even if both were already clearly very much present): it is precisely because of the belief that what existed, the selling of bulk products through a salesperson, could still be modernised, that we are led to do everything possible to improve the conditions of this type of mediation. The article is therefore careful to show the development of non-packaged sales over time. It points out that in the past, products as fragile as meat were handed unwrapped to customers, as if the bulk sales prevailing in shops continued on the consumer side. The proposal to wrap at the point of sale, once the merchandise has been chosen and sold, therefore clearly appeared not as a substitute for service but on the contrary, as an extension of the concern to help customers once outside the shop: it was a matter of ensuring that "When a customer purchases an article at your store he is entitled to have it wrapped in a manner that will enable him to carry the package safely home" (1923, 08, 50).

Far from being limited to a single article on paper-folding techniques and tying string, this type of concern recurs throughout an entire series of adverts for innovative devices such as sticky tape reels (1922, 08, 44–45), paper reels (1925, 08, 101), cylindrical cardboard packages (1923, 05, 77; 1924, 01, 102) or

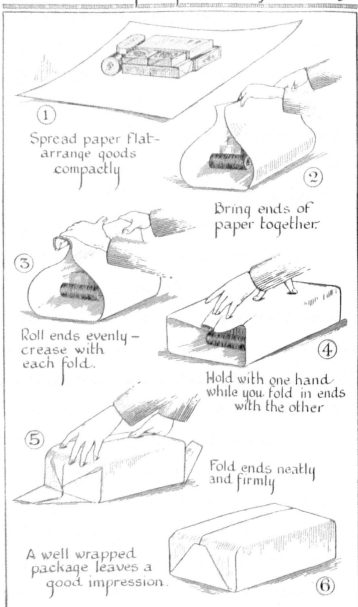

Figure 3.4 How to wrap a package neatly
Source: 1923, 08, 46

other "paraffined boxes" (1924, 06, 99) meant to store liquid or wet products, or Nashua gummed and coated paper (1922, 09, 83), which aimed really to emphasise that there was paper and paper, by specifying the financial risks of the choice involved: "Hundreds – thousands – of dollars are being wasted in your store every year through inefficient package wrapping." The article adds to its sales pitch, like so many other adverts for new products at the time (Strasser, 1989), by providing a small manual entitled "Save the waste" on how to make packages.

Nor can we forget the impressive advert by the Continental Paper & Bag Mills Co. for Flamingo paper, which is unfortunately impossible to show in its original form, despite that being what made the advert so striking: the advert actually consisted in printing the publicity as a costly four-page spread, on the very thick paper they were hoping to sell (1926, 07, 85) – a method predating a marketing use of language performativity which we come across much later in more contemporary forms, and which consists in mixing what is said and done in order to reinforce the effectiveness of speech (Cochoy, 2011a). This innovation was not, moreover, limited to advertising material and techniques given that it could be inverted: after having printed its own advert to sell its paper, the Continental Paper & Bag Mills Co. offered to print this same paper for advertising purposes. The company was in fact one of the first, together with its competitor Jap Rose (1923, 08, 35), to sell "advertising bags", meant to turn utilitarian packaging, for protecting the product, into a promotional vehicle aimed at informing the customer:[10]

> if your bags are just containers, they are only doing half a job. Continental Advertising Bags are better advertising than lots of space that merchants pay real money for. For your *printed* bag goes directly to the consumer. Into the home.
>
> (1026, 07, 86)

The task of improving a grocer's moves, ranging from training to the description of good practices and to their technical extension, with the help of paper and other tricks of the trade, makes us of course think of Taylorism, that essential component of the Progressive Era (Carson, 2011), a movement which we know was not only at the time taking over the world of American production but also that of marketing spaces and marketing (Cochoy, 1994). Nonetheless, apart from the somewhat anecdotal cases of "to-do lists" and the art of packaging just mentioned, as a whole *Progressive Grocer* offers little regarding the codification, standardisation and division of a grocer's work, other than when the magazine refers to major roles such as telephone operator or deliverer, with which we shall deal later. This relative absence of the Taylorisation of work is undoubtedly due less to a resistance vis-à-vis modern techniques, given that the magazine's profession is, on the contrary, to embrace and relay them, than to the erratic nature of commerce, far more subject to external hazards, to whims of demand, and thus to an ineluctable requirement to be versatile and flexible, in particular in the case of small shops, less suited than others to a division of labour.

As a result, optimising the grocer's work was less to do with codifying and dividing tasks and more with improving their efficiency, thanks to the labour-saving effect of certain pieces of equipment, as is incidentally shown by the increasing number of contributions dedicated to new tools that are likely to help shop owners in their daily activities. In fact, it is regarding these tools that the connection to Taylorism appears almost explicitly, particularly in a series of three articles dedicated to the subject of shop equipment. These articles, which appeared in the summer of 1926, were all written by Carl Dipman (1926, 07, 11 sq.; 1926, 08, 23 sq.; 1926, 09, 41 sq.). This author was a central figure in the magazine's history, who after writing his first text in *Progressive Grocer* as a simple journalist in November 1922, became associate editor in March 1923, then editor in June 1924 – in other words, two years prior to publishing these articles – remaining in this central role as editor until his death on 22 July 1954 (1954, 09, 36–37). Given that he knew the field of the grocery sector and the people involved,

> Carl Dipman reasoned that the food trade could be best served not by preachments, not by sermonizing, not by theorizing – but by seeking out successful men and ideas, by investigating and analyzing and by factual reporting to the readers of PROGRESSIVE GROCER.
>
> (1954, 09, 36)

As we shall see, Carl Dipman adopted an aesthetic and visual approach to retail sales: he was concerned with shop layout, improving displays, appropriate shop furniture and adequate lighting, rather than price setting, cost management, and other management strategies or economic issues.

The second article of the series of three that interests us is dedicated to ascertaining the optimal equipment for a given shop. This is the article where the link between new commercial equipment and Taylor's approach to the work of a grocer appears most distinctly, even though no direct reference is made to the father of scientific management. This connection can be seen in the title, which immediately presents the subject broached as a problem of optimisation: "How much – or little – equipment should your store have?" (1926, 08, 23 sq.). This point of view is even more clearly explained in the body of the text: "Over-equipment eats into the store profits. Under-equipment makes for inefficiency and waste. Somewhere there is a happy medium".[11] The article clearly links the question of equipment to that of labour efficiency, given that it examines "labor and time saving equipment, that is, *equipment that promotes efficiency*". The question of optimising salary costs is even more important, the text points out, as wage levels have never been so high. Carl Dipman then mentions the time factor, in the purest Taylorian style, by reminding us of the importance of every second, the problem caused by managing busy periods, the particular need to satisfy customers who come at the peak times. To assess these difficulties and the urgency of the solutions to be implemented, he calls on grocers to suggest to their local professional association that they acquire a pedometer. This device was to the grocery sector what the stopwatch was to Taylor's factory, in that it allowed one to record the number of steps taken by staff every day and thus to make comparisons between different shops. "You will find," assures Carl Dipman, "that in one store, the same amount of sales requires twice as many steps than in another" (1926, 08, 25).

We then have a better understanding of the paradox raised in the first article of the series, whose aim was to show that money could be made by spending a lot, given that it deals with the acquisition of new and expensive equipment (1926, 07, 11 sq.). Admittedly, this equipment represents a cost, but one should not ignore the symmetrical cost of service, in particular the time and workload of employees. Furthermore, states the author, there is equipment that *"keep[s] down the cost of selling"*, or more specifically, "equipment that saves your time, your clerks' time, or that eliminates waste *in the process of selling"*.

What equipment is Carl Dipman referring to? We discover the list reading through a slightly fanciful figure quoted in the previous article, based on a panel of undoubtedly large shops, if we refer to their average annual turnover of $60,000, but neither their number, nor the sampling principles involved are disclosed. These shops, which invested an average of $2,786 in their equipment, owned, again on average, 1.2 cash registers, 1.1 adding machines, 1 coffee mill, 1 meat slicer, 3 counter scales and 1.5 meat choppers (1926, 8, 26). The inventory of elements involved is much more important to us than the numbers. In fact, we notice that the items listed are above all service-oriented devices: they are tools that accompany, relieve and reduce work but which do not replace it; they are objects that in no way call into question the shop's general organisation and sales system, with its counter, bulk products, service, credit and delivery. In other words, we are clearly in the presence of tools aiming to improve rather than change what exists; the purpose of these machines is to extend and preserve the work of the grocer, and not replace it (admittedly, productivity gains always look to reduce the labour but at least this operation was not meant to change jobs or make them redundant).

Significantly, this list considerably increases the range of objects individually or collectively promoted throughout the pages, in adverts which are the life-blood of the magazine, and which include, for example, the almost complete collection in the catalogue of the equipment manufacturer Dayton, a branch of IBM, one of *Progressive Grocer*'s regular customers, with its scales, coffee mills, meat-slicing and chopping machines, and so forth.

No doubt, there was a risk that all these devices, meant to improve service, ironically would eventually reduce or even replace it in favour of an entirely different sales system, especially as, at the same time and as we shall soon see, they were accompanied by other supplies promoting the "display" – a type of visual presentation of products predating the sales without salespeople that would follow (Grandclément, 2008). However, for the moment, the work

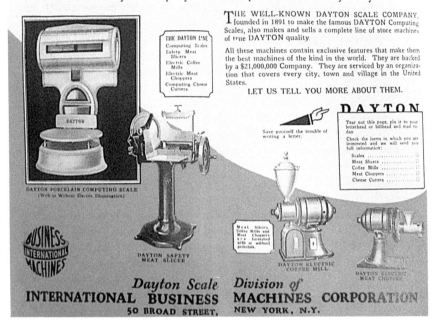

Figure 3.5 Dayton – A complete line of Store Equipment
Source: 1925, 11, 40–41

saved thanks to the equipment could be employed elsewhere, in places where other tools help reduce it.

Yet, of the tools able to extend and improve traditional service, none was more fundamentally human, modern and adapted to commercial interaction than the telephone (Mallard, 2011). This almost magical innovation only makes sense for the human voice because it has the ability to carry (and receive) it far beyond the confines of the shop limits, as a grocer from North Carolina proudly states in a personal testimony in which this professional intends to explain how he and his team sold "$100,000 worth of groceries by telephone", and to what extent "service is the keynote of phone selling" (1926, 10, 22).

From sales over the counter to sales over the phone

The telephone fitted so well in *Progressive Grocer*'s modern grocery project that the magazine, in its first year, did not hesitate to give it pride of place as the publication's front-page headline (Figure 3.6).

We are far too used to reading the history of business through the prism of the experience of very large companies, no doubt because these names have stuck more than those of smaller or shorter-lived actors, or simply because it is

The PROGRESSIVE GROCER

SEPTEMBER, 1922 $1.00 A YEAR

**A Butterick Business Publication.
Circulation more than 50,000 monthly**

Figure 3.6 The grocer on the phone as front-page news
Source: 1922, 09, cover

these behemoths whose archives are still available and are most accessible. Traditional studies of "business history" are thus brimming with stories where giants such as Sears, Roebuck & Company, Montgomery Ward, A & P, Woolworth or Macy's have starring roles (Chandler, 1977; Strasser, 1989; Tedlow, 1990). Nonetheless, even instances where sales activities supposedly focused on individuals, such as those of mail order houses or department stores, reveal a local history driven by smaller establishments, as shown notably by Joël Jornod's ongoing thesis on the case of Switzerland. The history of the American grocery sector allows us to go into much more detail, by teaching us that at least since the beginning of the twentieth century, many independent grocers made considerable efforts to present themselves as local-level micro mail-order companies. Therefore, the phone appeared as a powerful tool for improving and extending service, not only by making it possible to receive, prepare and deliver orders remotely, but also by promoting active customer market research or the sale of additional products, thanks to the development and use of sophisticated instruments and organisational principles, such as real customer files and organising telephone-assisted sales in quasi-call centres.

Just as we might have imagined that the telephone, in its early stages, was used above all by large companies, we might also think that at the time, the use of the telephone was in the main uncomplicated, sustained by demand: answering unexpected calls; serving customers by inventing a way of purchasing that had not necessarily been thought of until then. Yet, this is not the case, or rather, although it is impossible to measure the extent of its demand-driven use, it is nonetheless easy to understand the extent to which the telephone was promoted as an instrument for the supply side, and more precisely as a tool for professionals in the modern grocery sector (grocers and *Progressive Grocer* included), to act to acquire customers.

The use of the telephone as a market research tool was the subject of many precise personal testimonies. We can quote, for example, one of the very first articles by Carl Dipman, presenting the innovative methods of the Burns & Lutz Company of Kansas City (1923, 04, 16 sq.). The two former simple salesmen who founded the business, which employed no fewer than thirty people, "decided to take service into the very homes of the people of their neighborhood" thanks to the telephone, by calling their customers to inquire about their possible requests. Far from confining themselves to calling existing customers, this endeavour was, on the contrary, built on the resolute cold calling of new customers. They systematically used a grid system to identify potential contacts in the neighbourhood, and even identified new occupants after a move, first done door-to-door, then by telephone, after having asked people's permission to contact them directly, being careful to ask them when and how often they preferred being called (daily, two or three times a week). The company was thus able to add one to four customers a day to its previous clientele.

The concern to reach and serve customers from a distance, systematically and on a massive scale, shows once again how the idea at the time was not to reduce service, or even to preserve its current state, but rather to modernise and extend it. Cases similar to this abound. Elsewhere we learn that another shop made a habit of calling at least ten people every day who had not yet bought anything (1923, 09, 94). We discover that a grocer in North Carolina, whose personal testimony is proudly called "How we sell 100,000 dollars of groceries by telephone", deliberately chose "to go out after business in a most aggressive way", "instead of waiting for customers to come into our store, as many retail establishments do" (1926, 10, 22).

The actors at the time attempted not only to sell their products over the phone but, in order to do this, tried to promote the telephone to sell their products. This endeavour to "sell telephone sales" was the subject of individual initiatives, as seen with the example of a grocer who filled his window display with handsets and signs tempting customers to use this medium to do their shopping – an example that *Progressive Grocer* of course invites its readers to copy (1923, 04, 12). However, above all, it was the subject of a collective promotion endeavour, which in 1925 organised a major campaign entitled "Phone for Food".

This nation-wide campaign was first presented to grocers in an article whose title, once again, very clearly highlights the link between using the telephone and improving service ("Here's a campaign of tremendous importance to service grocers"), even if its promoters were careful to point out that the campaign had nothing to do with the issue of cash or credit sales, as the telephone could be used to support all types of sale (1925, 05, 9 sq.). More specifically, this was a campaign that had been launched and inaugurated by the National Wholesale Grocers' Association, and which also enjoyed the support of the executive committee of the National Retail Grocers' Association and the personal backing of the chairman and secretary of the Retail Association (1925, 05, 9). This campaign appeared as one of the most suitable ways of fighting competition, particularly that of takeaway sales. *Progressive Grocer* even presents it explicitly, in the very first lines of a second article, as a genuine counter-campaign aimed at adopting the opposite view of the government's effort which, during the war, had backed takeaway sales: "A few years ago, millions of housewives were taught to carry home their packages." The objective was to "re-establish" the demand for delivery that existed before the war (1925, 06, 23). The telephone was obviously promoted as an efficient weapon to achieve this: "The campaign is to popularize phoning for food and to teach the housewife the economies and convenience of service grocers." The magazine announced that "the country is to be flooded with advertising telling the housewives to 'Phone for Food'" (1925, 05, 9 sq.).

In order to achieve these objectives, the campaign suggested involving grocers in the promotion of the telephone by presenting them with "ways and means of increasing your telephone business" (1925, 06, 23 sq.), and by providing them with a set of materials likely to support this objective. More specifically, the committee responsible for the campaign made a whole range of window display decorations, posters, postage stamps on bills and letters, envelopes with the campaign's letterhead available to the participants, not to mention adverts to be reproduced as leaflets or small ads in newspapers. Of course, all of this was not provided free but even so, only at cost price: $2 for 1,000 stamps, $5 for 1,000 envelopes, $1 for a set of five posters, $7.5 for help installing a special display, etc. As we can see, it was not just a matter of promoting the telephone but the campaign that went with it as well, with one supposed to support the other.

What we are witnessing here is a typical case of an American movement that is both collective and individual, similar to what is described elsewhere regarding the history of marketing (Cochoy, 2014), and of which we shall discover another version later, with sales of canned food. This type of endeavour, far from consisting in projecting a collective watchword "from above", entirely funded by those at the top and which it was hoped would be obediently followed by those at the bottom, relied on the joint participation of both levels. It was more a matter of bringing together personal projects into a collective one, combining all of the participants' resources, including financial, without which nothing would be possible, ensuring top-down success by very actively motivating the bottom-up. Far from inventing the commercial use of the telephone, the campaign gambled more on a large number of actors broadly anticipating it, and on its ability to prolong, unite and bring about the convergence of the individual and pre-existing interests of these same actors, such as grocers, of course, but also wholesalers, the trade associations of both, not to mention manufacturers and consumers.

Progressive Grocer passes on a real avalanche of practical advice on how to give substance to the movement. Grocers are thus encouraged to speak about it locally, tell their customers that phoning for food saves both their time and that of the grocer, that the same care is given to telephone orders as to direct purchases, that they only have to give their shopping list over the phone and the shop takes care of the rest. The most diverse suggestions are given for further action: invite staff to call customers regularly, whilst requesting their approval and asking when they prefer to be contacted; use the campaign's stickers and material to popularise the slogan "phone for food"; use their delivery trucks as mobile campaign posters; display the campaign in shop windows; slip adverts on the campaign in with the post; use the campaign's model adverts for small ads in the press or leaflets; proscribe substitution and offer the best products over the phone; use the phone correctly, by calling customers by their name and adopting a very friendly tone; popularise the slogan, on the grounds that even famous slogans, such as "say it with flowers", have not been overnight successes (1925, 06, 23 sq.).

Not only does *Progressive Grocer* refer to the promotional material aimed at supporting the campaign, but it also, of course, mentions the arguments likely to convince grocers about the merits of telephone-assisted sales, without forgetting to mention comparable local initiatives, such as a shop's advert boasting about the ten reasons to "Phone for Food" (1925, 08, 78). However, contrary to all expectations, amongst all the motives referred to by the magazine, the argument of technological modernity is not put forward, given that its first rhetorical move consists, on the contrary, in admitting that "the telephone has always been used in the grocery business" (1925, 06, 24). Note in passing how much this surprising assertion reveals about the extent of the progressive fever at the time, given that one major innovation, certainly marketed since 1877 but which in the United States alone only began in earnest at the start of the twentieth century and whose use was still far from being widespread (see Figure 3.9), was already considered a legacy of an almost distant past. The argument is thus more reasonable than that of radical innovation – the telephone supports a modernisation based on improvement and not transformation – and focuses both on the obstacles that ought to be removed in order to develop it, and on identifying the previously untapped potential of this means of communication, which it would therefore be appropriate to highlight so as to increase its use.

Fulfilling the first goal leads us, in particular, to wonder about the reasons why certain "women" would not phone. In fact, these customers complained that they frequently received products of a lower quality when orders were given over the phone. In order to resolve this problem, a severe warning had to be given: "If you want to commit commercial suicide, that's about the easiest way to do it" (1925, 06, 24). The magazine recommends instead selling the best products over the telephone in order to reduce the suspicion of substitution, and clearing second-choice products as special offers.

As regards promoting the telephone's advantages, this involved presenting it as a means to develop sales, by covering a wider geographic area than simply waiting for customers to visit the shop (1925, 06, 23) and, paradoxically, as a cost-reduction instrument. In fact, "[t]he service grocer offers the housewife the saving effected through reduced store expenses, for, in the long run, less overhead is required to fill the telephone order than any other kind of order" (1926, 01, 32).

Two reasons are mentioned to explain the telephone's positive contribution to cost reduction. The first is that a shop focusing on service generally needs a less expensive location than that of a cash and carry, leading to a very substantial saving on the commercial lease. The second reason lies in the telephone's ability to bring about a more rational management of activity, thanks to sales being more regularly organised throughout the day. Indeed, a graph created by the campaign's committee shows that transactions over the phone were spread out more evenly than those over the counter. Whereas physical sales were busy between 10 am and 12 midday, and between 3 pm and 6 pm, and concentrated on Fridays and Saturdays, phone transactions, on the contrary, began from 8 am sharp and were then more evenly spread throughout the day and the week. Whereas peak hours in the shop often required hiring additional employees, at least for the time needed to deal with the heavy workload, the telephone made it possible to reduce or even eliminate such bottlenecks, thus making a positive contribution to reducing costs (1925, 05, 9–11).

This general argument in favour of optimising service costs by using the telephone was extended a few months later in an article suggesting not that grocers ease peak times thanks to the telephone, but rather that they "turn [their] telephone's idle hours into profits" by learning from the successful experience of a retailer from Indiana (1925, 09, 26). This shopkeeper, who offered twenty-four-hour service, seven days a week, noticed that the telephone was mainly used between 8 am and 9 am, and between 3 pm and 5 pm. This inspired him to use off-peak hours for cold-calling customers with a view to possible additional sales: in order to do this, he identified customers on the books who had not purchased anything for a while, by looking at the names of the main items each customer had recently bought, carefully noted beside their name and address, and contacting them to inquire about their possible restocking needs.

In addition to mentioning these advantages, the magazine describes methods of organisation required for efficient telephone sales, in terms of both division of labour and customer management, and offers other pieces of advice and examples of how to get the most out of this marketing method.

Even if it is impossible to measure the extent of this trend with precision, perhaps limited to a small group of avant-garde shopkeepers with above-average economic resources and a progressive ethos, it is nonetheless remarkable to note that from the 1920s, some grocers – admittedly of a substantial size but unlike mail-order houses, department stores or chains – already operated in a way that was a surprising forerunner to contemporary "call centres" which most specialists of the phone-based commercial relationship do not hesitate to present over hastily as an innovation that was exclusive to the very end of the twentieth century. In the grocery sector of the Progressive Era, the division of labour between physical and telephone sales was able to begin very modestly, as one short paragraph leads us to believe, suggesting assigning one employee to calls (1926, 02, 36), or mentioning a case where this wish has been granted, in a shop where a salesperson is actually responsible for calling customers between 9 am and 3 pm (1925, 09, 26). Even though it was limited, the division of tasks was able, nonetheless, to take a very sophisticated form not restricted to human activities, as in the case of the Burns & Lutz Company covered by Carl Dipman. The company, despite employing around thirty people, actually took care to assign two separate stocks, one to be sold in the shop, the other for telephone orders and delivered directly to customers, so as to avoid any interference between the two types of sale, which incidentally shows that the division of labour goes hand in hand with the division of objects (1923, 04, 18).

However, most of the examples given are noticeably different in nature. The personal testimony of a grocer from North Carolina teaches us that the remarkable annual turnover of $100,000 from telephone sales is the result of well thought-out organisation, based on employing a saleswoman responsible for the department and appointing two telephone operators under her management, as well as using six telephones, four of which were main lines and two were extensions. As two of the lines were reserved for internal communications, two other lines and both extensions were allocated to telephone sales. In the morning the operators called the customers who purchased on a daily basis and corresponded to a given delivery route, to take their usual orders. They spent the rest of the morning "pushing some special items", such as a new coffee, or a particularly beautiful fruit, and then remained available to take orders in the afternoon (1926, 10, 22–23).

The company owned by M. Kamper, who was none other than the chairman of the National Retail Grocers' Association, did even better. This shop had a telephone switchboard, with 18 main lines, connected to the shop's 25 departments. The salespeople, who were able to contact between 60 to 75 customers a day, were tasked not only with processing orders, but also with filling in a file recording customers' names and addresses, the time they preferred being called, and whether they were paying on credit or in cash. The Young's Market Company of Los Angeles, presented as the "world's finest grocery store" (see Introduction), assigned operators to taking telephone orders who carried out 3,000 to 5,000 transactions a day (1925, 09, 11–12).

The most impressive, however, was the system implemented by Wolferman's in Kansas City, which employed 450 people, 40 of whom were assigned to a department operating exclusively with the telephone. We discover a kind of service whose organisation was an extraordinary forerunner, almost a century earlier and apart from its heightened gender inequality, of the most sophisticated call centres of the twenty-first century: these employees – all female – "sit in glass-enclosed cages, where they may be visible to all who enter the stores", and also visible to *Progressive Grocer*'s readers in a photograph that is as enlightening as it is spectacular (Figure 3.7). We learn that this transparency is deliberate, but instead of being aimed primarily at the panoptic monitoring of the labour force, as with modern call centres (Fernie and Metcalf, 1998; Ray, 2006), its objectives were more market based: "We want them where they can be seen, Mr. Wolferman explains, so that telephone customers who occasionally do personal shopping may see the persons who have been dealing with them on the phone." The operators were held personally responsible for customer satisfaction and not only had to take incoming calls but also had to canvass around forty housewives every day in order to encourage them to buy (1926, 02, 11).

Lastly I can mention the way in which an article from November 1923 reproduced the Burns & Lutz Company photograph, shown a few months earlier in Carl Dipman's article dedicated to the company's telephone excellence (1923, 04, 16). In the November article, the original photograph, no doubt already "arranged", is once again the subject of a derived dramatisation: it is distorted (the original source is not mentioned) and takes the form of a cutout by processing the image in a way which today's most up-to-date infographics would not put to shame: the shop's particular environment and the salespeople in the background, previously responsible for taking products off the shelves to prepare orders, are erased, in such a way that the gaze inevitably focuses on the telephone sales alone. The first operator on the left, in the foreground, is rubbed out and his neighbour's arm, which he was concealing, is discreetly completed by subtly retouching the image to conceal its

*There are 450 employes in the Wolferman organization.
Forty of these handle the telephone trade. Note the
products for selection and inspection on the top of each
telephone operator's desk*

Figure 3.7 Forty employees appointed to telephone sales
Source: 1926, 02, 11

disappearance. Perhaps this sleight of hand is due to the impossibility of seeing his face, a wish to simplify the scenario, or even, you never know, a concern to ensure a very modern parity between men and women (1923, 11, 12) (see Figure 3.8). More fundamentally, rendering telephone service anonymous and generic leads to its imposition as an almost universal figure, decontextualised and thus applicable in many other shops (here to reinforce the effects of another campaign focused on selling tinned food, see below).

Admittedly, in light of these examples, we can clearly see that the most spectacular, systematic and efficient cases of telephone sales are most often found in large companies, halfway between a grocer's and a department store. However, publicly recognising these companies, as rare and atypical as they may be, is also intended to point out that some of them, such as the Burns & Lutz Company, founded by two ordinary salespeople, started from nothing, and thus suggest they can be profitably imitated by one and all. The idea behind presenting the telephone as a factor in such successes was to establish these companies as examples to be followed by all other grocers, and if possible, to rouse their hopes that adopting remote sales could be the means of, if not doing as well, at least following in their footsteps and finding an opportunity to progress.

The success of telephone sales not only depended on adopting the appro-priate organisation but also, as we had guessed, on using one's very precise knowledge of the customer base. There are two aspects to the latter, which it is of decisive importance to distinguish between and take into account.

Burns & Lutz telephone an average of 200 customers daily

You will be able to sell canned goods in big quantities by calling your customers on the phone, telling them about your sale, and soliciting their orders. This is one way to reach the people who do not visit your store every week

Figure 3.8 Staging telephone sales
Source: 1923, 04, 16; and 1923, 11, 12

On the one hand, the development of telephone sales was based on prior knowledge of the customer base. The idea that a food business could know all its customers by name might sound surprising today, at a time when entering into market relationships is in the main based on anonymity (Callon, 1998), where identifying customers is not the foundation but the horizon of contemporary marketing, with the help of relational marketing (Mellet, 2012), trace collection (Mallard, 2012) and loyalty devices (Coll, 2012). At the beginning of the twentieth century, loyalty was, on the contrary, at worst a benefit one was scared of losing due to the de-socialising attacks of cash and carry stores, and at best a legacy intended to be preserved and consolidated or even developed, thanks to new possibilities offered by technical communication. In fact, one must properly assess the importance and value attached to credit sales and to service, which we would be very wrong to reduce to an obligatory risk in the case of the former and an irrational cost in the case of the latter, and in both cases to a burden that some people wanted to preserve despite the prevailing rationalisation and development of types of commerce that were more flexible and economical in relational expenditure. Credit and service were risky and expensive, admittedly, but they were also the means to acquire an intangible treasure, a kind of "secondary good will", measured in terms of dependence and mutual knowledge, and hence as powerful tools allowing market relationships to be created and maintained.

On the other hand, telephone sales could use this relational capital to extend it even further. This is in any case the stance adopted by *Progressive Grocer* and other promoters of remote sales, which made an effort to list the initiatives in the same vein. Earlier we discovered the extent to which, in the 1920s, the organisation of telephone sales was based on the implementation, before their time, of genuine telephone platforms. Similarly, we soon learn that the origin and purpose of this operation was to maintain and develop authentic customer files which can also easily stand comparison to their contemporary equivalents.

In 1922, the magazine reported the case of the Fanestil Store of Hoisington, a rural town in Kansas, which launched a telephone sales system aimed at its customers, most of whom were farmers, by sending a letter that first indicated the postal charge for sending a package weighing between 1 to 50 pounds so that the customers could estimate how much it would cost them for a delivery made by the postman. This piece of information was followed by an invitation to place an order by phone and have it delivered free of charge. By calling the shop early, every consumer could receive the products requested on the same day. In fact, the shop became specialised in this service and developed a substantial telephone business, backed by an efficient delivery system, covering the town eight times a day. After that, the company sent monthly canvassing letters to its customers based on a file covering the entire county (1922, 04, 57).

Even more elaborate than this was the case of a grocer from North Carolina, whom we came across previously, who tasked a commercial manager to study consumers, keeping a record of their purchasing habits in order to be able to call them whenever the business received goods to their taste. The company therefore had updated lists of people who were particularly fond of certain types of bread, ham, cheese, and so on. When fresh arrivals of these goods came in, these lists were acted on and customers called. The telephone was also used when tastings were organised in the shop, even if sales were often concluded over the phone (1926, 10, 22–23).[12]

Lastly, I can mention the case of an anonymous grocer who described the successful experience he had with telephone sales by highlighting, from the outset, that "the very first requisite is a well-compiled list of customers and prospective customers to telephone to". This was not all. Every name had to be recorded on a separate card, specifying the customer's surname, address and telephone number, together with a pre-filled out list of the days of the week, on which one marked a cross on the days when he/she wished to be called, not forgetting the preferred times for calling. In order to complete this file, the company sent a standard letter to its customers advertising telephone sales, accompanied by a government postcard written in such a way that the customer only had to tick the days "she" wished to be called and indicate the preferred times. Those who did not send the card back were not forgotten but called. Lastly, a "comment" section was included, giving people the possibility of notifying the grocery store that, for example, they wished to be contacted if a promotional lot was being sold. Maintaining these accounts made it possible to see if a customer did not buy her coffee at the shop, so that a special effort could be made to sell a particular brand.

Note, in passing, that the reference (already encountered many times) to the gender-based division between housewife (meant to do the shopping) and "male breadwinner" (supposedly absent as a customer) is favourable to telephone sales as the wife was generally reachable at home: thus, it is not in the least bit paradoxical to note that an archaic (social) practice serves as a (transitional) medium for (technical) modernity (1927, 02, 14 sq.). This is because telephone sales were clearly resolutely modern, as is shown (as if it were necessary) by the reference to relational and marketing know-how that was increasingly original and sophisticated, anticipating all the modern techniques of call centres, perhaps with the exception of a comment paradoxically noting (and incorrectly, as we shall see much later[13]) that "you cannot depend upon facial expressions and smiles" when on the phone (1925, 06, 80).

Amongst these innovative techniques is the visionary codification of the "telephone rebound" described and analysed by Christine Licoppe (2006) at the beginning of this century. It should be recalled that this technique consists in relying on an ongoing exchange in order to slip in a commercial proposal at the right moment, in the hope of, if not circumventing, at least reducing the "annoying" nature of "blind" cold calling, of which the actors at the time were well aware, knowing that the need to be "very tactful" and efforts to "keep their voice pleasant and cheerful" (1926, 10, 100) were not always enough. Therefore in 1923 the Burns & Lutz Company recommended drawing customers' attention, when placing orders, to the availability of fresh produce and special offers (1923, 04, 16).

Three other variants of this technique can also be mentioned. The first, proposed by a grocer from Indiana, consisted in creating the rebound based on an *ex nihilo* call, in order to give pure cold calling the appearance of being a spontaneous exchange, in the hope of course that this way of operating would reduce the impression of intrusion and maximise the chances of a positive response. The clerk calls the customer, asks him diplomatically if a mistake has been made regarding one of the most recent items bought, and once the consumer has answered negatively, he assures him that the shop will always take care to satisfy him and then gives him suggestions of possible purchases (1925, 09, 26).

The other technique consisted in orchestrating the rebound by coupling it with the activation of a customer file, as we saw above, or a file containing specific offers, such as described by Alexandre Mallard (2002) regarding the online sales of the beginning of the twenty-first century. Thus, a short item entitled "A Pointer for the Phone-Order Clerk" recommended having a pad next to the telephone and writing down the day's special offers and all the products they wanted to "push". The trick consisted in avoiding ending the conversation with "Anything else today, Mrs. Armstrong?" but by mentioning the items that might be likely to interest the customer (1927, 08, 33).

The third rebound variant consisted in linking possible purchases to the items actually requested by the consumers, by playing on the association between products in a way that would thrill the promoters of the most up-to-date data-mining software (Coll, 2012): "If he calls for a box of cake flour we know he is going to bake a cake, so we suggest baking powder, cocoanut, eggs, butter, etc." (1922, 05, 31). Another way of playing the same game consisted in suggesting recipes over the phone, like the grocer from North Carolina, meaning that if the customer was missing an ingredient, it could be added to his list (1926, 10, 24).

In fact, the grocers' imagination as regards the commercial uses of the telephone was almost boundless, as will be shown in these last two examples. The first consisted in using the appliance as a customer "captation" device,[14] very similarly to the most contemporary tools (interactive displays, two-dimensional barcodes; Cochoy, 2011b). The source of this new use lies paradoxically in an initial endeavour to counteract the telephone's disturbing effect on in-store sales, when customers asked to make private phone calls from the receiver on the counter. In order to overcome this problem, a grocer from Ohio had the idea of placing a telephone extension at the opposite end of the shop, thus offering an additional service to the clientele whilst freeing the sales area from any unwanted congestion (1924, 05, 35). Elsewhere, a shopkeeper from the Midwest put forward a similar solution based on an inverted organisation of the space, deliberating using the telephone to ensnare customers. This professional, having observed that customers often asked for permission to use the shop's telephone when doing their shopping, decided to prioritise the provision of this service: he moved the telephone from the back to the front of the shop, to ensure the appliance could be seen from the street, with a sign saying: "This phone is for our customers. Make use of it." The grocer concluded that he had everything to gain from such a device, given that the shop, with unlimited phone calls, had no cost to bear for this service that was offered to customers free of charge, whilst, however, attracting an additional clientele (1923, 09, 22–23).

The second innovative use of the telephone consisted in using it as an instrument for recovering credit, long before specialised companies turned it into their preferred means of applying pressure, due to the unique emotional control allowed by this form of communication, described so well by Joe Deville (2012) in his survey on credit recovery in England at the start of the twenty-first century. The Hunt Grocery Company of Texas reports that, in its experience, "Telephone beats letters for collecting slow accounts" (1925, 08, 25). In fact, the telephone allowed for a more personal contact than the post, as well as the possibility of reaching, at the end of the conversation, a tacit mutual understanding and an assurance of a promise of payment.

From the ensnaring of customers to recovering their debt, via sales, the circle is complete: the telephone ensures customer seduction and service and maintains the quasi-exclusive personalised relationships one builds with them. The old interpersonal relationship of sales on credit with delivery is preserved, but above all modernised by improving the technical conditions for it to be maintained.

However, what should one make of this set of stories collected from a limited group of innovative companies, whose unilaterally positive tone seems too good to be true to reflect all of the underlying practices, whose selection methods remain opaque, and whose experience tells us, of course, nothing

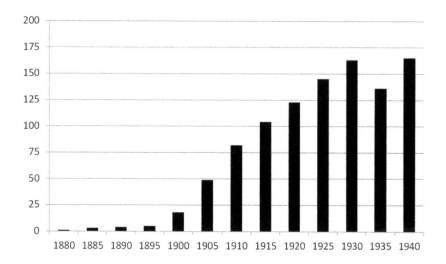

Figure 3.9 Number of telephones per inhabitant
Source: According to the US Census Bureau, quoted in Fischer, 1988, p.35

about that of the vast majority of their more silent colleagues? *Progressive Grocer* is professionally committed to a progressive rhetoric, in other words, hemiplegic: the magazine's discourse operates using a ratchet effect, just like any process intending to progress, by reporting only what works, and by carefully selecting the most spectacular and effective cases. In order to obtain an idea of the more general expansion of practices, one solution is to search outside the magazine (in other sources, completing the medial focalisation with an external eye); another is again to ferret elsewhere, but in the magazine, on the pages not directly dedicated to the telephone but likely to report certain uses, with no demonstrative intention (enriching the central vision thanks to the peripheral vision).[15]

The first strategy, for example, is to link the uses of the telephone described in *Progressive Grocer* to the more general place of this tool in America at the time. As shown in Figure 3.9, towards the 1920s, when the magazine was starting up, the telephone had already spread considerably.[16] Generally speaking with less than 15% of inhabitants owning one, we are still far from quasi-market saturation, but if we think in terms of households and not individual users, and if we accept the reasonable hypothesis for the time of four people per household, we realise that probably more than half of Americans already had access to a home phone in the 1920s. The conditions for telephone sales were therefore broadly in place.

The second strategy, which I chose to prioritise in this book, confirms the first finding. As always, *Progressive Grocer*'s contributions on a given subject are even more reliable if they appear beside another, given that in this case the peripheral object is not the subject of a promotional endeavour. The use of the telephone emerges discreetly, for example, when leafing through the publication of the accounts of a grocer from New Mexico: we see that telephone communications feature as an ordinary expense and amount to $120 in average monthly expenditure, when the spending on delivery is more than four times higher ($582). These are modest expenses, particularly when related to total salaries ($6,714 a month, admittedly no doubt for many employees) (1924, 10, 76; 1922).

Another indicator showing how common the use of the telephone was is provided in a series of articles dedicated to a promotional campaign for selling canned goods, which we shall examine later. One example of an advert that could possibly be placed in the local press recommends writing this type of small ad as follows: "Phone us for special prices and other particulars" (1922, 10, 11). Other advice calls on grocers to "tell 'em over the phone" (1923, 11, 18). Lastly, and perhaps above all, given that the advertisers were generally very cautious regarding staging the conditions of felicity likely to carry their message or not, concerned as they were to place their products in a very widely acceptable context of use, we see indirect and "eloquent" traces of telephone use being trivialised in adverts featuring a grocer on the phone (1926, 06, 97; 1926, 07, 130), a customer placing orders (1925, 12, 35), or a dialogue between them (1924, 08, 35; 1926, 07, 72–73; see Figure 3.10).

Figure 3.10 "Yes, we always have Jap Rose"
Source: 1924, 08, 35

However, these adverts are of interest for another reason: they also demonstrate that the brand is a means of referring to foods without using their generic name, by offering the customer the possibility of naming a specific product, whose make, flavour and appearance they know, of course, as long as they have tried it beforehand. This approach makes it impossible to assess physically the quality of products, using sensory experience, during distance communication, and eliminates all risk of substitution by the retailer. The brand in fact establishes a new type of close relationship between market actors, which is just as tight as the connections maintained thanks to credit and delivery, but in which the traditional link between retailer and customer is replaced by a new tie between customer and manufacturer. Thus the phone turns out to be particularly suitable for promoting brands, which can forge direct relationships with consumers and free them from the control imposed by the seller (Lury, 2004). This was clearly understood by the manufacturer of Quaker Oats, with its advert asking the grocer: "when she telephones, can she be as certain of getting what she asked for as she could by coming into your store?" (Figure 3.11).

The sales pitch that follows this question is particularly subtle:

> Where does a woman make her decision to replenish her morning cereal supply – in her home or in your store? Home, of course. That's where the shortage is noticed. And it's a simple matter to 'phone in the order for Breakfast Foods. No shopping or selecting is required. The kind, quality and price are firmly fixed in her mind and have been for years. Offering a substitute is upsetting an old habit – and people don't like to have their pet habits upset. Again, the new food may not agree with the baby. Who gets the blame? You – never the manufacturer. Much easier and safer to give a woman what she wants when she wants it. If you don't, she'll look around for some one who will. Quaker products have been the choice of American mothers for over 50 years. They are safe *and profitable* to feature.
>
> (1925, 12, 35)

Underlining that purchasing decisions are "of course" made "at home", clearly implies they are made there "rather than in the shop". Presenting substitution as an act of violence against "an old habit" means reversing the order of history, presenting consumers' preference for brands, still in its infancy, as already deep-rooted in habit, and the traditional offer of products from an unknown source, which grocers had always proposed, as a new twist in the "new-old" order of things. "Blaming" the grocer for a person's dissatisfaction in case of substitution, and alluding to the threat of customer flight to the competition, so much easier in times of telephone communication, leaves the grocer no room for manoeuvre. Does this mean, then, that he was excluded? No, not yet. The grocer remained an obligatory partner whom manufacturers still intended to pamper, as is shown with the sweet promise of profit that concludes the sales pitch. Although the packaging promoted by the brand in fact appeared an opportunity for selling without the salesperson (Grandclément, 2008) and thus one of

When She Telephones

Can she be as certain of getting what she asked
for as she could by coming into your store?

WHERE does a woman make her decision to replenish her morning cereal supply — in her home or in your store?

Home, of course. That's where the shortage is noticed.

And it's a simple matter to 'phone in the order for Breakfast Foods. No shopping or selecting is required. The kind, quality and price are firmly fixed in her mind and have been for years.

Offering a substitute is upsetting an old habit—and people don't like to have their pet habits upset. Again, the new food may not agree with the baby. Who gets the blame? You—never the manufacturer.

Much easier and safer to give a woman what she wants when she wants it.

If you don't, she'll look around for some one who will.

Quaker products have been the choice of American mothers for over 50 years. They are safe *and* profitable to feature.

Quaker Cereal Products

Quaker Oats	Quaker Egg Noodles
Quick Quaker	Quaker Farina
Mother's Oats	New Pettijohn's
Quick Mother's Oats	Quaker Best Corn Meal
Puffed Rice	Quaker Hominy Grits
Puffed Wheat	Scotch Pearled Barley
Quaker Milk Macaroni	Quaker Flour
Quaker Milk Spaghetti	Mother's Flour

The Quaker Oats Company, Chicago, U. S. A.

Figure 3.11 Quaker Oats, "When she telephones …"
Source: 1925, 12, 13

the vital props for the self-service of the future, using the telephone to sell brands and their packaging still recognised the central place of the grocer and thus of service. The grocer lost his status as a mediator able to redefine the terms of trade, as his power of substitution was drastically diminished, but remained an unavoidable intermediary, admittedly restrained but nevertheless necessary, between customers and manufacturers: the fact that he is the one being addressed ("your", "you") is sufficient to demonstrate this. As it was less brutal than self-service because it required the grocer's active cooperation, the telephone undoubtedly played a non-negligible role in brand acceptance and thus, later on, in promoting methods of sale relegating human mediation to back-office organisation. That said, the grocer is, however, an essential element that is ignored by the Quaker Oats advert: as opposed to what is claimed in the manufacturer's sales pitch, accepting telephone sales no doubt relies to a considerable extent on trust in the salesperson and recognising his power of substitution. Indeed, we are more inclined to order by telephone the products we cannot see because we consider them generic, or because we accept the advice of the person serving us and who can see them. Therefore and paradoxically, besides the new brand loyalty, traditional commerce based on the sale of bulk products and/or on human service, without a doubt strongly supported the use of this very modern telephone, which some people intended to use, if not to remove it, at least to control it. At the end of the day, or rather the end of the line, the telephone, far more than being a mere extension of service, proved a powerful means of further embedding independent business socially (via the local "community", closely bound to its grocer) and economically (via the dependence of customers on credit) – a business founded on service, to which it offered the means for its "penultimate modernisation".

Motorised delivery as the final modernisation of service

The telephone was only the "penultimate" modernisation of service, as the final modernisation was yet to come, at least in my account, though it actually accompanied it simultaneously. In fact, after orders had been given by telephone, there was, inevitably, the moment of delivery: these operations were almost inseparable, as is incidentally clearly illustrated in a Ford advert for delivery vehicles, which proudly proclaims, quoting statistics for the Springfield Tea Co.: "Salesmen with Ford trucks Average 125 Calls and Deliveries Per Day" (1924, 09, 41).

The association between telephone and delivery can of course be found in the grocery store itself. We can thus refer to the case of the Weber shop in Kansas, whose success was due to speedy deliveries, supported by a "telephone system" in contact with all of the shop's departments and with salespeople who were specially qualified to take remote orders (1922, 08, 7 sq.). The shop, which only sold "high-grade products" – an option which we saw was particularly adapted to telephone sales, given that it cannot survive with disappointed customers – was equipped with a battery of telephones and a fleet of very carefully liveried and maintained vehicles. It is interesting to observe the extent to which this example conforms with a modernising dynamic that was thought of in terms of incremental service improvement rather than the radical transformation of commerce, given that the introduction of attractive, motorised vans merely reiterates and extends the company's "fine horses" logic, which it considered "walking advertisements" that were now on wheels. Moreover, we would be wrong to interpret motorisation as a dehumanised technicisation of transport, given that new vehicles, although free from the animals pulling them, were nonetheless inseparable from their drivers and thus from service – drivers whose behaviour was also meant to be optimised by training them in courtesy and efficiency, in line with the company's motto, "Speed, efficiency, accuracy" (1922, 08, 11).

The limits to this kind of modernisation were obviously those imposed by the competition and by cost pressures. The question had already been asked in relation to the telephone and became even more pressing with motorised delivery, which implied investment and expense that were *a priori* much higher than those required for using the telephone. In the case of the Weber shop, however, the writer of the article states that "[t]he time and cost of delivery is cut down". Other contributions attempted to support this kind of statement and used several types of arguments to this end. One consisted in pointing out that the supposed savings from takeaway sales were exaggerated. Thus, the 1925 article that launched the "Phone for Food" campaign also claims that delivery is not an "extravagance", and for this reason draws attention to the fact that an average basket bought from a cash and carry came to $0.81, whereas the average amount for an order made by telephone and delivered to the customer was $1.91. Now the management of large orders was apparently less costly: it took 4 minutes and 26 seconds, on average, for a cash and carry order to be sold, compared with 1 minute and 57 seconds to handle an order by telephone. Moreover, the article reminds us that cash and carry was a temporary solution invented by the federal government to overcome the difficulties of the war (see above), that its advantages had thus been exaggerated, and that a return to delivery therefore had to be defended (1925, 05, 9).

A second argument pointed out that like the telephone, the intensification/ modernisation of delivery could be presented not as an increase in costs but as a way to reduce them, thanks to productivity gains made through mechanisation: "*one dependable man and an inexpensive motor truck can economically replace the boys you use now*" (1922, 05, 7). Thanks to the positive externalities linked to using a van, such as free benefits or other savings, having a van actually made it easier to supply fresh produce, and meant one could negotiate a discount with the wholesaler on the grounds that one was responsible for transporting the goods oneself. Above all, it offered ambulatory advertising space that was able to ensure the shop's promotion in town on a daily basis, without involving any additional expenditure on advertising (an argument that is repeated on numerous occasions in the magazine; see Figure 3.12; 1924, 10, 15; 1925, 02, 18).

A third argument consisted in putting into perspective the initially high cost of motorisation by observing that actually, not one grocer in one hundred had any idea about the true cost of delivery, and by developing, on this basis, clever calculations to show that the cost "per delivery" was in fact very modest. Stating that the price of a van lay between $800 and $1,500 and that its shelf life was estimated to be three years with a use of around 35 miles a day or 35,000 miles a year, the article assesses monthly cost, including amortisation, taxes, maintenance, insurance, not to mention the driver's salary ($104) at $248, in other words 27.5 cents a mile for 50 daily stops, and concludes that the price per delivery is 19 cents. It does not stop there, either, encouraging routes per area and avoiding special deliveries to reduce costs (1922, 05, 62). Advertisers developed similar sales pitches, particularly Ford, which, not content with promoting its slogan, "To Fordize is to Economize", made an effort to explain "How Fords cut food delivery costs" with the help of a calculation that was similar to the previous one, but which managed to get a far lower result than 9 cents per mile travelled.

With this kind of argument, we are confronted with a logic of "longitudinal improvement", given that the reasoning compared the current state of a particular practice with its past, so as to guarantee that the changes introduced really had made a positive difference. Therefore, we are not entirely in a logic of "lateral transformation", which would consist in changing practice by looking to the side (examining one's competitive position) rather than behind (measuring one's personal progress).

The improvement of the delivery service did not stop with mere ownership of a van but came with a whole series of suggestions about organisation, commercial activity, staff training, maintenance of equipment, and so on. As regards organisation, the magazine advises, from 1923, scrupulously planning one's routes (1923, 11, 14), and points out to its readers that "[h]aving a separate stock for deliveries saves time for clerks and delivery men and eliminates any interference with the customers at the counters", thus inventing in passing, long before their time, the principles on which the back-office management of today's supermarket "drives" is based (1923, 03, 23).

In commercial terms, *Progressive Grocer* refers to the case of a company that managed successfully to link a driver-deliverer to a salesperson, with the salesperson canvassing neighbours on every delivery (1923, 07, 44). In terms of training, educating deliverers is encouraged, to avoid allowing a draught into their customers' houses by leaving the door open, to be careful not to dirty the floor, to make an effort to deliver at times that are convenient for the customers and try to drive at a reasonable speed (1925, 12, 30–31).

On the subject of vehicle maintenance, the magazine refers to the example of Goldberg, Bowen & Co. in San Francisco, which equipped itself with a special maintenance service for its fleet of vans and had a repair workshop to work on them, including at night, thanks to powerful lighting (1925, 04, 12). Nor can one overlook the advert by S.F. Boweer & Co., Inc., offering a private petrol pump system that was meant to give its users the benefit of

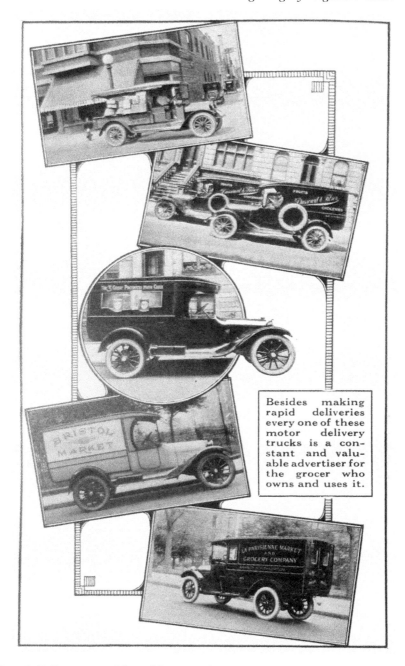

Besides making rapid deliveries every one of these motor delivery trucks is a constant and valuable advertiser for the grocer who owns and uses it.

Figure 3.12 Every one of these delivery trucks is an advert
Source: 1922, 05, 8

How Fords Cut Food Delivery Costs

One of the most convincing examples of cost-cutting in food delivery by the use of Ford Trucks in the experience of the H. Piper Company, wholesale bakers, Chicago.

Beginning ten years ago with one Ford Truck the Piper Company built up a fleet of 40 One-Ton Trucks, each of which today is delivering baked goods to an average of one hundred stores and restaurants daily.

An average truck of this fleet is operated 306 days a year, traveling 10,700 miles, making 30,600 stops and carrying 229½ tons, at an operating cost of just a trifle over 9 cents a mile, including maintenance and repairs, depreciation, tires, oil, gas, fixed expense, garage and insurance.

The fact that the Piper Company has re-ordered Ford Trucks year after year, and continues to re-order, is the most practical proof possible as to their satisfactory performance.

See Authorized Ford Dealers for further facts about this and other examples of Ford operation.

To Fordize is to Economize

CARS · TRUCKS · TRACTORS

Figure 3.13 How Fords cut food delivery costs
Source: 1924, 02, 45

wholesale prices for fuel as well as better quality control (1925, 08, 50). The different advantages of motorised delivery are moreover repeated, fine-tuned or completed[17] in the myriad adverts by various delivery van manufacturers – Ford of course (e.g. 1924, 01, 49; 1924, 02, 45; 1924, 03, 59), but also, sometimes before Ford, Garford (e.g. 1922, 09, 39; 1923, 03, 103; 1923, 04, 83), Graham Brothers (e.g. 1923, 12, 73; 1924, 11, 74–75; 1925, 02, 92), International Harvester (e.g. 1924, 06, 104; 1924, 12, 78; 1925, 02, 102) and Chevrolet (1926, 01, 77; 1926, 02, 43; 1926, 07, 115) – adverts that colonised the magazine throughout the 1920s but which became less frequent a few years later with the progress of takeaway sales and the corresponding shrinkage of service.

Service improvements that hint at its transformation

Motorisation was, in fact, like the telephone, a very particular improvement given that it won over both shops and customers equally. Admittedly, it was only after the Second World War that almost all American households came to own a car. However, from 1925 the percentage of ordinary citizens with a car, at 0.15 vehicles per inhabitant and 0.6 per household,[18] was significantly already equal to what we saw for the telephone at the same time (see above, Figure 3.9). Nevertheless, whereas telephone equipment at both ends of the line of communication was the *sine qua non* condition for the development of service, the generalisation of motorised transport produced the completely opposite effect: the same motorisation allowing service to be improved, simultaneously weakened it, by making it easier for customers to transport goods themselves. The switch from the motorisation of professionals to that of individuals is beautifully illustrated by the experience of the Los Angeles grocer who, after buying tyres for his own fleet of vehicles, realised it was in his interest to market this kind of item to his ordinary customers as well (1923, 12, 60). Customer motorisation thus reduced the relative interest in home deliveries and, consequently, the usefulness of the kind of telephone-assisted sale that yet seemed so modern.

The modernist grocer, on the lookout for all the movements likely to affect his activity and all innovations able to respond to them, did not fail to notice the motorisation of his customers, take an interest in it and take advantage of it. Thus *Progressive Grocer* notes that from the early 1920s, "the question, 'where shall we buy the groceries?'" is often answered by "Where ever we can park the car!" The magazine mentioned new services aimed at meeting this expectation, such as making car parks available (1923, 12, 60).[19] One article asks about the traffic law and its possible effect of eliminating commerce – "Are traffic laws driving trade away from your store?" – in particular because of a rash of signs saying "No Parking". It immediately gives the example of a solution tried by a grocer from Houston, Texas, who rented land, offering 2 cent parking spaces for his customers, paid a security guard, and turned this system into an advertising ploy by offering a ticket to everyone who visited the shop, without any obligation to buy, whilst making it clear that such a system para-doxically achieved its objective, that of generating sales. The article concludes by referring to a project by an engineer in Houston, who proposed the grocer's experiment be extended by bringing together a cooperative of shopkeepers who would join forces to manage a shared car park, with a free parking ticket given every time a person entered one of the participants' shops (1925, 07, 33 sq.).

In fact, motorisation was not the only factor demonstrating the emergence of a shift from improving service to its more radical transformation, with the advent of a transfer of tasks formerly performed by the grocers, to the custo-mers themselves. Upon closer inspection, we notice that what is true for motorisation is also true for all the improvements to service that I have already described: they are all ambivalent in that they all lead to service being opti-mised then superseded. We saw that even the telephone, *a priori* inseparable from human service, surreptitiously competed against it by teaching customers to name products by brand, and considering this the surest way to avoid increased risks of substitution in remote, asynchronous sales. The need to improve shop hygiene and the introduction of new equipment, initially aimed at assisting the labour force, also led to a new, more direct relationship with merchandise.

Earlier I mentioned a series of three articles that Carl Dipman, in the summer of 1926, devoted to the subject of new equipment likely to improve service, but I – deliberately – did not present the third one because, without giving up on service, it goes far beyond its simple modernisation. Whereas the first two articles were based on the potential of new equipment in terms of increasing the productivity of service, the third is an attempt to connect the choice of equipment to the more general development of commerce, and particularly to the increasing pressure of competition from chain stores. The article is entitled "The right equipment will help you meet changing conditions" (1926, 09, 41), but the proposals it puts forward, whilst providing solutions aimed at supporting service, back a sales approach that make it, at least partially, unnecessary.

In order to withstand the competition from chains, Carl Dipman suggested independent grocers focus on supplying what chains did not – in other words, providing fresh produce such as fruit and vegetables, and meat. Carl Dipman did not claim to "provide" these solutions, given that he presents them, on the contrary, as two of the "changing conditions" affecting the grocery store world. He therefore notes that although 90% of grocers sell smoked meat, 35% to 40% of grocers now supply fresh meat, which is no longer exclusively sold by butchers with an abattoir, thanks to the development of modern establishments specialising in the distribution of this merchandise. Similarly, he observes that "[a]nother changing condition is in the increasing importance of fruits and vegetables in the grocery store". The author attributes this development to competition from chains, given that as they manage a reduced and standardised stock list of 700 products, they would find it difficult to supply this kind of product, whose provenance and appearance vary considerably. Thus he presents fruit, vegetables and meat as among the best weapons for protecting independent grocers from the pressure of integrated distributors.

However, although Carl Dipman did not invent this weapon, he made an effort to emphasise the conditions for its success – according to him, the need to acquire an appropriate piece of equipment. This is where once again we come across the question of hygiene, given that fresh produce, no doubt more than any other, is fragile, perishable, subject to damp, rot and all kinds of contamination. It was therefore very logical for the author to insist on the need to acquire modern devices for refrigerating merchandise:

> the well-run meat department must have, first of all, proper refrigeration and, secondly, facilities for display. To meet both of these requirements you need refrigerated display cases.
>
> (1926, 09, 44)

By noting that "[e]lectric refrigeration is one of the new things" whose "use is spreading rapidly", Carl Dipman is merely paying reflective attention, as a specialist journalist, to the countless examples of refrigerated furniture produced by McCray (e.g. 1922, 04, 43; 1922, 05, 41; 1922, 06, 57), Hussmann (e.g. 1922, 05, 58; 1922, 07, 53; 1922, 08, 69), Ligonier (1923, 06, 102; 1923, 07, 92), Gruendler (e.g. 1924, 05, 73; 1924, 07, 64; 1924, 08, 71), Thesco (1925, 08, 93; 1925, 09, 95), Brecht (e.g. 1926, 03, 94–95; 1926, 06, 54–55; 1926, 07, 77), Holcomb and Hoke (1926, 03, 128), Weber (1926, 06, 102–103), Hill (1926, 08, 45) and, of course, Frigidaire (1926, 02, 81; 1926, 08, 87), as well as other ice-making machines labelled Lipman (e.g. 1922, 05, 57; 1922, 06, 84; 1923, 07, 83) or Baker (e.g. 1924, 05, 68; 1925, 09, 68; 1925, 12, 88) which had been spreading in the adverts on the pages of *Progressive Grocer* since it began.

Nonetheless, Carl Dipman also emphasised the fundamental ambivalence of the new equipment, which was inextricably linked to preservation tools ("proper refrigeration") and stands for exhibiting merchandise ("facilities for display"), an ambivalence that we had already come across in previous adverts, such as the advert for McCray refrigerators in Figure 3.14, whose sales pitch in 1923 promoted a performance directed towards the grocer, their ability to "stop loss from spoilage by keeping your perishables pure and wholesome", and the visual appeal directed at customers, with their ability to "increase your sales by enabling you to display this stock attractively, keeping it fresh and tempting". In order to illustrate this two-pronged argument, the models presented fell somewhere between shelves or back office cupboards to be used exclusively by the shopkeeper, and the most modern displays, wide open and in view of customers, particularly in the form of a hybrid compromise between the old-style counter and glazed furniture to whet consumers' visual appetite.

As preservation tools, the new refrigeration equipment assisted but did not replace service; they were tools for improving the old grocery store world. In fact, the idea was precisely to draw a clear line between displaying merchandise and handling it, the latter being strictly reserved for the professional, while increasing labour productivity, as refrigeration was just one tool amongst many

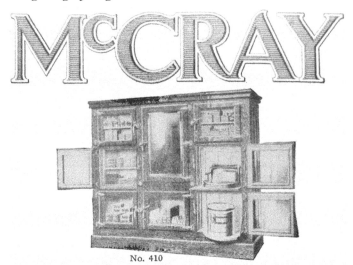

No. 410

One Mark of the Progressive Grocer

The fine exterior of the McCray Refrigerator adds to the attractiveness of any store. Its appearance is a mark of up-to-dateness which gives your patrons confidence in your sanitary standards, and helps you make the casual buyer a regular customer.

And the promise of its appearance is fulfilled by its performance. The McCray stops loss from spoilage by keeping your perishables pure and wholesome, and it increases your sales by enabling you to display this stock attractively, keeping it fresh and tempting.

The efficiency and economy of the McCray are the result of—

Care in selecting and seasoning the best materials obtainable;
Our patented system of construction, which insures a constant circulation of cold, dry air through every part of the refrigerator;
Skill in manufacture, devotion to every detail;
Our steadfast purpose to make the best refrigerator it is possible to build.

You can buy a McCray with the profit that it saves you. Ask about our easy payment plan. Send now for further information.

McCRAY REFRIGERATOR CO.
2330 Lake Street   Kendallville, Indiana

No. 1042

Figure 3.14 McCray refrigerators
Source: 1923, 05, 0

that could assist the grocer to supply meat-based products: "Now meat, both smoked and fresh, requires efficient cutting, slicing, grinding and weighing equipment" (1926, 09, 44).

However, contrary to knives, slicers, grinders and weighing scales, which merely prolonged and optimised the grocer's moves, as is clearly shown in the US Slicer advert in Figure 3.15, refrigerators belonged to a family of tools capable of acting independently of the work force, not just assisting it, and thereby pointed to a new type of market organisation. This development can be seen in Carl Dipman's previous hesitation between two uses for the equipment: "The right kind of fixtures may enable fewer people to carry on the work in your store or enable the same number of clerks do more work" (1926, 07, 12).

By dint of helping work, we end up by making it disappear, at least in its previous form, such is the paradox. We move from assistance to substitution, from improvement to transformation and, in this switch, refrigeration devices play a pivotal role, not only because they mean, as Carl Dipman is careful to point out, that people can do without the "ice man" and save on the corresponding "ice bill", but above all because, unlike simple tools-prostheses, they are able to operate without the help of the grocer and even in his total absence, in order to sell merchandise more efficiently.

In fact, these same refrigerators which, as conservation devices, were the grocer's loyal assistants, were also, as display tools, independent instruments of seduction – "equipment that *sells goods*", according to the beautiful motto Carl Dipman had the good fortune to use in his first article on new commercial equipment (1926, 07, 11, emphasis in original). In other words, refrigerators introduced an obvious tension, which in itself brought about an entirely different future for commerce.

They allowed one to imagine a new way of selling, one that was almost entirely delegated to technical devices, whereby one capitalised on the statement that *"people buy food with their eyes"* (1926, 07, 13), an expression repeated three times in the text. In principle, "there should be no barriers between your customers and your merchandise. Theoretically, open display[20] should prevail throughout" (1926, 07, 13). However, what was good in theory was not always the case in practice:

> Practically, you cannot display all items in the open. Some goods, for sanitary reasons, must be kept free from handling. Sanitation and cleanliness are big items in the grocery store, and if you display goods in an unsanitary manner, open display will do your store more harm than good.
> (1926, 07, 13)

The new refrigerators specifically made it possible to overcome this particular tension: thanks to their glass cases, aimed at protecting the grocer's goods, merchandise could be kept cool, clean and away from any undesirable dirt, but thanks to these same windows facing the clientele, they encouraged the visual

Fenske's Market at 804 Thirteenth Ave. S. in Minneapolis, Minn.

"I Like the U. S. Best of All"

A. H. FENSKE, 804 Thirteenth Avenue S., Minneapolis, Minnesota, past president of the National Association of Retail Meat Dealers, has this to say about his experience with U. S. Slicer in the retail meat business:

"I have had four different makes of machines in my twenty-three years of retail meat business and can tell the World I like the U. S. best of all."

That statement coming from a man of Mr. Fenske's long experience will help you in selecting the right slicer for your market—a slicer that will insure profit where loss was evident before.

Take no chances—insist on having the best. The best costs less in the long run. Ask anyone who owns one.

Send for the circular "How a Modern Slicing Machine Opens the Way to New Profits." It's free for the asking. Write direct to the

U. S. SLICING MACHINE COMPANY, La Porte, Indiana

U.S. SLICER
The World's Best

A   S L I C E R   T O   F I T   E V E R Y   N E E D

Figure 3.15 US Slicer meat slicers
Source: 1927, 06, 126

enhancement and thus the desirability of the products. To put it another way, the refrigerated cabinets meant one could keep goods cool (inside) and heat up their sales (outside). This is why Carl Dipman suggested, unsurprisingly, choosing "the display-case type" as much as possible.

Were these refrigerators the only things working in this way and, moreover, was visual selling really new? In her survey dedicated to the emergence of sales without salespeople, Catherine Grandclément (2008), rightly notes that there was no brutal transition between counter and self-service sales, pointing out that with the old way of selling, goods could be viewed and touched, since they were available in baskets and crates and displayed in other ways around the shop, on the other side of the counter. However, Carl Dipman has an even more precise view on the vestiges of the first art of the display:

> Partly filled boxes, baskets and barrels have no place in the grocery, because the container surface occupies more of the area of vision than the articles displayed. Containers made for display purposes are much better.
>
> (1926, 07, 70)

He recommends, where hygiene is important, using glass display cases, specifying:

> be sure the show case is of the modern type – one that works from the floor up, and not one that sets on top of the counter and wastes some of the most valuable display and selling space. The simple rule, then, is this: display as much merchandise in the open as possible, and display under glass only merchandise that must be protected from the customer for reasons of sanitation, cleanliness or refrigeration. Always remember that people buy groceries with their eyes. [...] And don't forget it's the groceries that are to be displayed and not the fixtures. That's why the clumsy, old-fashioned, wooden displays, with heavy overhangings must give way to the simple, modern kind.
>
> (1926, 07, 70)

In order to convince grocers of the benefits of glass display cases, Carl Dipman mentions their ability to increase sales by 33% and refers to the cases of the Woolworth shops which "would lose half of their volume if they stocked their merchandise in bins and on shelves, as most grocers do". The author insists: "remember the first principle: people buy food with their eyes – and they cannot buy with their eyes what they cannot see. Sight is by far the most important selling sense, but there are still four others" (1926, 07, 74). He alludes to the market benefits of each sense that would be encouraged by an open display, not restricted to glass display cases, including hearing, since he urges grocers to talk to their customers about products they are holding, incidentally laying the foundations of the sensory marketing that modern marketers believe they invented (Hultén et al., 2009). Nevertheless, Carl Dipman's merit, visionary and decisive as he was, was also very modest, given that the author only opened people's eyes to all the new equipment for merchandise display of which the trade magazine had been full from the outset, and which can be divided into two categories.

The first, mainly intended for fruit and vegetables, is the new metallic shelves, very light and almost transparent, offering a panoramic view of the merchandise, and whose origin also lay, as with refrigerators, in the two-fold concern to limit the hygiene risks threatening fresh produce, thanks to the metal (possibly enamelled), a material whose surface and properties were less likely than the wood of traditional furniture to be contaminated, whilst favouring the broadest visual display possible of the merchandise. This was particularly the case of products by the United Steel & Wire Co. and its competitors, American Wire Form Co. and Union Steel Products Co. These companies supplied, which we can guess from their names, openwork baskets (e.g. 1923, 06, 92; 1923, 07, 101; 1925, 06, 85) or perforated shelves (e.g. 1925, 04, 47; 1925, 05, 94; 1925, 06, 59) made from metal tubes and wires.[21] The main argument they put forward was the hygienic nature of their installations ("no germs" would be, from the beginning and for decades to come, the American Wire Form Co. motto), but they also boasted about the aesthetic value, solidity and very broad visual access that their products guaranteed.

This was also the case of the Dayton Company – a branch of IBM which, we discover incidentally, manufactured commercial equipment long before designing computers. Not only did Dayton also supply, since the magazine began, shelves made of enamelled metal for protecting and showcasing fruit and vegetables (e.g. 1922, 04, 52–53; 1922, 05, 54; 1922, 06, 0), but it went even further, inventing and codifying the notion of open display in March 1926 – four months before Carl Dipman adopted the concept (only to attempt to turn it later, together with *Progressive Grocer* as a whole, into the standard bearer of the modern grocery sector). Dayton roughly defined open display as the art of maximising the relationship between the surface for visual display of the product and the place occupied by the sales furniture.

The second type of furniture appeared in the form of glass cabinets with no refrigeration devices and thus far from being restricted to displaying "naked" perishable food, such as meat, fruit and vegetables, were suitable for presenting all kinds of products. In fact, these "show cases" were themselves also present from the magazine's beginnings, promoted by companies such as Hunt Show Case Co. (1923, 06, 96), Duluth Show Case Co. (e.g. 1924, 04, 97; 1924, 06, 86; 1924, 06, 86), Weber Showcase & Fixture Co. (e.g. 1926, 01, 33; 1926, 02, 67; 1926, 03, 79), Columbus Show Case Co. (1926, 05, 136; 1926, 06, 114), Walker Bin Co. (e.g. 1926, 05, 144; 1926, 06, 79; 1926, 07, 109), and could be found in the sales area of a number of avant-garde grocers (e.g. 1922, 04, 8; 1923, 06, 9 sq.; 1924, 08, 22–23), even if the sale of more traditional furniture, equipped with opaque drawers and cupboards, had not yet completely disappeared (1924, 02, 70–71).

The A-B-C of
Open Display

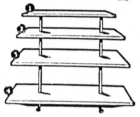

This Is the Dayton Method

It occupies 14 sq. ft. of floor space. It provides 41 sq. ft. of display space. Three times as much as a table, counter or case of the same size.

3 Times the Display Space

3 Times the Selling Power

That's the Dayton Method in a nutshell. Is it any wonder Grocers are turning to the Dayton for greater sales?

Two Models for the Grocery

One for fruit and vegetables—one for canned, bottle or package goods; both for quicker turnovers.

THE DAYTON is a silent salesman. People see—handle—want—buy the merchandise it displays. It makes customers shop. They buy 2, 3 or 4 items when they come in for one.

Increases Floor Space

—three times. Makes every inch sell. Helps clerks sell more—moves "stickers"—makes your store attractive.

Guaranteed in Writing

We issue an iron-clad profit guarantee on every Dayton Method. It must increase turn-overs and profits.

Thousands of grocers say, "It is the best salesman in my store." Make us prove it to you. Your name and address will bring full information and our Warranty Bond.

THE DAYTON DISPLAY COMPANY
Dept. 102   DAYTON, OHIO

THE DAYTON DISPLAY METHOD
The All-Steel Patented Display Stand

Figure 3.16 Dayton: the A-B-C of open display
Source: 1926, 03, 132

It is even more remarkable to observe that despite the coexistence of refrigerators and show cases, it was above all the former that Carl Dipman chose for visual sales. As a good analyst, the author perceived that fresh products corresponded to the interests of his audience, given that independent grocers were better suited to selling these products, while refrigerators, as they were closely linked to service and to back-office concerns about hygiene, were the best way of introducing this other "display" logic, which they also promoted and would in the end, in subsequent years, no longer improve service but rather change the retail trade very significantly.

Despite the initial efforts on the part of the Dayton Company or the journalist Carl Dipman to produce a theory of display, it is important to note the extent to which the gradual addition of "objects that sell" to the "service of salespeople" was an emerging effect, pushed less by a limited and clearly identifiable list of actors or very visible institutions (particularly innovative companies, large chain stores, journalists, professional associations), and more by a host of anonymous innovators, concerned to place their products with all possible customers, drawing no distinction between chain stores or small, independent businesses. The equipment makers knew that all sorts of customers, all acceptable targets, were involved in the infernal movement of modernisation, and were thus also concerned not to "drop out", especially in the context of increasing competition (Deutsch, 2001). They therefore gambled on the fact that their customers were more or less prepared to adopt any tool that was able to guarantee their progress in the general race towards modernity and economic success.

In order to include their products in this movement and to demonstrate that they were the very condition on which it depended, they honed all possible and conceivable arguments in their adverts. More specifically, they used the particular style adopted in copy writing, taking as much care with the text as with the image, always presenting the same object, but using slightly different text and reasoning every time. By refining and accumulating sales pitches, they thus laid the foundations for a broader and more comprehensive theorisation, able to link the innovations together, and giving them meaning, as was shown by the "display" topic. However, they did not stop there. They also implemented an inverted performativity, in which the effect preceded the narrative, by taking care to show their products being used in up-to-date spaces, as shown by the frequent presentation of new products such as electric lights (1924, 01, 93; 1926, 03, 140) or packaged products (1922, 04, 51; 1923, 09, 0; 1926, 02, 37; 1926, 02, 107; 1926, 03, 69; 1926, 07, 99) on the antique counters of old-style shops.[22] This type of advert, particularly innovative in itself, was at the same time conservative in other ways, by virtue of its conviction that innovation would be more acceptable if they had a place and significance in the existing environment. In other words, the components of the old sales context were perceived as necessary props, similar to the lateral felicity conditions of an efficient modernity. In fact, the lateral felicity conditions of the adverts, and thus the performance of the equipment they presented, became themselves the very longitudinal felicity conditions of the magazine's articles given that it is easier to perform a discourse that has already produced at least pictorial effects, as we have already seen the world it promoted a thousand times in previous adverts.

From this point of view, it is fascinating to note the extent to which the progress of commerce as a whole did not solely depend on what history records as major innovations remembered because they have remained, such as cash registers and supermarket trolleys (Grandclément, 2008; see Chapter 5), so much that they are presented as the causes or symbols of self-service. It also relied on innovations which, while they have not disappeared, have at least been forgotten and rejected, pushed to the background of the transformation of commerce. I would like to show these as having played just as important a role by paving the way for their luckier and longer-lasting peers, and thus laying the foundations of the self-service of the future, in line with the more general logic that I presented in further detail elsewhere (Cochoy, 2011b).

First we shall mention false-bottom baskets. This device, as clever as it is elementary, prolonged in archaic fashion the displaying of products beyond the counter, in containers Carl Dipman believed to be too opaque, but developed the modern concern to make merchandise visually accessible by ensuring that products, even if few in number, were always displayed close to the top of the basket – the area that was most visible.

Something similar but more sophisticated was the hybrid containers, associating back-office barrels and crates aimed at maintaining sales of bulk products, and a removable aluminium lid (Inland MFG. Co, Inc., 1922, 10, 92), or

These false-bottom baskets aren't sold, but are used merely for displaying fruit

Figure 3.17 False-bottom baskets
Source: 1924, 07, 22

better still, one of "convex glass strong enough for a man to stand on" (Sanitary Cover Co., 1925, 03, 97). Such equipment was meant to ensure the protection of goods against maintenance risks and vermin (both companies used the same slogan, "keep the kitty out of the prunes"; Figure 3.18), and at the same time cater for the more modern demand for displays.

However, the transitional innovations that were most able to ensure the switchover between the old and new ways of organising commerce were undoubtedly those on the "knife edge of the counter" – a counter which adopted the service logic and the concern for hygienic protection, whilst directing it towards the new demands of the display. This is the case of the "display computing cheese cutter" of the Computing Cheese Cutter Co., which linked a cheese-cutting tool to a predetermined weight scale meant to improve service, while a glass cover aimed equally to protect the merchandise and promote it to customers (see Figure 3.19).

This is also the case with the Panay Company's wonderful globular glass containers, which sat on the counter with their futuristic, transparent, closed front facing the eyes of the customers, and their flap-opening rear at the service of the grocer (Figure 3.20).

However, the most fascinating of these innovations, as well as being one of the most ephemeral and anecdotal, despite it being declared that 7,000 had been put into use when it was marketed, is undoubtedly the machine for distributing cool bottles, made by The Liquid Carbonic Co. This machine made it possible to cool a large number of bottles by sliding them into tubes that were plunged into a tank filled with ice. As the caption states, "[p]ush a warm bottle in and out comes a cold one". This device combined the increasing concern for refrigeration with the old ice box technique, the modernity of packaged drinks and the service tradition, the traditional appearance of a counter and the modernity of a display – like any good technology without a future, this machine was without a doubt one of the devices that best prepared it (Figure 3.21).

Like the glass refrigerators, this last innovation and all those that we have just (re)discovered in fact shared a characteristic: hesitation between the two worlds of service and display, of bulk and packaged products, generic and branded

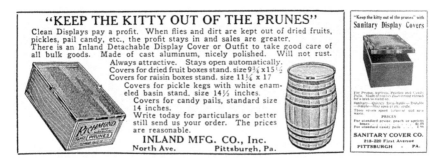

Figure 3.18 Keep the kitty out of the prunes
Source: 1922, 10, 92; and 1925, 03, 97

Figure 3.19 The display computing cheese cutter
Source: 1923, 10, 96

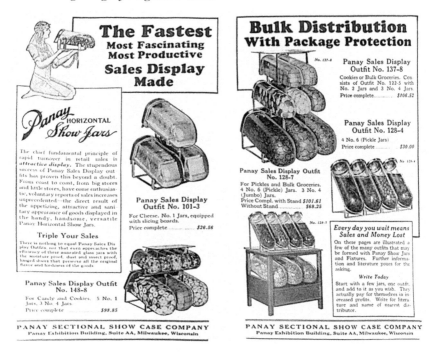

Figure 3.20 Panay display cases
Source: 1924, 02, 86–97

products, counter and shop, product safety and the visual seduction of consumers ... By offering a new way of doing things, while basing it on the old
way, they had the advantage of calming people's fears, respecting habits,
prolonging know-how, and thus enabling the transition from one to the other,
at the risk of their own rapid demise, given that the advent of the world they
contributed to creating would soon ungratefully relegate them at worst to the
dungeons of the past, and at best to the margins of the history of commerce
and shops.[23]

Following in the footsteps of modern commerce, or how to progress with cans

With the introduction of scientific management, the presentation of new
methods of communication and delivery, and the promotion of innovative
equipment able to ensure better merchandise protection and optimum display,
Progressive Grocer resolutely supported the modernisation of service ... but not
only that – far from it. Although the magazine tried its hardest to support and
improve service, above all it made a more general effort to help grocers make
money. In fact, symptomatically, the article launching the series by Carl
Dipman on commercial equipment was titled "Is your store's equipment

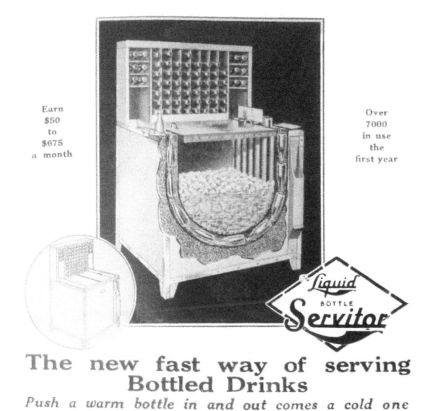

Earn
$50
to
$675
a month

Over
7000
in use
the
first year

The new fast way of serving Bottled Drinks

Push a warm bottle in and out comes a cold one

Figure 3.21 The bottled drinks distributer
Source: 1926, 04, 71

making or losing money for you?" The theme "making money" is in fact repeated three times in the text, as though it were important to underline that the intended aim is clearly more important than the methods used to achieve it (1926, 07, 11 sq.). More generally speaking, almost all of the magazine's pages have but one obsession: reflecting on what to sell and how to sell it, for what level of profit. Service and its improvement, but also the furniture we have encountered, oscillating between service and display, constituted only a few of many responses to the economic questions raised by the magazine.

Among the other responses were the products themselves, especially canned goods. I would like to show that these items played an unexpected role but one that was perhaps more decisive than other elements in changing independent grocers into modern businesses.

From its earliest beginnings, *Progressive Grocer* paid special attention to cans – more attention even, from a certain point of view, than that given to improving service or adopting new equipment. As we shall see, the magazine of course dealt with cans in the same manner as with other subjects, with the help of articles about their advantages, how to promote them and the profits to be expected from them. However, *Progressive Grocer* did a lot more for cans, moving from words to action, from speculative rhetoric to performative narrative. In October 1922, its first year, in an article called "Put on sale of canned goods in dozen lots this month" (1922, 10, 7 sq.), the magazine, despite being extremely new and undoubtedly little known, was unafraid of linking its reputation to its commitment to promoting them: it took the risk of launching a sales promotion of batches of cans, destined for the "Canned Foods Week" in following years, a national campaign whose ambition was to include all American grocers in a seasonal effort to promote canned goods (and, if successful, to promote the magazine itself).

The arguments used by *Progressive Grocer* for selling as well as using canned goods are, above all, deployed in articles specifically aimed at preparing and accompanying the campaign every year (1922, 10, 7 sq.; 1923, 10, 23 sq.; 1924, 09, sq.; etc.), but we also find them in other texts, admittedly rarer and forceful, dispersed throughout the year (1923, 07, 90; 1923, 12, 24–25; 1925, 01, 20; 1925, 09, 13 sq.; 1926, 11, 92; etc.).

The more general arguments, and those less related to the practical aspects of the campaign, consisted in defending the quality of canned food (the content) and promoting the use of this type of packaging (the container). In order to support the quality of these products, the magazine used arguments that were both offensive and defensive, all based on scientific authority, a guarantee that fits so well with its declared belief in progress. On the offensive side, the magazine cleverly used the nascent fashion of vitamins (discovered during the previous decade) by reporting the results of a study demonstrating that canned food was richer in vitamins than food cooked at home (1926, 11, 92). In this respect, it tries to address the Levenstein paradox, along which the discovery of vitamins paralleled that of the evils of industrial production and food conservation techniques (Levenstein, 2003).[24] On the defensive side, it made an effort to provide its readers with counter-arguments that could be used against "customers who think canned foods are unsafe". It thus reported the results of another study, carried out jointly by the National Canners' Association, the University of Chicago and the United States Public Health Service, which showed that 97% of complaints involving canned foods were unfounded, and added arguments favourable to the idea that tinned goods were safer as they were canned at the production site, heated to eliminate germs, and were banned from using preservatives or dyes that were dangerous for this kind of product (1925, 09, 13 sq.). The magazine also promoted the correct use of tins. In fact, it knew that opening them posed risks and difficulties.

In order to overcome these problems, potentially damaging to the product's widespread commercialisation, *Progressive Grocer* armed its readers with a real education on the tin opener, based on a solution that seems odd to our contemporary eyes, of holding the edge of the can and cutting the side of the cylinder rather than its lid (1926, 08, 44), at a time when the first cans,

Little Boy: "Ma wants to know if you'll take that thing and open this can for her."

Figure 3.22 "Ma wants to know if you'll [...] open this can for her"
Source: 1926, 08, 44

formerly with a stopper at the top, had disappeared thanks to (or because of!) the introduction in 1897 of their contemporary, completely hermetic version (Twede, 2012; see Chapter 4). With this innovation, the idea of progress falters, rather ironically, given that we see how a major industrial step forward becomes, at least for a time, a step backwards for the market: the new cans, easier for the manufacturer to make and fill, were harder for the user to handle and empty. Nevertheless, when *Progressive Grocer* was making an effort to relay a clumsy solution to this difficulty, the manufacturers of the accessories Blue Streak (1925, 02, 103; 1925, 08, 86; 1926, 07, 112; 1926, 12, 135) and Star Can Opener (1926, 04, 61) began publishing adverts in the magazine presenting tin openers that were very similar to today's solutions.

This interesting difference between what the magazine said and what was shown beside its progressive narrative by advertisers, which were in fact more "advanced", makes it possible, if not to catch *Progressive Grocer* in the act of professional incompetence, like a teacher whom we discover should himself be learning what he claims to be teaching to others, then at least to assess how new the canned goods market was (at least regarding the second generation) and to evaluate the real obstacle, in the absence of a solution or information, caused by the problem of opening them. Above all, it allows us to observe, once again, that it was the equipment manufacturers – in other words, those with new innovations that came from outside, in a dispersed manner – that were often the first to propose solutions able to carry the grocery store world

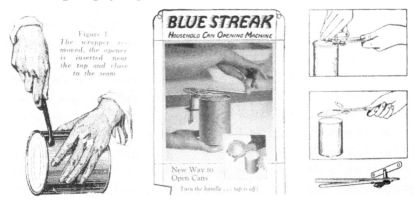

Figure 3.23 The art of can opening
Source: *Progressive Grocer*, 1926, 08, 444; Blue Streak, 1925, 02, 103; Star Can Opener, 1926, 04, 61

forwards, solutions which the actors "on the inside" did nothing more than adopt and integrate, at an earlier or later stage, with varying success.

Progressive Grocer's most fundamental arguments in favour of selling canned goods were linked to the campaign's objectives and presented within its context. The campaign in itself was not exceptional. *Progressive Grocer* in fact willingly recognised, in the first article launching the idea of selling canned goods on a seasonal basis, that it had absolutely no intention of starting to market these products, which were already well established, nor of inventing their promotional sales. In fact, the magazine quotes from someone who testifies "[having] been doing this for the past ten years" (1922, 10, 8) and explicitly points out that, until then, this kind of promotion occurred in March (1924, 12, 3). Therefore, *Progressive Grocer*'s innovation was more modest, yet nonetheless decisive, given that it consisted in moving this kind of promotion from the spring to the autumn, and in focusing very much on sales in lots. Through this double shift, *Progressive Grocer* intended to exploit and promote two distinct advantages of cans: their propensity to overcome a problem of seasonality, and their ability to store food.

Emphasising, or rather building, the seasonality of canned goods on the principle that "every business has its harvest season" (1924, 10, 9) might seem completely paradoxical. In fact, were these cans not, on the contrary, aimed at transcending the seasons, at allowing fresh produce to last for months or even years? Yes, obviously. However, the marketing genius of *Progressive Grocer* consisted in observing that the natural seasonality of fresh produce could serve as the basis for the commercial seasonality of cans responsible for preserving it, and could thus act as a relay. It is precisely because a time is approaching when fresh produce is rare, precisely because in autumn the season for fresh fruit and vegetables was coming to an end (1923, 11, 11), that we can identify the emergence of a period that was more favourable than others to selling solutions intended to replace them. By virtue of the logic, inherent to all operations for ensnaring customers, which invariably consists in developing technical devices aimed at taking advantage of people's dispositions (as I attempted to show elsewhere, Cochoy, 2007a), *Progressive Grocer* invented the annual autumn fair of canned food as a device designed, according to a sexist and almost animal anthropology, to seize upon the sleeping squirrel lying in every female consumer: "Even in this day of prompt delivery, women have a feeling of security if they have a well-filled cellar or pantry" (1923, 11, 11). In the autumn, "[t]he old nesting instinct arises in the breast of the housewife and she wants to fill the larder" (1924, 10, 10).

In support of this chauvinist prejudice,[25] according to which there would be an autumnal mood, leading female customers to stock up for the winter, *Progressive Grocer* highlights that mail-order shops sell more products in November than at any other time of year (1922, 10, 8), therefore implicitly suggesting that if one does not pre-empt this need, there is a risk of seeing the purchasing power involved go to the competition.

Autumn, and more broadly speaking the 1920s, were in fact favourable to the consumption of canned food. Having only been introduced during the previous decade (Anderson, 1953), domestic refrigerators were still very rare; freezers would only be invented much later (Shove and Southerton, 2000). Thus, most consumers continued, as they had always done, to put up with the seasonal eclipse of fresh produce. For a long time, people had the habit of preparing preserves for the winter. At the turn of the century in America, the consumption of dried fruit and smoked meat was still very much a way of life. Thus, the weight of the past created the conditions for the development of a future market. With cans, it was specifically a matter of associating an old practice with its evolution, by making the most of a favourable environment, but turning it in another direction. However, this association was not self-evident: although the broad acceptance of fresh food substitutes created a propitious context for canned food, the habit of preparing preserves at home was clearly an obstacle to its marketing. However, once again the general development of the American economy and society changed the game: *Progressive Grocer* noted that more than half of the population lived in towns, far from individual gardens required for home-grown produce, which is why there was hope of a decline in "home-made" preserves and a corresponding development of the market for their industrial substitutes (1923, 10, 23). This conviction was based on tangible data, such as statistics showing the spectacular progress of canned food sales since 1889 (Figure 3.24).

The magazine also points out that this general tendency towards the development of the tinned food market conceals important differences, particularly those of a social nature. Contrary to its contemporary image, the canned food market was initially directed more towards the upper classes, due to the high price of this kind of product at the time (Mayo, 1993), but also, no doubt, due to the traditional propensity of wealthier social classes to adopt innovations as a way of differentiating themselves and their economic ability to free themselves

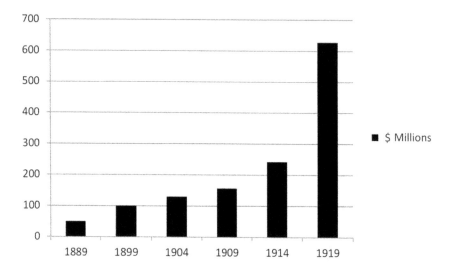

Figure 3.24 Progress of production of canned foods
Source: Production cost, according to 1923, 10, 23

from domestic chores, by adopting more expensive substitutes. Nonetheless, the magazine also featured data demonstrating the very speedy democratisation of industrial preserves, once considered an extravagance reserved for the richest. Thus, a study by the United States Bureau of Labor Statistics, involving 12,000 working-class families, shows that 60% of them buy canned milk, 60% canned salmon, 58% canned sweet corn, 55% canned peas, 50% canned tomatoes, 36% canned cooked beans, 25% canned peaches and 22% canned pineapple (1924, 11, 20).

Although the autumn of 1922 was the best time to promote sales of canned food, batch sales were the best way of ensuring success (1924, 10, 12). One conditioned the other: buying a product at a specific point in time rather than continuously meant spacing purchases and thus storing the acquired goods in the meantime. Although economic and social conditions at the time were favourable to seasonal sales, it was the technical qualities of cans – their propensity to be accumulated and stored without damage to their content or external integrity – which made it possible for them to be "mass" marketed. Batch sales reinforced the seasonal device of seduction with another whereby the logic of calculation was added to the logic of time: the new component of the seduction device in fact consisted in giving buyers of lots a better price compared with the unit price. This time the idea involved gambling on a new version of the sexist animal reference previously drawn on to choose the best season for selling canned food. In fact, in addition to the squirrel Progressive Grocer was trying its hardest to ensnare earlier, here the magazine was making an effort, during this autumnal hunting period, to trap the economic wolf also lurking in all female buyers:

The average woman is a bargain hunter. It makes no difference how much money she has, she is interested in making a saving. It is the hope of making a saving that releases her buying impulses. It is the appeal to her savings instinct that will make her take your sale seriously. Appeal, then, to the *saving instinct*. Therefore the keynote should be *saving*.

(1926, 10, 14–15)

However, the arithmetic of batch sales did not stop there. The calculation proposed to the consumer serves as support for a secondary calculation aimed at grocers, according to another traditional logic in which the first aim and effect of devices for ensnaring customers is always to captivate the captivators (Cochoy, 2011a). In the end the relevance of atavistic or calculating dispositions attributed to the clientele[26] is of little importance if their promotion makes sense to retailers and wins their approval. What counts the most is the idea of first arousing the more predictable and plausible tendency of grocers to take an interest in all things likely to make them money. This is why *Progressive Grocer*, far from settling for telling its readers they must sell lots more cheaply in order to seduce their customers, takes great care to explain why lowering prices will paradoxically increase their profits. Batch sales follow the "profit through volume" strategy – a new strategy that Richard Tedlow (1990) showed had played a decisive role in transforming old-style commerce into mass distribution. Nonetheless, far from presenting the financial issues involved in batch sales in such abstract terms, at the risk of not necessarily being understood, *Progressive Grocer* deploys treasures of arithmetic instruction in order to translate the components and foreseeable profits into terms that were understandable to the men in the trade.

A first argument is based on increasing volume. It claims that batch sales are likely to lead female consumers to consume more than they had intended, basing this assertion on the adoption of anthropological hypotheses. The American housewife, the magazine assures us, is more inclined to prepare her meals by looking at what she has in the cupboard than going to (making someone) buy something else.

When the housewife thinks of supper or lunch, she goes to the larder and looks it over. There, staring her in the face, is a can of appetizing succotash[27] or baked beans or asparagus. She makes a meal of it instead of sending down to the meat market for a pound of beef.

(1922, 10, 9)

Therefore, everything that was already stored at home is more likely to be consumed: "She will use twice as much [of the product] as though she had to buy it from day to day" (1924, 10, 11). A second financial argument can be split into two points. The first points out that batch sales save on service costs by saving the time and energy devoted to sales:

If you can get your customers stocked up in the fall, you will save many deliveries during the winter months. You will save the trouble and expense of selling hundreds of small orders.

(1922, 10, 11)

The second point emphasises that batch sales mean one can increase merchandise turnover – "[y]ou will cut down your inventory" (1925, 10, 10) – and thus earn liquidity – "you will also have considerable extra cash in hand" (1922, 10, 11). In doing so, this type of sale implicitly avoids banking charges: "Instead of your carrying the burden and the investment over the winter, your consumer does it for you" (1924, 10, 10).

However, the effort *Progressive Grocer* makes to list the slightest advantage of batch sales and more generally of canned food sales only makes its complete silence regarding two other savings even more remarkable – savings which are nonetheless equally or more important than all the others put together, and which the same cans can also provide. First, because this kind of packaging can be displayed in stacks and requires no particular protection, whether by a refrigeration system or the intermediary of a display case, it requires less furniture, or furniture that is less costly compared with the marketing of other products. Second, and above all, because tins can be easily handled by the customer at no risk, and because their labels describe the exact nature of the product, its brand and origin, the cans "sell themselves", and thus save on part of the service. It is undoubtedly because they were not aware of these two advantages, or more likely because they were concerned not to frighten the grocery store world which they knew was still deeply attached to customer service and to product substitution, and wary of the universe of brands which reduced their importance and room for manoeuvre, that *Progressive Grocer*'s journalists still preferred, in the 1920s, not to highlight the most distinctive marketing assets of the products they intended to promote.

This promotion, far from being solely narrative, relies on concrete actions, and far from being limited to the efforts made by a single magazine, consists in mobilising the active participation of a large number of actors around this publication. More specifically, the "Canned Foods Week" campaign that *Progressive Grocer* organised every year from the autumn of 1922 combines, according to a pattern we had already encountered with the "Phone for Food" campaign, an effort of collective organisation, driven and maintained by the magazine, with the personal commitment of stakeholders, of which the grocers were of course the protagonists. In order to seduce them, the magazine not only used the aforementioned sales pitches, but two additional devices as well.

The first device is an avalanche of suggestions and advice with which the magazine showers its readers, one campaign after another. They are encouraged to organise preparation meetings with their employees (1926, 10, 16), set dates and a time frame for the special offer, design appropriate advertising, arrange their window displays accordingly, announce the event on the sides of their delivery vans (1924, 10, 29). They are provided with examples of possible window displays, posters, adverts or letters (1924, 10, 12 sq.). In particular, they are advised to invest massively in batch sales and, to this end, emphasise the savings that one can make from this type of sale (1924, 10, 15), to install suitable shelves, for example by "[h]av[ing] plenty of cases of goods in sight to put over the quantity idea", increase the number of signs, distribute leaflets beforehand (1923, 11, 17), etc. Participants are invited to draw inspiration from the "atmosphere" of department stores, given that "[one must not] forget [that women] are used to [their] sales methods" (1924, 10, 16). Similarly, with an opportunistic transposition used by their competitors, the magazine suggests backing batch sales with credit purchases, proposing, for example, instalments of between $10 and $20 a month, proceeding "just as vacuum cleaners or sewing machines stores do".

"Why let other merchants take your customers' money first?" (1924, 10, 49). This last suggestion is a particularly clever way of prolonging the old tradition of credit whilst renewing it, and of finding an appropriate solution to the unusually high cost of batch buying. Lastly, the magazine encourages its readers to use different media to reach out to their customers, such as the telephone ...

> The telephone can be of great assistance. You can call up your customers in advance. Give them a good explanation of your sale and you can call them again when the sale is on, getting their order. The telephone will do much to bring the people in your store.
>
> (1924, 10, 19)

... but also the post, presented as one of the most efficient ways of reaching customers, particularly if they are able to make the most of public systems established to tackle the isolation of rural areas ...

> If you are located in a small town your post office will deliver one of these letters [about the campaign] to each box in the Rural Free Delivery route and all you need to do is address the envelope to the box number.
>
> (1926, 10, 19)

... not to mention, of course, direct contact, vital for ensuring the relatively recent promotion of these food cans whose inaccessible content still worried customers, used to the sensory relationship with products sold bulk (Strasser, 1989), and whose clear and non-negotiable presentation continued to worry grocers, keen to retain their function as mediators. From this point of view, the appeal to "sell [cans] through demonstration", in other words opening a few samples, placing the contents in glass containers and allowing customers to taste them (1924, 10, 17), not only brings promises of profit – "Seeing and tasting will make lots of extra sales" (1924, 10, 18) – but also, probably, an implicitly reassuring message aimed at customers and above all professionals.

The second device used by *Progressive Grocer* to enrol as many grocers as possible in its campaign is the regular organisation of a competition with a $100 prize, half of which was given for the best letter of personal testimony on the subject "[h]ow I (or we) conducted a Fall canned foods sale", and the other half for the best photograph of a display featuring cans of food (1923, 10, 24).[28] Here the magazine launches the method it will use again for the twin campaign started two years later on telephone sales (see above), and which makes it possible to multiply the effect of an almost non-existent budget to a vast territory without having to canvass anybody directly, either upstream or downstream of the operation: upstream because people are committing themselves in the hope of making profits; downstream given that the actions to be taken allow the magazine to obtain, for almost nothing, a huge number of spectacular illustrations, personal testimonies, stories, experiences, "evidence" of efficiency. Countless contributions that it makes a point of publishing and which inevitably (without anyone being coerced, and this is the trick – letters written for the competition make up a kind of readers' letters section and are necessarily laudatory and positive!) celebrate the spirit of the campaign, consider it justified and effective, give examples to follow for the following session or even provide new ideas.

Thus, for example, the prize-winning letter for the 1924 edition of the competition recounts the experience of W. Brown Chiles of the Render Grocery in Texas. His shop achieved a turnover of $9,000 in one week from canned food. Not only does his story appear to validate all the advice given by the magazine, but it also contains an original course of action, consisting, in an astonishingly reflective manner, in using the leverage effect of competition to influence people's commitment on the customers themselves: "Our customers were asked to register their names as they entered the store and each day we gave to some lucky one a No. 3 can of coffee [with no obligation to buy]" (1925, 02, 18).

This collection of responses, far from taking the form of a simple proclamation of results, feeds into other articles: for example, in October 1926 the photos for first and second prize of the previous year (see Figure 3.25) are shown as an example with another shot of a way of preparing the new campaign, but with no mention of their origin. The captions read, "Here are some displays that will sell goods in big quantities", and "Give your store a sales atmosphere by, first of all, displaying canned foods in quantities" (1926, 10, 13). The results of the competition are of course not the only "feedback" to be exploited in such a way. Year after year, the magazine endeavours to point out successful enrolments in order to better prepare the following ones: in September 1924, just before the next campaign, it points out that professionals, canning factories and distributors had followed in the footsteps of *Progressive Grocer* by deciding to adopt the principle of the November campaign, and it makes a point of publishing personal testimonies and letters of thanks (1924, 09, 9 sq.). The same year (1924, 12, 2–3) it mentions that jobbers requested 25,000 reprints of the articles on the previous campaign and then 63,000 reprints of the money-making, "How you can build up quantity sales in Canned Foods Week" (1924, 10, 9 sq.). At the end of the day, the impression (observed and given) is precisely that of progress:

FIRST
PRIZE

(Left) Won by
V. A. Miklas,
The Economy
Store, Man-
istee, Mich.

SECOND
PRIZE

(Right) Won
by McM. Cox,
Flemingsburg,
Ky.

ADDI-
TIONAL
PRIZE

(Circle) Won
by Julius L.
Straus, Straus
Brothers, Dan-
ville, Ill.

ADDI-
TIONAL
PRIZE

(Left) Won by
H. E. Marsh,
Medford, Ore.

ADDITIONAL PRIZE

(Circle) Won by A. J.
Filicsky, 20 W. Main St.,
Danville, Ill.

Figure 3.25 List of winners of the "Canned Foods Week" photo competition
Source: 1925 competition: 1926, 01, 29

> A few years ago Canned Foods Week was more or less an experiment. It was a time when grocers, and only a few of them, put a banner in their windows and piled a few dozen cans around it. [...] But today all is changed. Canned Foods Week has become a national event.
>
> (1926, 10, 11)

Therefore, the advertising of the campaign and its various results have the effect of promoting the event and providing a measure of its success but also of the magazine's audience. This device thus gives credit to *Progressive Grocer*'s authority in its role as a central driver of the progressive grocery world, by virtue of a kind of performative loop where the announcement of a programme is completed with the staged production of its *results*.

This success does not, of course, rely on mobilising grocers alone, but also on the mobilisation of all other actors likely to be involved, such as the middlemen and wholesalers we have just come across and, soon, because of a knock-on effect, the local press and brands. This effort to engage them is based, from 1924, on establishing local committees that the magazine, skilfully optimistic, encourages its readers to contact: "No doubt there is one in your town" (1924, 10, 13). These committees are responsible, as with the telephone sales campaign, for helping and accompanying initiatives on the ground, by suggesting possible campaign actions, promotional material, etc., to grocers wanting to become involved in the campaign. However, once again, this mobilisation does not in any way consist in "prescribing, from above" the implementation of a centralised and hierarchical programme, but instead in defining and creating a common cause and timeframe which it is hoped will simply contribute to the convergence, articulation and success of everyone's well understood interests, while recording and publicising the actions to this effect in the hope that such publicity will encourage other potential participants and thus lead to a snowball effect.

The most obvious organisation of interests is among the grocers themselves, connecting interests that are initially similar yet independent, or even opposed in terms of competition. Therefore, the magazine deliberately points to the case of joint initiatives, such as the cooperative marketing endeavour by grocers of Fremont, Ohio, who joined forces to fund and carry out a shared advertising campaign in the local press (1924, 10, 14; 1924, 10, 17). Another construct consists, on the contrary, in gambling on the possible complementarity of interests among highly dissimilar actors, as is perfectly illustrated when *Progressive Grocer* suggests its readers involve the press, highlighting the convergence between the former's demand for publicity and the latter's need for information ...

> Get your local newspaper to cooperate. The editor will, no doubt, be glad to run some editorial material, telling the people in your community of National Canned Foods Week and what it means to the housewife.
>
> (1925, 10, 14)

... and by offering itself as an example, given that the magazine announces its campaign will be covered by the main American magazines (1924, 10, 11).

A final construct is to make the interests of distributors and suppliers converge, in the name of a common commitment to promote the same products – for example, when the magazine recommends its readers contact canned food manufacturers in order possibly to work with them (1925, 10, 10). Despite appearances, this last convergence is not at all spontaneous, particularly as some manufacturers, because of their size and thus their concern to promote their products as a priority, might have already engaged in an initiative similar to that the magazine intended to promote, but with a different timescale and on their own account.

Indeed, in May 1923, half way between *Progressive Grocer*'s 1922 and 1923 campaigns, the Van Camp company, specialising in the preparation of canned food, did not hesitate to use the cuckoo strategy by advertising in the magazine's pages its own "National Van Camp Campaign", aimed at retailers, with the specific slogan: "Something Good for Every Meal". According to a pattern that was astonishingly similar to the event *Progressive Grocer* planned to develop, the canned food company highlighted that its campaign-produced two-page adverts in colour in the *Saturday Evening Post* were "sending hundreds of thousands of women into grocery stores all over the country to ask for Van Camp's". Moreover, it invited retailers to "cooperate with [it]" and for this purpose offered promotional material, such as a branded placard for window displays and shops, as well as a book with cooking advice – "What to Serve and How to Serve it" – written by "Mrs Harriet Ellsworth Coates", "an international authority on domestic science and good foods" (1923, 05, 50). Two months later, Van Camp struck again, this time by suggesting creating displays using stacks of cans and by presenting no fewer than three booklets. Added to the previous collection of cooking advice came a publication aimed at children, "making thousands of mothers extremely friendly toward Van Camp's entire line of food products", and a booklet for professionals to use, "More Profits for Retail Grocers", which promised "a veritable mine of practical selling suggestions" (1923, 07, 48).

Thus, by 1923 *Progressive Grocer*'s action was not a guaranteed success. Having only recently been launched and therefore still lacking scope, results and renown, the campaign could have found itself facing competition, even threatened by similar initiatives led by the sector's manufacturers. It was therefore with certain pride, no doubt mixed with relief, that in 1924 *Progressive Grocer* declared the cooperation of several canning factories in its own campaign (1924, 10, 11), including, in the following year, Libby's, one of the market leaders, and announced that this manufacturer would undertake a campaign in women's magazines in October to support *Progressive Grocer*'s week. Incidentally, the magazine invited its readers to "write for free display material on the Libby's Foods [they] carry" (1925, 09, 87), thus demonstrating the success of its effort to aggregate different interests, no doubt in the hope of completing the synchronising of all private initiatives to promote sales of canned foods which to a large extent it was responsible for initiating.

In the final analysis, the *Progressive Grocer* campaign appeared as a genuine "private policy" effort. It involved a political effort, in the sense of governing the markets, taking initiative, sidelining laissez-faire and moving from a purely individual entrepreneurial movement to one that was more collective and coordinated. At the same time, this political effort imposed nothing in political terms, but on the contrary, endeavoured to promote the convergence and coordination of the local initiatives and interests of all the actors involved – grocers, wholesalers, press and brand names – and to achieve this not by mobilising considerable or compulsory resources, but instead lighter mechanisms such as narrative and competitions which themselves draw on the logic of information, competition and the market. It was also, simultaneously, an entirely private approach where public authorities only appeared in the background, for example when the magazine mentions food safety measures sanctioned by law, or when it suggests opportunely making the most of the free rural postal service to relay advertising messages cheaply. We are therefore in the presence of a typically American movement, one that is not entirely market based, not completely collective, neither top-down nor bottom-up, and consequently one that is rather a "cross-over", based on competition and cooperation – the "coopetition" (Bruno, 2012) – and which thus manages, through the intentional aggregation and synchronisation of interests, to create a joint movement in favour of a shared object.

This was not just any old object, either. By virtue of their ability to take over from seasonal products and be neatly stocked, canned goods were particularly suitable for selling in batches, which itself supported the development of "profit per volume" strategies. Soon we shall also discover that cans, because they were sealed, because of their labelling and their propensity to be easily stacked up en masse, not only facilitated the art of the "display", but also the direct manipulation of products by consumers, and thus the advent of self-service.

In this respect, canned food ironically caught on the back foot the grocery world promoting it. In fact, the beginnings of *Progressive Grocer* played on a wide gap: on the one hand, the new magazine immediately gambled part of its credibility on the seasonal sale of these canned goods, pointing to a world beyond service; on the other, the rest of the time, it put a lot of energy, as we have seen, into modernising this world, with the help of food safety policy, tools for increasing labour productivity (in the shop), or telephone sales (at the entrance) and motorised delivery (at the exit). If things went in another direction some time after, and to a certain extent simultaneously, if the transformation of commerce soon replaced service improvement, it is therefore perhaps not (solely) because service was facing external competition from other actors, systems and structures. The development of service itself favoured the generalisation of methods that would make it less useful, through the *progressive* (gradual and modernising) introduction of a whole series of small technical innovations, including canned goods, but whose inventory it is necessary to consider if we are to understand better the "other reasons" behind the advent of self-service.

Notes

1 See the Introduction.

2 Tracey Deutsch rightly emphasises that the "community" and "interpersonal" relationships of traditional business could be oppressive, particularly for women, and that price uniformity, cash and carry stores and the generalisation of self-service in chains contributed to loosening this constraint (Deutsch, 2001). However, establishing a radical opposition between outdated small business and modernising chains, as well as attributing innovations almost exclusively to chains, should in my view be subject to caution, if only due to the emergence across the board of these innovations, in particular the open display, at a time when chains were no more quantitatively significant.

3 I shall expand later on the role the telephone played in modernising service.

4 The author of the article only refers to the period that is favourable to his argument: contrary to what he leads us to understand, credit sales were not a "very widespread" characteristic of large shops: on the contrary, they initially began with cash sales in order to lower prices, before reintroducing credit later on (Crossick and Jaumain, 1999).

5 The article about cash and carry sales mentions a hybrid system of the same kind used by a grocer in Arkansas, who also set his prices based on cash sales and added 3% at the end of each month for delivery and credit services (1925, 01, 74).

6 See below for more on the professional use of the phone.

7 A fairy tale character whose strange proximity to the world of grocers I highlighted elsewhere (Cochoy, 2006). This close association is brilliantly confirmed by the very origin of *Progressive Grocer*, given that the Butterick Publishing Company, which launched the magazine, was founded by a tailor and his wife, and had initially specialised in distributing sewing patterns (see Chapter 1).

8 Note that these adverts do not exclusively target the needs of grocers but often present the insecticides they promote as some of the products they are likely to stock. It should also be noted that the subsequent disappearance of these adverts, very present during the magazine's early issues, is an indirect measure of the progress of pre-packaged or tinned products, which significantly contributed to improving shop hygiene (on this progress, see Chapter 4, Figure 4.4).

9 In addition, we find other advice elsewhere. The magazine points out that paint offers good protection by specifying that using a spray gun, when possible, mean cracks in the walls and shelves can be reached. It also shows devices aimed at keeping mice away, such as tin-lined drawers (1923, 03, 24).

10 On systematisation and issues involved in this method, see Chapter 4.

11 In the original, the sentence is in bold.

12 Another case of the same kind was that of a Long Island grocer who kept updated lists of consumers who were especially interested in certain fruit and vegetables, and who were called as soon as a special delivery of their favourite products had been received (1924, 01, 24).

13 See for example: www.tacamor.com/talkamore/does-it-really-matter-if-you-smile-on-the-phone/.

14 By captation (a French word which as no satisfactory English equivalent), I mean the set of operations that tries to exert a hold over, or attract to oneself, or retain those one has attracted, but without resorting to any coercion, especially in market settings where "free entry-free exit" is the rule of the game (Cochoy, 2007a).

15 On these two points, refer back to Chapter 1.

16 Note that farmers and rural America, which we might have considered to be backwards, on the contrary particularly supported the adoption of the telephone, which they quickly identified as having a strong power to open the area up (Kline, 2000, quoted in Spellman, 2009, p. 173).

17 In terms of the additions put forward by the advertising sales pitches, we can mention fewer stock losses and a reduction in maintenance (1923, 09, 101).

18 Data from the USDOT Federal Highway Administration and the US Census Bureau, quoted in Tang, 2011. For a more detailed history on the rise of the car market in the United States, see Flink, 1972.

19 On the generalisation of car parks, see Chapter 4.

20 Here Carl Dipman uses this crucial expression for the first time, one which will play a decisive role in the magazine's policy and the subsequent transformation of commerce (see below, and Chapter 4).

21 This list of companies is of course not exhaustive: the Jabobs Bros. Co. offered similar products (e.g. 1925, 07, 104; 1925, 08, 104; 1925, 10, 69).

22 For an example and analysis of this advertising strategy, see below.

23 In order to be (almost) complete (given how many innovative proposals there are), we cannot leave out the astonishing machine for printing advertising messages on wrapping paper as it was unwound (1923, 04, 87), but which wrapped its own demise by bringing with it the idea that a shop's packages should bear the name of the grocer. And above all, there was the "Step-in-and-shop Serve Self Store" – an extraordinary concept of a truck-shop, which associated traditional delivery with the most modern kind of shopping, by inventing in a single move shop on wheels and self-service, long before the idea emerged, with trolleys, of putting wheels in shops (1923, 06, 66–67).

24 "Apparently crucial in maintaining vision, vitality, and even life itself, these tasteless and invisible items had gradually come to world attention from 1911 to 1921, and they proved to be a boon for food advertisers in the 1920s. Because so little was known about what they did and how much of them was needed for good health (there were no standardized methods for measuring them), they provided immense scope for exaggerated health claims. Thanks to food advertising and home economics in the schools, vitamin-consciousness was wide spread by the end of the 1920's" (Levenstein, 2003, p. 13).

25 For a detailed and fascinating account of gender and social aspects of early American grocery stores, see Deutsch, 2010.

26 The drafting of wording on consumers' efficiency is particularly enduring, as shown by its constant presence in the modern distribution world (Koch, 2012).

27 Traditional American dish made from beans and sweet corn.

28 The competition involved additional prizes from the following month (1923, 11, 9).

4 Transforming commerce

A business of pens and brands

The innovations that transformed the American grocery store world occurred in the market place, in places of competition. According to neoclassical economic theory, speaking about "places of competition" is an oxymoron, a contradiction in terms: there can only be pure and perfect competition in the absence of a place, when the entire market is reduced to a single point, and products can be instantly traded, without any obstacle; competition has no location, other than the theoretical market that is everywhere and nowhere. At the same time, beyond the theory, everyone is perfectly aware that the game of competition is inseparable from the "marketplaces" (Strasser, 1989), organised so as to resolve the following riddle: how is it possible to assign a (real or virtual) location to property rights, whilst simultaneously organising their trade and thus their physical movement in the economic world?

It is remarkable to observe that the two main, generic solutions that were invented to overcome this hurdle – enclosures and brands – were developed for managing cattle – in other words, to control the mythical farming market that contributed to forging the American nation, its culture and, of course, its economy.[1] As the philosopher Olivier Razac (2002) showed, barbed wire fences were initially created to reshape, quickly and constantly, at the lowest cost, boundaries for herds on the prairies, a form of property that was extensive, mobile and temporary. As Jean-Claude Thoenig and Charles Waldman (2005) recalled, the etymology of the term brand comes from these same herds, referring to the branding iron: the brand was invented as a means of tracing the origin of merchandise quickly, cheaply and permanently, either to avoid theft or losses, or to respect and promote property rights on the market, within or beyond the enclosures. Whereas the flexible enclosures helped to gather and maintain the livestock in a specific place so that they could be sold, brands on the same head of cattle promoted their marketing and their tracking accompanied them in the open and external economic space. Bringing together these two stories and two solutions – which are in a way two sides of the same cow! – helps us to understand that markets are a matter of managing property and space; these are matters of "territory", to put it in the terms of Thoenig and Waldman. In a way, the location side of markets is a matter of "penning" and "branding" goods.

More specifically, I would like to show that this dynamic of pens and brands, far from being restricted to the rural world, has also been a motive force in the competitive economy by, for some time, driving the operation of ordinary markets. I shall focus on the spatial methods of these transformations, as used by *Progressive Grocer*, by showing that they relied entirely on the games of penning and branding. These games, which increased in speed and diversity from the 1930s, began by defining the boundaries as well as the signs of recognition between the street and the shop, then between the consumer and the product on the packaging. They continued with technical arrangements for the movement of people and things in the commercial arena, with the help of turnstiles, trolleys, rails, divisions and checkouts. They were integrated into a wider area where manufacturers, the press and *Progressive Grocer*'s adverts attempted in turns to rework the boundaries of commerce, and they ended by redefining and relocating shops themselves, with new stores in the middle of car parks.

We could reduce the history of the modern grocery store world to different kinds of containers, referring to the commercial locations that were transformed at the turn of the twentieth century (Péron, 2004), and to the jars, cans, packets and other recipients used and displayed in commercial spaces, in the hope of moving them. However, not only do both these elements fit into each other but they also share common characteristics: they are both enclosures, hermetic pens aimed at protecting the property of shops and product integrity but they are also spaces for branding, surfaces where one can display the owner's identity and the nature and origin of the foodstuffs. Each kind of enclosure also operates in its own way in transforming the grocery trade, beyond merely improving it, and it is these differences that I would now like to specify.

Real estate: playing within four walls

Let us first consider the real estate aspect. What makes the grocery store different from other kinds of food business is precisely the place, shape and size of the shop. They are parked in the urban space, at the foot of buildings, often all along "Main Street" (Longstreth, 2000), whose area is as precious as it is limited (Mayo, 1993), and their walls cannot be pushed back. The immobility of the commercial premises is self-evident, which makes all the difference with respect to supermarkets. Grocers are in fact proprietors who pass on their business from father to son, as is shown by a number of articles aimed at retracing the enlightening development of the same shop, from generation to generation (1923, 05, 53 sq.; 1929, 12, 30 sq.; 1931, 04, 22 sq.; 1932, 12, 16 sq.; 1939, 03, 40 sq.; 1931, 04, 22 sq.; 1932, 12, 16 sq.; 1939, 03, 40 sq.; etc.). This is no doubt why in most cases and until about just after the Second World War, the physical limits of the shop shown by *Progressive Grocer* were of a kind that had not been designed, that were self-evident, something that could not be modified. The area was arranged but not its boundaries; blueprints could be drawn up, but within the framework defined by the building. The only detours towards the outside were intended to show window displays or the front of a shop, whose name was interchangeable with that of the owner (1946, 10, 76–77), as if businesses were seeking really to distinguish themselves from chains and show that the identity of the independent grocer went hand in hand with the "immobile property".

The blueprints displayed by *Progressive Grocer* in the 1930s and 1940s therefore seem like a kind of secondary architecture, using the traditional architectural sketch as a starting space that could not be modified or discussed, but in which and with which one attempted to play by artfully arranging new equipment and furniture (see Figure 4.1, where the walls are a background against which one moves furniture represented by cut-out pieces of cardboard; 1944, 05, 58–59). Therefore, the logic promoted was clearly based on rearranging what existed rather than radical innovation, as is seen with the obsessive repetition of the topic of "modernisation". The magazine defends a superb model of progressive, qualitative and intensive grocery store transformation, consisting – contrary to the alternative model of extensive growth that was being experimented with at the same time in nascent supermarkets – in rearranging the same number of square metres and the same sales volume, in the hope of increasing the flow of customers and products, and thus boosting sales and turnover.

This rearrangement was based on the invention of the art of "faire (doing) laissez-faire" (Cochoy, 2004), allowing more customers to enter and move around the shop thanks to withdrawing salespeople and thus making products available ("laissez-faire"), whilst efficiently and discreetly organising the new spatial and commercial situation ("faire"). In line with the "faire laissez-faire" logic, promoters of the modernist grocery store devised a very subtle two-fold transition between over-the-counter sales and self-service, with the first stage involving the introduction of a fleeting and quickly forgotten innovation called "open display", which we already briefly encountered in Chapter 3. This open display strategy (1930, 06, 22–23), energetically supported by *Progressive Grocer* throughout the 1930s, consisted in putting forward the idea of "free looking" as an ambiguous kind of modernisation, presented as both an "alternative to" but also a "step towards" the subsequent "free movement".

From free looking to free moving: from "open display" to self-service

Progressive Grocer's big idea involved bringing people and things closer together, making access to products easier, transforming the grocery store so that its customers could take merchandise themselves, without embarrassment or obstacle, in the hope that this closer, more direct and more comfortable relationship between supply and demand would increase purchases (Cochoy, 1999). However, the magazine anticipated that its readers would consider this a risky operation.[2] Accustomed to serving their customers from behind their counters, with most products well protected behind them, grocers might have feared that giving consumers immediate access to the foods displayed could

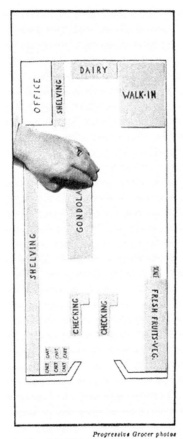

5. AFTER YOU TRY a number of arrangements, you may decide this general plan meets your particular needs best. When you have made that decision, you have but to work out the details, such as whether to let the frosted-food cabinet stand as is, or square it up to the meat case, whether to move the dairy case forward, or whether you have the right size gondolas. After you have placed all the equipment items to your satisfaction, sketch them in by drawing a pencil around the cardboard blocks (or paste in), and you will have a permanent floor plan your workmen can use.

Figure 4.1 Arranging one's shop
Source: 1944, 05, 58–59

only lead to the goods being stolen or damaged (1929, 09, 24 sq.; 1939, 07, 42 sq.; 1941, 10, 481 sq., etc.). Thus, in order to overcome this fear, without for all that abandoning their project of giving consumers more direct access to products, *Progressive Grocer*'s journalists endeavoured to promote the (re-)penning of products behind glass cases meant to support the new "open display" strategy.

These pieces of furniture, called "islands", appeared as shelves, low tables or glass chests, which systematised the direct visual access of customers to products that had previously been unwrapped but hidden in opaque containers, or far from people's eyes, behind the counter and the grocer.

Although the open display marked a clear development compared with over-the-counter sales *stricto sensu*, there are two reasons why it cannot be mistaken for self-service. On the one hand, although both formulae aimed to provide consumers with a more direct access to products, the first tried to do so cautiously, by limiting this access to viewing and thus (more or less) forbidding people from touching the produce. On the other, the open display, favourable to gradual improvements to what existed rather than breakaway innovations, did not involve removing the salesperson and his counter, as with self-service, but in redistributing the material elements of a shop differently, changing the look of some of them and using them in different proportions. In fact, the open display, far from being no more than a new type of furniture, implied, on the contrary, a total reorganisation of shop layout, in the hope of diversifying browsing and thus consumer purchases, as the possible routes clearly attempt to suggest, represented by lines and arrows in the first of two diagrams reproduced side by side in Figure 4.3.

As we can see in the left-hand picture, showing before and after the open display was introduced (Dipman, 1935, p. 12),[3] the double counter, which prevented the consumer accessing products displayed on the shop's wall shelving, has not been removed, but it has been partly moved away from the shelves in order to give the consumer a broader view of the products, and it has been reduced to a minimum, pushed to the back of the shop, so as to ensure that the consumer – in order to access the salesperson, obtain and pay for his products – has first to look at everything the shop has to offer. This offer is now more extensive and more open, thanks to the introduction of a new type of furniture, laid out throughout the central space, extended and unencumbered as the counters have been removed.

Open display consisted in suggesting grocers rearrange commercial fences: the barrier (the counter) was reduced and relegated to the back of the commercial space according to the logic of a pen (the glass cases and the shop equipped with a window). With the external or internal glass divisions, it was not yet a matter of initiating the physical removal of commercial barriers but, on the contrary, of transforming these barriers in order to organise their cognitive transgression: the window display was to the grocer what electrified pens were to barbed wire in the cattle farming sector: it appeared a more discreet yet equally efficient way of preventing undesirable behaviour. Above all, the display also offered customers the chance to "touch with their eyes" what was not

One Big Jump...

*From
This* →

*To
This*

↓

By arranging an "island" in the middle of the store, opening up the shelves along the sides, and locating the meat department behind a wide arch in the rear, an effect of spaciousness before almost unbelievable has been achieved

Figure 4.2 One big jump ... from this to this
Source: 1930, 01, 29

yet directly accessible to them. By doing so, the open display managed simultaneously to preserve the traditional grocery store (the medium of a salesperson was still necessary), whilst modernising it (the direct and visual choice of products was made possible).

However, the right-hand drawing (1946, 05, 55) marks a subsequent step, taken about ten years later: it is supposed to show that self-service (on the right) is superior to over-the-counter and open display sales (significantly, the picture depicting how shops were previously organised features both: a counter on one side and islands on the other). In the organisation of the self-service shop, the counter

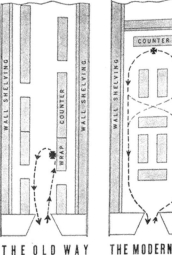

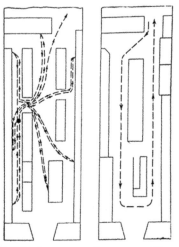

THE OLD WAY

Store No. 1—A typical layout of the old-style store. Most of the activity is in the front of the store. Long counters and show-cases separate customers from most of the merchandise. About half of the merchandise cannot be seen and less than a quarter of it can be handled. The result is that the store's sales expense is high.

THE MODERN WAY

Store No. 2—The store opposite arranged the modern way. The counters and show-cases have been removed and the side walls opened. The center of activity has been moved to the rear. The equipment and displays have been arranged into islands. Now most of the merchandise can be seen and handled. Sales will increase and expense decrease.

LEFT: In counter-service store assembling delivery order takes many steps. RIGHT: In self-service store but one trip (with carrier) through salesroom is necessary.

Figure 4.3 The development of shop routes
Source: Left: Dipman, 1935, p.12; right: 1946, 05, 55

has disappeared and been replaced by a new type of furniture, a "checkout", not placed at the back of the shop but at the entrance (at the bottom of the picture).

Until the arrival of the open display, the grocery store consisted in organising peaceful trade relations between the inhabitants of each territory – the grocer's territory and the territory granted to the customer – each on either side of a boundary indicated using variable markers: the counter and other display cases. With self-service, the boundary is abolished, both territories merge, one moves from the line (of the counter) to the pen (of the shop); between the grocer and his customers, we move from an interface relationship to one of inclusion. Inside the common territory there are fewer hermetic islands; to be more precise, they have been replaced by a single "aisle-end display shelf" which is now not only visually accessible but from which things can be taken too, as we can understand from the circular, single, simple and complete route allowing the same person to remove the products he is looking for – a route which is in strong contrast to the incessant comings and goings of people gathering together to place an order at the counter.

However, who is this person? From one scenario to the next, the subject has not changed: far from showing the linear progress of a consumer in the new self-service space, as opposed to the "radiating" comings and goings of the grocer who had previously been responsible for serving at the counter, both scenarios depict the development of the routes ... taken by the same grocer in both forms of commercial organisation. This is when the elucidation of one anomaly raises a new one: is ensuring service in self-service not nonsensical? Here, the magazine *Progressive Grocer*, aware of its audience's reluctance to introduce self-service as such, resorts to a ruse consisting in promoting the new sales method by reversing the roles: it is a question of showing that the spatial arrangement of self-service, far from removing the grocer and the "service" to which he is committed, allows it paradoxically to continue, to be strengthened and rationalised. The magazine's message is as follows: "grocers, rest assured that the new linear and simplified routes, made possible by removing the counter and using a checkout, open display shelves and a trolley will mean you can prepare your orders more quickly and more easily!" However, the route that the magazine is looking to sell to the grocer as being his own, is also (with the exception of the inversion of the exit) identical to that of the consumer, whom we are of course trying to position behind him.

Packages: from canned goods to cellophane

The second component of the double transition towards self-service was introduced along with the open display, and relied on the role, as remarkable as it was decisive, of packaging innovations. These innovations in fact constituted another way of reinventing the boundary of the counter, which had previously forbidden all direct contact between the consumer and the goods as long as they were still the property of the grocer, no longer at the global level of displays as the glass cases of the open display, but at a local level for each of the products. I am thinking in particular of packaged products, bottles, canned food and cellophane.[4]

With the exception of cellophane, which appeared in 1908, these different packaging techniques emerged long before *Progressive Grocer* – in particular glass, which had been used for millennia. Nonetheless, as soon as we take more of an interest in the market than in the technique, the emergence of innovations matters far less than their extent. Or rather, one should distinguish between two types of innovation, the first being the invention of a new object, the second allowing it to be produced and marketed on a large scale. From this point of view, as old as packaging techniques might have been, they all underwent very significant improvements at the end of the nineteenth century, which managed to change radically their importance and use, as was very clearly recounted by Diana Twede (2012). In 1879 the paper bag manufacturer Robert Gair devised a way of mechanising the cutting out of cardboard for producing packing boxes on a large scale. This first mechanisation was perfected between 1894 and 1900 thanks to the development of machines which, by automatically folding and gluing the boxes, paved the way for modern packaging, and through this to brand promotion.

In 1881 in the metal can sector, the manufacturer Edwin Norton invented a machine that was able to move from 1,500 units by hand per day to manufacturing more than 100,000, contributing to the advent of a new mass market, and to the success of famous national brands, such as Libby's and Campbell, and one industrial giant, the American Can Company.

Then Charles Ams, an engineer with the competitor Sanitary Can Company, revolutionised the design of the cans themselves in 1897 by abandoning welding their parts, which had meant that they had to be filled through a small hole on top (which was then closed using a cork). This was a much more effective method for crimping the parts in a far more practical way, at the risk of squashing the merchandise during filling.

Lastly, the glass industry, which was much older, was paradoxically the last to undergo similar progress: the former self-taught glass worker Michael Owens managed to develop a machine in 1910 that freed glass workers from the age-old blowing of bottles, paving the way for their large-scale production. The standardisation of bottlenecks and bottles served, respectively, to permit the automatic filling of containers at a rate of up to 200 units a minute from the 1930s, and, thanks to the design, the rise of leading brands such as Heinz, Ball fruit jars or Coca Cola, from 1915.

Generally speaking, and as was shown particularly well by Thomas Hine (1995) and Susan Strasser (1989), all of these packaging innovations meant that self-production decreased, products circulated more easily on a national scale, the advent of branded products was boosted and the agrifood industry developed. *Progressive Grocer* thus intervened at a very particular time that was not industrial but rather market based. The magazine began its activity at the exact moment when methods allowing different kinds of packaging to be mass produced and the appearance of a "packaged" economy led, at the beginning of the 1910s, to an invasion – as brutal as it was spectacular – of the American market by packaged products, as is clearly shown in Figure 4.4.

The 1920s and the years that followed thus constituted a period when room needed to be made, not only physically but socially, for these new product presentation methods which, far from being solely additional products in relation to what was previously on offer, on the contrary brought with them a new kind of commercial relationship in terms of merchandise traceability, manufacturers' legal liability, information and consumer choice, product definition, transformation of service, etc. (Cochoy, 2002). In order for these "alien packages" to be welcomed by shopkeepers, the manufacturers concerned and *Progressive Grocer* had to use an art and specific precautions which were particularly well illustrated by the example of food and beverage cans.

Cans helped the actors at the time to understand that the open display glass cases were perhaps redundant, useless. Admittedly, in the adverts reproduced in Figure 4.5, these containers are still quite modest: most of the food cans only appear behind the counter, in the traditional way, according to the traditional sales routine mediated by the grocer, no doubt because the advertisers who designed these small ads knew that most of the professional customers targeted

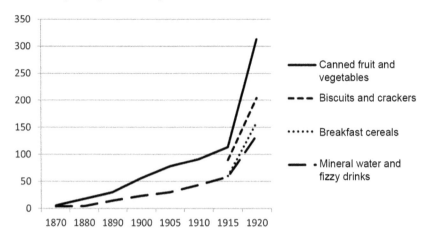

Figure 4.4 Growth in value of packaged products ($ million)
Source: According to the US Census Bureau, quoted in Twede, 2012, p.265

still operated in this way, and that it was therefore sensible, in order to win them over, not to propose anything too far removed from their habits and to strive to operate "all other things (in the grocery store) being equal".

However, upon closer inspection of these adverts, which all used the same narrative, we see that the cans display their propensity not only to stand as a self-supporting stack, without the help of shelves (as areas in which products can be penned), but also to promote their content themselves, speaking at the same time as or instead of the grocer (as displays of branded foodstuffs). Therefore, by virtue of their greater ability to "display" (positioning and exhibiting), food cans were able to move surreptitiously from the silent background of shelves to the chatty forefront of the counter, and thus relegate the grocer to somewhere in between, between the over-the-counter sales of the past and the self-service of the future. This development then increased, particularly with the introduction of merchandising techniques such as the "Monarch way" display (Figure 4.6).

This technique suggested going one step further, jumping over the barrier of the counter by using other enclosures – low tables – in order to make cans even more accessible, and thus operating a shift, as subtle as it was discreet, towards self-service. The Monarch way attempted to make shopkeepers understand that food cans were not only stackable, as was highlighted by the previous advertisers, but could also be directly handled by customers, without the shopkeeper having to fear that such manipulation would cause material (cans are solid) or health risks (cans are hermetic).[5] The standardised size and flat top of metal cans were far more suitable for stacking than the disparate jars, boxes and bins that preceded and/or accompanied them.[6] Their cylindrical shape and modest size encouraged people to pick them up. The two-fold

Modern Merchandising

THE old-time store-keeper kept only what he knew people wanted to buy. The modern merchant makes people want to buy what he has to sell. That is modern merchandising.

Your own customers, Mr. Grocer, buy ten times as much milk from others as they buy from the grocer.

There are greater possibilities of increased business for the grocer on milk than on any other item in your store.

More than half of your best customers are reading Pet Milk color pages in national magazines. On those pages we are telling your customers why they should buy their milk from

the grocer—telling why Pet Milk is the safest, most convenient, and most economical form of milk for every household use.

Pet Milk displayed in your store and window reminds your customers of the story we have been telling them—makes our advertising your advertising—tells them again in your store why they should buy their milk from the grocer.

When you display Pet Milk you appeal to people who are "almost persuaded." You tell them once more to buy their milk from the grocer—and you sell them.

That is modern merchandising.

PET MILK COMPANY
(Originators of evaporated milk) Arcade Bldg., St. Louis, Mo.

Put them on the counter every Thursday!

During Lent, display B & M FISH FLAKES and take the extra profit that the Season offers. B & M FISH FLAKES supply the Sea Food that your trade desires — Cod and Haddock, cooked, seasoned, broken into flakes and sealed in parchment lined tins, shutting out air, from the cold deep sea.

Most grocers know the success of B & M Fish Flakes — your customers by displaying and featuring this delicious Sea Food during Lent.

B & M FISH FLAKES

"The Most Profitable Space in my Store —
—is the space I use for Blue Ribbon Malt Extract."

"Every can of Blue Ribbon Malt represents so large a profit compared with the small space it takes up and it sells so fast that I've dropped slow-moving brands. From now on—it's Blue Ribbon for me!"
—So writes Jos. Sanguinetti, dealer, of San Francisco.

A tip for you—friend dealer! Protect your shelf space. Stick to the brand that sells—and sells fast—Blue Ribbon Malt Extract... "America's Biggest Seller."

Premier Malt Sales Co.,
Dept. C-567
720 N. Michigan Ave., Chicago

Blue Ribbon Malt Extract

America's Biggest Seller
and getting Bigger every Day!

"Sales jumped to 10 cases a month . . .

when we put Jolly Time Pop Corn on the counter" *Says E. M. Schafer*

THE grocer in the picture is Mr. E. M. Schafer. H. M. and his brother John operate the famous Schafer Brothers store in the university section of Minneapolis, specializing in better class goods, and figure that show a real profit. They buy Jolly Time Hulless Pop Corn in ten-case lots.

"Jolly Time is a year-round seller with us," says E. M., "and putting it out where people can see it, has pushed our

sales up over ten cases a month in the winter season. There's room for a ton or two of Jolly Time in nearly every order-bag these days, and by having Jolly time right on the counter, it's no effort to make the extra sale."

The experience of Schafer Brothers, duplicated in thousands of stores, has made Jolly Time the national leader in hulless pop corn. It is an extra-fine grade of corn, specially cleaned and cured to insure perfect popping condition, then hermetically sealed in tin to retain its freshness indefinitely. Being absolutely guaranteed to tollers, and being familiar to millions through national advertising. Jolly Time is proving a rich source of extra profit for grocers.

It is well worth while to feature Jolly Time right now. Get it out where your customers can see it, and just see how fast your stock will turn.

AMERICAN POP CORN COMPANY
World's Largest Exclusive Pop Corn Dealers
Box 784-L, Sioux City, Iowa

FREE TO GROCERS

JOLLY TIME HULLESS POP CORN
Guaranteed to pop

Figure 4.5 Food cans and counters
Source: 1926, 02, 37; 1926, 02, 107; 1929, 08,51; 1929, 11, 127

ARE YOU READY?

HOME from vacations come the American people.
Back to work--"settling down." Factories, workshops and stores take on a busier hum.

Getting ready for school is next on the program.
That in itself means increased buying demand.

Modern stores will profit. Are you ready?

Grocery stores equipped the Monarch Way have an
advantage. New and better foods displayed attractively introduce themselves, make their own sales
appeal, and build sound and profitable business.

Make it a pleasure and a satisfaction to shop in
your store. Mail the coupon and learn how little it
costs to install "The Monarch Way—See It in Glass,
Buy It in Tin."

THE MONARCH WAY

See It in Glass-Buy It in Tin!

▲

**For Independents
Only**

"The Monarch Way — See
It in Glass, Buy It in Tin"
is only for merchants who
own and operate their own
stores. You pay no profit.
You make no contract ex-
cepting your purchases. You
are free and independent.

▼

Quality for 77 Years

REID, MURDOCH & CO.
Established 1853
Main Offices: Chicago, U. S. A.
Branches:
New York   Boston   Pittsburgh
St. Louis   Wilkes-Barre
Jacksonville Tampa Los Angeles
San Francisco

MAIL COUPON TO

REID, MURDOCH & CO.   Dept. R-9
P.O. Drawer RM, Chicago, Ill.
Gentlemen: I am an independent grocer.
Please send me full information explaining
how you will loan me your patented Mon-
arch Display Brackets.

Name ....

Street ....

City .... *State* ....

I do
I do not ☐ handle Monarch Foods.

MONARCH FOODS

Figure 4.6 The Monarch way
Source: 1930, 09, 86–87

suitability[7] of cans to be stacked and manipulated was enthusiastically received
by shopkeepers, who threw themselves into building "mass displays". The
invasion of grocery stores by impressive pyramids of metal cans (see Figure 4.7),
encouraged by canned food retailers (1929, 08, 6–7), food can manufacturers
(1947, 10, 102) and the organisation of display competitions (1939, 07, 117),
strongly contributed to the generalisation of mass consumption, showing incidentally that pyramid sales, long before referring to an abstract form of commercial organisation (Clarke, 1999), initially described a very tangible and
concrete type of distribution (1941, 01, 179). There seems to be little doubt
that pyramids of food cans were one of the decisive props behind the mutation
of grocery stores into self-service: the more products were protected behind
armour, the less the shield of the counter was needed.

The examples of selling cans over the counter and the Monarch way nonetheless show us that the actors involved in this development proceeded very
carefully and gradually. Whereas the first adverts attempted to reach a very
measured compromise between the "open display" of cans and over-the-
counter sales, Monarch was just as cautious whilst focusing its restraint

Figure 4.7 Can pyramids
Source: 1931, 04, 24

elsewhere, in the form of a clever device involving a display of merchandise samples under glass, in order to encourage the sale of the same product in cans: "See It in Glass – Buy It in Tin." This way of operating reminds us of the extent to which the acceptance of products concealed behind opaque packaging was far from self-evident (Strasser, 1989). The Monarch way replays the strategy of the invisible enclosure of the showcase at the level of the product itself, in order to show customers that the opaque cans did indeed contain what they concealed, that cans showed more of their product and displayed it differently rather than hiding it, by using another of their remarkable properties – their ability to operate as a writing space that was simultaneously descriptive and contractual, able to lead consumers to exchange the advice of a grocer with vested interests for the promises of a brand committing its name and responsibility in the long run.

The cans' opaqueness, far from contravening the open display, in fact helped with the invention of a new transparency, that of packaging, which paradoxically allowed the consumer to learn more about each product than from direct contact with it, thanks to the description about its content and origin (Cochoy, 2002), while doing without the previously necessary mediation of the salesperson (Strasser, 1989). Thus, the generalisation of food cans was inseparable from the promotion of leading brands such as Monarch (1929, 08, 62–63), Libby's (1929, 11, 6–7) or Gerber's (1930, 01, 74–75), and from the emergence of new preferences, such as a taste for vitamins (1937, 03, 10; 1941, 03, 142–143; 1942, 09, 97).

Lastly, food cans completed and accelerated the entire development thanks to the activation of a final property, more discreet but no less significant: their ability to introduce a barrier capable of slowing down the progress of time. By making it possible to preserve goods for longer, food cans deformed the competitive space. Henceforth, products from further afield or that were older could compete against fresh produce from local markets. Food cans thereby contributed to the disappearance of the segmented markets of the past and to the unification of the mass American market (Tedlow, 1990). They played a part in replacing bulk products controlled by the salesperson, with branded products supported by manufacturers' advertising (Grandclément, 2008). They led grocers to grant more concessions to their suppliers, to the extent of rearranging, step by step, the entire point of sale.

Cellophane – an innovation dating back to 1908, industrialised from 1917 (Horowitz, 2006; Bowlby, 2001; Grandclément, 2008), and promoted by Dupont in *Progressive Grocer* (1932, 02, 68–69; 1932, 12, 6–7; 1950, 08, 185) – completed this development. Thanks to its transparency, this new packaging in fact supported the open display logic, increasing and extending to other categories of products (such as dried pasta and vegetables) one of the characteristics of glass jars, which were widely disseminated for the same reasons (1924, 04, 87; 1925, 02, 97; 1925, 03, 90; 1929, 08, 56–57; etc.). However, cellophane's waterproof quality (admittedly also a characteristic of glass) and above all its flexibility (a characteristic of its own) ensured its transition towards self-service by offering the consumer, from then on, the chance to see and touch products without risking dirtying or breaking them.[8]

Furniture: adjustable shelves and baskets

Far from stopping at the edge of the commercial enclosure or the surface of packages, the logic of penning, filtering and channelling customers extended

CELLOPHANE DOUBLES *and* TRIPLES SALES *of*

GROCERY STAPLES –SOMETIMES AT HIGHER PRICES

Safeway Stores find visible packaging a remarkable sales stimulant even for bulk items having little eye or appetite appeal

SAFEWAY STORES are very much pleased with results from their present use of Cellophane. They find that Cellophane is a perfect medium for merchandising, particularly in a self-service store. They plan to use it in *every* store and on many additional products.

This great Western organization presents an outstanding example of the new trend in merchandising food staples which is sweeping rapidly throughout the country. It took bulk products out of bins, barrels and burlap bags and put them up in small Cellophane units. The new packages

proved ideal for displays on island counters, and were more convenient for the housewife to buy.

Overnight these homely staples in Cellophane acquired attention value. Sales increased at an almost unbelievable rate, *sometimes at higher prices.* In some cases sales were doubled, even tripled.

The sales value of Cellophane as a wrap for **food products of** nearly every kind has been proved by stores everywhere. A folder called "Proof" contains evidence gathered in actual retail store tests. Write for a copy to Du Pont Cellophane Co., Inc., Empire State Building, New York.

Cellophane

MADE ONLY BY DU PONT

Cellophane is the registered trade-mark of the Du Pont Cellophane Company, Inc., to designate its cellulose films.
In Canada the trade-mark Cellophane identifies the same products manufactured exclusively by Canadian Industries Limited.

Figure 4.8 Cellophane
Source: 1932, 12, 6–7

itself, on the contrary, to what was in between. Taking up space with display shelving and "islands" created the only route possible for re(viewing) all or almost all of a commercial offer that was in full view.[9] Other "flexible penning" devices on the supply side, such as vertically adjustable shelves but also mobile, lateral dividers between products, encouraged the regular adjustment of products according to customers' flow and their choice,[10] just as barbed wire had made it possible quickly to reshape enclosures according to herd size and movement.

The problem with penning objects cannot, however, be stated in the same terms as penning people. Whereas channelling the flow of customers consisted, as we saw, in finding a way of making them easily walk through the entire space of a shop where the crossing point of the counter has disappeared, in favour of a checkout which only intervenes at the end of shopping, generating the flow of products meant reconciling the former need to stock (according to the grocer) with the new logic of removing items (linked to the customer's point of view). The change was considerable: proper storage not only had to allow the grocer to locate his merchandise easily, but synchronically also allow the customer to find what he was looking for by himself and, if possible, draw his attention to what he was not looking for! Diachronically, storage also had to make it possible to follow closely customer movements and ensure product renewal, not only so that the grocer could make the best use of a limited space (from a logistical point of view), but also in order to offer the customer a visually saturated space, with no gaps (from the aesthetic point of view).[11]

Overcoming all of these difficulties involved finding a way to separate products (in order to keep order and favour stock legibility), whilst making these divisions mobile (in order to optimise storage space and ensure the visual continuity of supply). The means of doing this was found by bringing back and moving the frontier-based logic, no longer as the old frontier of a single and fixed counter (responsible for separating people), but as numerous new and mobile frontiers (meant to put products in order). From the beginning of the 1930s, vertically adjustable wooden shelves could already be seen (1931, 04, 26). However, in the 1950s, this type of system was generalised and perfected thanks to the emergence of metal furniture (1951, 02, 54 sq.) with lateral supports (1951, 03, 50–55). This made it possible to adjust more freely the lateral space occupied by different groups of products on one shelf, while (above all) removing opaque obstacles that were particularly annoying as the consumer could now move freely, adopting different viewing angles which under no circumstances were to be obstructed.

The use of metal wire – derived from the old barbed wire industry! – also made it possible, in the 1950s, to invent mobile lateral divisions, which were very useful for adjusting the supply of loosely sold products more efficiently, such as the "endless baskets" of the Tote-Cart Co. (Figure 4.9).

Such innovations, which allowed shelves to be adjusted vertically, laterally and in depth, were as discreet as they were crucial. They were discreet: the first was based on thin perforated toothed racks which could change everything; the second only appeared at the bottom of an advert mainly dedicated to a trolley (the Tote-Cart Co. was, as its name suggests, a company that mainly specialised in manufacturing this latter type of equipment); the third was merely a

"ENDLESS" makes the DIFFERENCE

THE MODERN METHOD OF
SHELF   MERCHANDISING

**ENDLESS
DISPLAY BASKETS**

Tote-Cart patent No. 2868391

TOTE-CART
COMPANY

226 West Superior St., Chicago 10, Ill.
WHitehall 4-4440

Figure 4.9 Endless Tote-Cart baskets
Source: 1959, 12, 142

variation of equipment that was already old. They were crucial: they made it possible to continuously reconcile and adjust the two apparently opposing worlds of organisation and market, frames and flows, property and moving entities (products, customers, money ...).

All in all, everything was arranged so that one could move effortlessly from one pen to the next, not only from outside to inside the shop but above all, once inside, from the fixed enclosures of shelves, islands and display shelves to the mobile enclosures of trolleys and cars, similar to the way in which cattle were transferred from pens to wagons when changing owner. Nevertheless, we cannot confuse products and customers. The latter, far from passively surrendering to being channelled by their surroundings, were themselves involved in the game of penning and branding, and called on to brand their property by placing the chosen items in the trolley's pen. Inside the shop, the clientele were in some way "penned in and penning": they were allowed to move whilst being directed; they were led to enclose products whilst being given more freedom to do so.

Checkouts: mobile barriers

This logic of transferring from one place to another (pens) and from one owner to another (brands) is of course applied at a crucial point, at the till, whose successive improvements attempted to overcome the difficulties of shifting places and identity. Here again, the problem consists in reconciling the smooth flow of traffic with tightly controlled operations, and the exact and exclusive attribution of baskets of products to their respective customers, despite the increasingly rapid succession of both. Managing the flow appears to have preceded the control of its sequencing with the emergence, during the post-war period, of tills equipped with rotary trays (1953, 02, 179; 1953, 05, 114) or conveyor belts (1950, 10, 220–221; 1953, 04, 162). However, the increased speed allowed by these devices soon led to a possible confusion of tasks ... and thus to a solution being proposed that was able to resolve it (or display it). This solution took the form of a small, very simple bar, connected to the conveyor-belt tills and intended to mark, when passing through a till, the boundary between different customers' purchases. Whereas the conveyor belt facilitated the flow logic, the small bar made it possible to re-establish the order and discontinuity needed for control.

In the Zephyr advert (see Figure 4.10), the commercial argument clearly gives priority to addressing the grocers it was trying to persuade to buy the whole device, by emphasising the importance of the part (the bar) to the whole (the conveyor-belt till), and by stressing in bold type that the former "prevent[s] check-out errors automatically". As a contemporary reader, I almost recognised this bar as being the first occurrence of these small mobile enclosures intended to mark the temporary property boundaries between different customers which we have today. However, upon closer inspection, we see the Zephyr bar is different: it is, instead, a small, single, fixed barrier intended to protect the

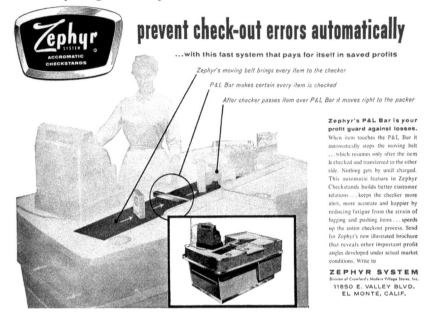

Figure 4.10 The Zephyr till prevents check-out errors automatically
Source: 1955, 10, 229

cashier's calculation by blocking each product at the "control point", without actually hindering the movement of the conveyor belt.

However, just as the preparation of orders had a few years earlier been a ruse for selling self-service and trolleys that were mainly aimed at the customers (see above), the argument for preventing checkout errors was also a clever way of presenting an object from the grocer's point of view that was just as useful for preventing possible conflicts between customers ... conflicts which for that matter had arisen following the introduction of another kind of mobile barrier which intervened downstream, separating the purchases of two different customers at the checkout whilst preserving, as far as possible, the continuous movement of the conveyor belt as before (see Figure 4.11).

With such devices, we finally discover that the wonderful expression "mobile counter", used by Catherine Grandclément (2008) to describe shopping trolleys, can also be applied to checkouts: whereas the trolley means chosen products can remain immobile (in relation to each other) while the customer moves about, the conveyor belt means products can move forward while the consumer remains immobile. The till is precisely the place for penning products and for marking property rights. One does not go without the other: although the products move from one pen to another (from shop to trolley, from trolley to conveyor belt, from conveyor belt to bags – see the "loading stand" arranged below the "moveable partition" in Figure 4.11), at the same time they move from one brand to another, one owner to another,

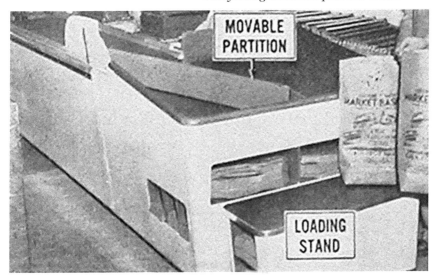

Figure 4.11 A moveable partition
Source: 1951, 07, 84–85

from hand to hand (from manufacturer to grocer, grocer to customer). For all that, the shift between brands and pens is far less radical than we might think given that professionals endeavoured, at every transfer of location and owner-ship, to preserve the trace of the previous allocations, in the hope of encoura-ging a subsequent repetition of the same circuit. The grocer's products carried the manufacturer's brand, just as the consumer's bags – acting as a new enclo-sure intended to prolong/relay the trolley – would soon bear the brand of the grocer ("your name goes here", states the paper manufacturer's advert aimed at retailers, see Figure 4.12).

Turnstiles and magic doors

The art of "faire laissez-faire" thus consisted of re-installing everywhere the general barrier of the counter which we thought had been removed: between products, in the form of adjustable shelves and partitions; between customers and products, in the form of wrapping or boxes able to prevent deterioration and to distinguish clearly between times of purchase and consumption. All of these barriers, which were very effective in channelling the lawful uses of self-service, were nonetheless often ineffective in terms of preventing unlawful behaviour, particularly theft (1941, 10, 81 sq.). Here we find the central dilemma involved in managing self-service: how can one allow customers to move about as much as possible in order to increase sales, whilst preventing this free movement from leading to the disappearance of a large number of pro-ducts (in an open universe people are more daring)? In a less dramatic way and regardless of all fraudulent customer behaviour, it was also necessary to find a

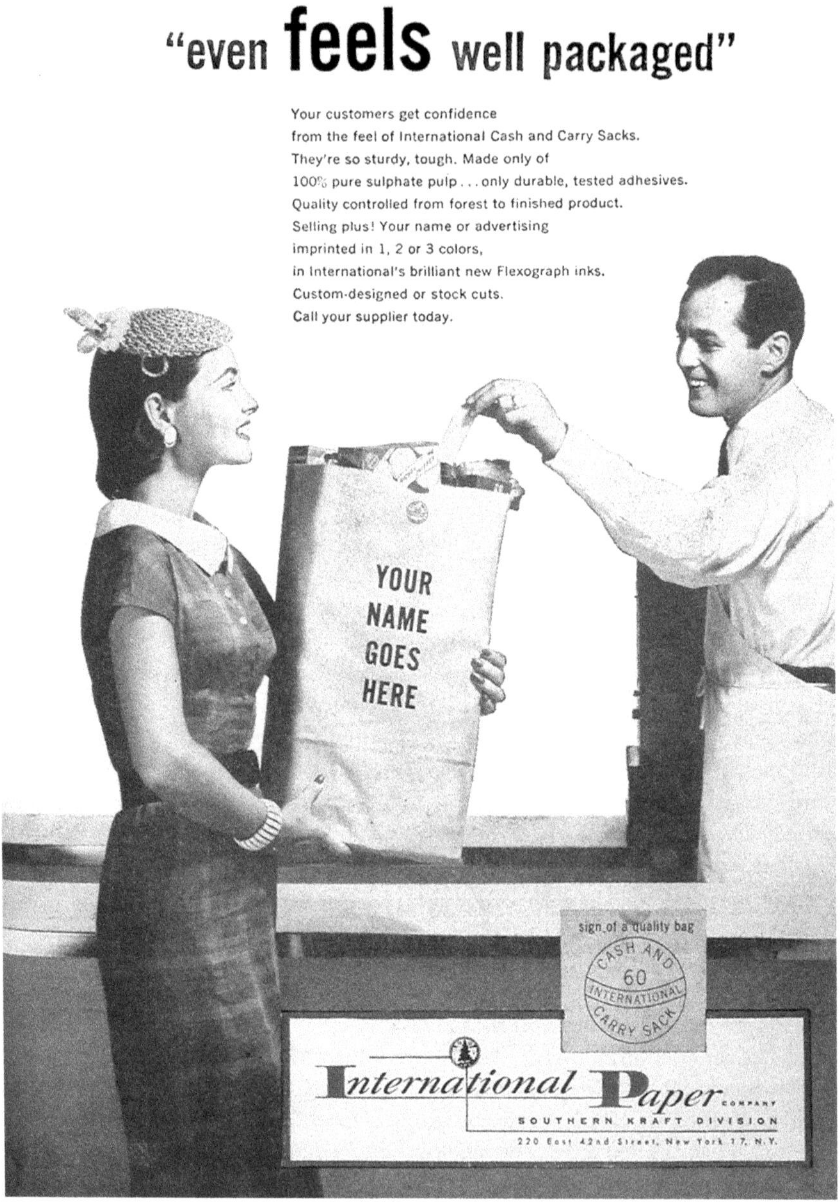

Figure 4.12 "Your name goes here"
Source: 1955, 12, 1

way of organising the maximum commercial openness whilst preserving the identity, atmosphere and thus enclosure of the shop.

Inside the shop, self-service appeared the cause and solution to the risk of theft, and of course also a means of facilitating product access. *Progressive Grocer* suggests that the best (anti-theft) barrier is paradoxically the absence of one: the adoption of lower furniture is meant to give customers a more panoramic view of what is on offer and thus better access to products, and allow the grocer to watch over the sales area and thus the consumers (1939, 07, 43).

At the shop's boundary, "free entry, free exit", the monitoring of customers and the enclosure of the shop are finally reconciled as a double reinvention of the door. Bruno Latour (1988a) demonstrated that the age-old device of the hinged door was the invention of an unlikely "hole-wall" – an arrangement that spares the person wanting to enter an enclosure from having to make an opening, and exempts the person wanting to isolate himself from building a partition. Now, grocery equipment manufacturers found a way of splitting this device and slightly modifying its properties, at both the shop's entrance and its exit.

At the shop entrance, setting up open display was accompanied by the installment of "turnstiles" (1938, 04, 94), a kind of almost invisible door which, despite offering no resistance when customers entered, did resist when they exited, thus breaking from what had until then perfect reversibility of the door on hinges, whilst also to some extent filtering customers.

Contrary to the doors equipped with mechanical door-closers (Latour, 1988a), the turnstile imposed no physical discrimination – it turned without the slightest effort, with no particular gesture being required even to push it – but it did create a deliberate cognitive and technical discrimination targeting children and their mischief and pilfering (I shall come back to this). The discrimination was cognitive given that the presence of a turnstile conveyed the image of control and of something forbidden. If this image was not enough, the equipment manufacturer Boston Metal Products Inc. suggested adding technical discrimination in the form of an "apron below the turning arms [which] keeps children from crawling through the gate" (see Figure 4.13, left-hand image).

In the grocery store the reversibility of the hinged door was broken: turnstiles only turned in one direction. Thus, the aim is less to close the door again (an action to which, for that matter, it is only complementary, as the traditional door was still nearby) than to enclose customers, so as to oblige them to exit somewhere other than the entrance, to overcome the difficulty of surveillance resulting from moving the counter to the back of the shop at the time of open display (or to the removal of this counter when switching to self-service), but also to lead the customers to browse as much of the shop as possible whilst going around the islands and display cases they encountered on their route, and thus to encourage them to make, if possible, several stops and purchases. This programme was particularly likely to be successful given that making a purchase was the best way, for those who had entered the shop and could therefore no longer leave discreetly, to avoid the discomfort that was always felt of being

Offers New Turnstile

Boston Metal Products Co., Boston, Mass., announces it is now filling orders for this all-purpose turnstile. The unit features a flexible railing arrangement that can be made to fit any requirement for complete self-service or semi-self-service markets, large or small, it is said. As a consequence, any number of individual entrances can be set up. The apron below the turning arms keeps children from crawling through the gate. The turnstile works either clockwise or counterclockwise, turns at a touch, and is said to be of unusual strength and durability.

Figure 4.13 Turnstiles and magic doors
Source: Left: 1945, 11, 206; right: 1941, 05, 177

empty-handed when passing the grocer (at the time of the open display) or the cashier (at the time of self-service) before reaching the exit. In other words, turnstiles contributed to converting the visitor into a buyer.

The exit was also the object of particular care given that in the 1940s it was equipped, like the entrance, with new ad hoc doors of a completely different style. It was still a matter of installing a "quasi-barrier" – one for marking property boundaries, avoiding draughts and maintaining an ambient temperature – but also, as with the case of the turnstile, preventing undesirable intrusions. A "quasi-barrier" obviously allowed people to leave as easily as possible, whilst ensuring that the door closed every time. It is as if an attempt were being made to rediscover the hinged door whilst ridding it of its greatest flaw, the need to push or pull it, which Bruno Latour (1988a) demonstrated could never be perfectly obviated by any kind of mechanical door closer. However, here, achieving such an objective was even more urgent and necessary as no compromise was possible. It was no longer a question of making do with a partial solution, which only allowed adults to pass unhindered whilst ignoring their less energetic ascendants and descendants, but rather of allowing everyone to leave and letting nobody in: the strong and weak, young and old. If everyone had to be allowed to leave, it was because every customer, no matter who, left with his arms full, and therefore found himself in an awkward position once the door had swung back. Shopping trolleys, which could have helped to overcome this difficulty by acting as a battering ram, did of course exist, but we shall see in the next chapter that for a long time they were retained within the shop, consequently leaving the consumer to face the problem of being overloaded alone, as soon as he had gone through the door, or rather encountered it once again. The reason no one was allowed to enter was to prevent two opposing flows from hindering surveillance by the staff and thus increasing opportunities to steal.

It was precisely these two difficulties that the invention of "magic doors" managed to overcome, as they were able to open by themselves, or nearly – in any case without anyone needing to push them (1941, 05, 177), thanks to simply moving a foot (recognised by a "magic carpet"; 1951, 02, 201) or the body (identified by a "magic eye"; ibid.), and only doing so in one direction, from the shop towards the street. The magic door thus managed to do away with all its ancestor's little flaws, identified as problems by Latour, since for the first time it was able to create a perfect and completely universal "hole-wall" requiring no particular intervention of the person wishing to go through it to open or close it. Nonetheless, we should observe that although the "hole-wall" was perfect, it was not reversible, given that it borrowed its ability to work in one direction only from the turnstile. As is summed up in this commercial sales pitch by the manufacturer, Stanley, magic doors are designed to offer "greater customer convenience", "faster traffic turnover", "extra pilferage protection" (1954, 05, 226).

Turnstiles and magic doors were nonetheless devices that were not only mobile in space but also in time: their properties only made sense when in reference to the characteristics of the technical system they conditioned but whose developments they also followed. When magic doors were first put in place in the 1940s, it seemed that only shop exits were equipped with them, whereas entrances had to be content with a traditional door followed by a turnstile. However, in the 1940s some grocers began to remove the latter.

Why? A first reason is that the presence of a turnstile, although more discreet and silent than a suspicious grocer, demonstrates a suspicion which, despite dissuading certain people, such as children, from doing stupid things, also appears unpleasantly out of place to customers devoid of any dishonest intentions, especially at a time when this kind of surveillance device was certainly not generalised. This is recognised by a grocer who decided to remove them: "I never liked them anyhow. They always made the store seem kind of unfriendly" (1947, 07, 59).

However, behind this "anyhow", we can guess that there were other reasons behind the removal of turnstiles and these were probably more decisive. A second reason relates to the intrusion of trolleys into the grocery store world, which began at the end of the 1930s (Grandclément, 2006) and became irresistible in the 1940s (see Chapter 5). These vehicles could not go through the turnstiles at the time ("How are the customers going to get the carts through the turnstiles?"; 1947, 07, 59), causing a dilemma: either the turnstile was retained and the shop's useful space beyond was invaded by stored trolleys, or trolleys could be pushed near to the entrance and the sales space thus preserved at the cost of removing the turnstile. It was the choice of the latter option, when it was selected, that lay behind a third reason calling for turnstiles to be removed.

In fact, the use of trolleys in itself led to a shift from the open display towards self-service. Why have a mobile basket if not to move it effortlessly throughout the shop and fill it yourself? The shopping trolley brought a predatory affordance into play: it was no longer a matter of just looking, but of taking too, since now people were equipped with a receptacle for instantly and effortlessly transforming each impulse to buy into an actual removal. The use of self-service "by trolley" changed methods of payment: first, as we saw, in a limited space the counter becomes an obstacle to customers' movements, particularly when they are encumbered with their new vehicle; second, giving over the commercial space to customers soon makes it clear that the best place to pay is not the old-style small counter at the back of the shop, but rather a checkout near the exit.

The low height and increased storage capacity of trolleys at the time (equipped with two baskets, one on top of the other, with one very near the ground) in fact worked together to create conditions that were favourable to the generalisation of a new kind of furniture – checkouts – which were like lowered counters, better suited to unloading trolleys. It was no longer a matter of taking the products that a grocer had gathered and placed on the counter, but of emptying the contents of a trolley filled by the consumer, meaning the cashier had to bend down, hence the need to shorten the gap between the level of the trolley and that of the till. Tills were soon equipped with "tunnels" (1940, 05, 93; 1948, 04, 72; 1951, 09, 96–97; 1952, 09, 78–79) or "rails" (1940, 10, 98; 1941, 01, 46; 1948, 12, 63; 1956, 03, 130; 1956, 05, 114) to ensure that trolleys were returned in an orderly fashion, and that conveyor belts or rotating discs were better able to absorb the increasing flow of goods.[12]

However, the use of one or several tills and above all their location at the shop's exit soon made turnstiles redundant, especially in very small grocery stores, given that these tills allowed those working at them a place from which to observe incoming flows and an efficient way of monitoring the exits, and also the ability to observe and monitor these flows discreetly. The installation of tills thus constituted a third reason arguing in favour of removing turnstiles, as our witness tells us: "both entrances are right next to the check-out counters. The checkers can see anybody trying to use them for an exit [...] What other reason is there for having a turnstile?" (1947, 07, 59).

We thus see how a change to a technical system of the grocery store world led to a cascade of changes to other elements. The introduction of the trolley brought about the move from the open display to self-service, and thus to a change in the technologies linked to these two forms of sale: the counter disappears in favour of the till and, with the till, the turnstile becomes a hindrance and loses its usefulness. Meanwhile, the magic door becomes more interesting: it discreetly reinforces control whilst allowing customers to move around with their arms full of bags, which the use of trolleys tended to increase in number and volume. As things progress, thanks to the continuous combination and rearrangement of these innovations and the corresponding purchasing system, we see a complete change to the movements of consumers who are both more mobile and more independent.

All in all, the interlocking dynamic of pens and brands that I have just brought to light completes the problem of "faire laissez-faire" already encountered. On the one hand, the gradual introduction of self-service created the liberal utopia of unhindered action by economic agents on the market ("laissez-faire"); on the other, and paradoxically, the professionals were well aware that this kind of utopia could only take shape through very strict guidance and control operations, with the help of devices that ensure smooth movement (conveyor belts), channel (rails, display cases) and control (cashiers) – devices that subtly connect these three operations, such as trolleys, turnstiles and tills. This is why we can refer to actions aiming to "faire laissez-faire".

Interlocking brands

The question that then arises is of course the identity of the agency responsible for "faire (implementing)". Was it a single actor, driving the fiction of the market alone, or was it a series of actors? Were these actors all human agents or did they include technical devices? In other words, who were the actors who wanted or were simply able to manage the enclosures where the market operated? The use of pens provides us with a clue: they were the means to and thus witnesses of the remote action required. Our agents can be found far from the commercial scene. Beyond the cans, shops and devices linking them, beyond the barriers and pens, but also paradoxically on the surface or close to each of these elements. We find, first, commercial brands that made themselves conspicuous to place their name within the commercial enclosure as well as to cross the barriers marking their boundaries, to promote the fact that they belong to a circle (see Figure 4.14) to unlock another (fighting against grocers replacing your brand with their own (Strasser, 1989), or to prevail against competing brands).

However, immediately after coming forward, one actor shows us that paradoxically, in order to stay afloat alone, it was better to act as a group. In order to promote itself Coca-Cola was careful to use all commercial mediators. In the space of a single-page advert, all competing locations and actors are summoned: Coca-Cola, of course, whose product, message and logo occupy the centre and half of the scenario, but the press as well, in two ways if you will. Closer inspection shows us that we are not in the presence of a Coca-Cola advert, but rather, using a dizzying mise en abyme, a Coca-Cola advert carried by a magazine that is open on the right page, which itself is featured in the magazine … *Progressive Grocer*. All of this is emphasised by the impressive circular "portfolios" of the magazines where Coca-Cola adverts appear, and explained by the message "Full pages in leading magazines are selling Coca-Cola for the food store".

The food store (and its owner) is therefore clearly present – not only by delegation, with the discreet depiction of a small display case for a six-bottle

FULL PAGES IN LEADING MAGAZINES ARE SELLING COCA-COLA FOR THE FOOD STORE

Month after month, striking full-page advertisements in full color are telling home-makers everywhere that hospitality begins at the food store. That ought to mean *your store*. And it can —if you stock and display Coke in cartons and cases . . . and if you use Coca-Cola display material for food stores to identify your place as refreshment headquarters. Ask the Coca-Cola bottler how you can tie in with the whole great program of Coca-Cola advertising to add traffic, volume and profits to your present business.

*   *   *

"Coca-Cola" and its abbreviation "Coke" are the registered trade-marks which distinguish the product of The Coca-Cola Company.

Figure 4.14 The circularity of magazines
Source: 1948, 08, 97

pack (a reduced reflection of a shop in which every grocer should be able to recognise their own), but also directly, given that it is precisely the grocer (on the other side of the advert) who is being addressed, as a reader and recipient of the advice given in the second person plural: "That ought to be *your store*. And it can – if you stock and display Coke [...] ask the Coca-Cola bottler." Lastly, in order to whet the grocer's appetite, he is shown smiling customers with a Coca-Cola (almost) at their lips, ready to consume the many bottles that are bought directly from his shop, if he ensures he can provide them.

However Coca-Cola (and of course many other manufacturers[13]) was far from being the only actor playing the same game of exhibiting and articulating marketing mediations in order to "take (or rather impose) its brands" on their market place.[14] Each type of marketing mediation involved, penned into Coca-Cola's advert, played a similar game to support its own interests, starting with newspapers (particularly *Life*) which insisted on their talent for selling products and being seen in retail outlets (see Figure 4.15).

In the *Life* advert, the kind of media and actors that Coca-Cola had placed in the background to distribute its products come to the fore, to sell *Life*'s own products: the mainstream magazine is promoting itself to sell its advertising

LIFE MAGAZINE... LIFE DISPLAYS...
sales maker!   sales booster!

Every week, LIFE presents the world in a unique combination of pictures and words . . . pictures and words that are crammed with interest . . . that are alive and meaningful.

Here is thrilling journalism that has won LIFE a larger weekly audience than any other magazine . . . a reading audience of *1 out of every 3 families in communities throughout the nation!*

Is it any wonder then that LIFE's advertising pages continually create sales for the LIFE-advertised products you sell?

The picture below shows a typical advertised-in-LIFE display that follows through on the initial buying impulse created by LIFE!

These LIFE ad reprints, streamers, posters, and stickers that say *"You saw it in LIFE . . . you can buy it here!"* constantly remind customers of the ads they've seen in LIFE and of the products they've been meaning to buy.

Point-of-sale material like this—thousands of grocers agree—increases traffic, points out their stores as headquarters for nationally advertised brands, and brings ADDITIONAL sales!

Are *you* making these *additional* sales!

LIFE, 9 Rockefeller Plaza, New York 20, N.Y.

Andrew Williams, San Mateo, California

Figure 4.15 Life magazine ... *Life* displays
Source: 1949, 10, 154–155

power. Since the modern market emerged, brands and the press have been indivisible: the press supports advertising and advertising supports the press (Cochoy, 1999). However, here the sale is indirect: what *Life* is selling is not its own issues or even the advertising space for advertisers. Admittedly, the latter are clearly present in the picture but they feature as quasi-generic "products they've [consumers] been meaning to buy", with the example of tomato juice cans that are difficult to identify unless "advertised-in-LIFE". No, what *Life* is looking to sell is the power the magazine has to accompany products from the home of the consumer (who buys the magazine on the left for 20 cents) to the point of sale (as merchandising devices that are able to remind people of the initial branding of products, in a way from the domestic pen to the commercial one[15]). Therefore and once again, a same kind of enclosure and brand – the magazine *Life* as an advertising pen – promotes itself by relying on all the others: the manufacturers' brands they are promoting, the grocers they are offering to help, but also *Progressive Grocer*, to whose accounts and modernisation efforts it contributes (see the discreet mention of the magazine's name in the bottom left-hand corner of the page), not to mention the consumer-reader who is the basis of the entire sales pitch ("a reading audience of *1 out of 3 families in communities throughout the nation!*").

The examples of Coca-Cola and *Life* give the impression that the fight for first place was always between manufacturers and the press, relegating other actors – shopkeepers and consumers – to the background, to the periphery. This is both true and inaccurate. It is true because neither consumers nor even independent grocers had the means of expressing themselves directly in the space of *Progressive Grocer*. It is inaccurate because *Progressive Grocer* precisely presented itself as the spokesperson for grocers (and occasionally consumers seen from the point of view of the grocery store). In all the adverts I have presented and from the outset, *Progressive Grocer* was always present, given that it is this magazine's physical pages that bear the narrative of all those who think they are expressing themselves in the first person (as is emphasised by the discreet running head bearing the magazine's name as close to each advert as possible[16]). Sometimes, and noticeably in its early years, *Progressive Grocer* spoke clearly and deliberately, by including within the enclosure of its pages inserts such as "Read the advertising pages" (1929, 08, 1), or "Always mention THE PROGRESSIVE GROCER when writing to advertisers", as a means of involving grocers in promoting the advertising space on which the magazine depended (1930, 01, 102). In addition, *Progressive Grocer* of course inserted, from its inception (see Chapter 1), regular adverts in its own pages and for itself (see Figure 4.16).

This time, it is no longer the branded product or magazine that occupies the front of stage, but *Progressive Grocer* presenting itself as a press organ in its own right – "The National Magazine of the Grocery Trade" – with a broad readership – "*75,000 distributors that handle 60 to 90% of the volume of nearly every manufacturer*". Here, *Progressive Grocer* promotes its own brand to draw manufacturers into its pen, using a very subtle strategy consisting in first making

WHEN a grocer speaks favorably of a product, five out of ten women will buy it.

If he puts it on display where people can see and handle it, sales always move ahead. If he puts it under the counter or in the back room to be sold only on demand sales always fall off

The more a grocer displays a product, the more he pushes it, the more he suggests it, the more he advertises it, the more of it he will sell.

This is an elementary principle of merchandising. You know it. We know it. Every grocer knows it.

Obviously every manufacturer wants to have the grocer on his side. How can you win the grocer's interest? The same method that gets the pull of the consumer will get the push of the retailer.

Advertise to the grocer. Tell him about your product, ask him to display it, tell him why, keep telling him, and he will display it and push it, and sell more of it.

THE PROGRESSIVE GROCER will carry your story to the 68,000 leading grocers, to all the wholesalers, to the leading brokers, to the buying executives of all the chain store organizations to the 75,000 distributors that handle 60% to 90% of the volume of nearly every manufacturer.

THE PROGRESSIVE GROCER

The National Magazine of the Grocery Trade

79 Madison Avenue   New York

Figure 4.16 Is the grocer on your side?
Source: 1931, 02, 2–3

manufacturers face the anxiety of Buridan's donkey:[17] between "your product" and "your competitor's product" (implying "which are as alike as two identical haystacks", note the strange similarity between the right- and left-hand pictures in Figure 4.16), which will be chosen? However, the way this dilemma is represented then aims – and herein lies the trick – to focus the worried manufacturer's attention on another, more fundamental choice, undermining the first – in other words, the choice of the farmer who sets the scene for this impossible choice and thus makes it possible for the consumer, if not to be freed from his indecision, at least not to choose at random: "Is the Grocer on Your Side?" This is precisely the question. And for the grocer to be on your side, *Progressive Grocer* suggests that one must of course work on him, in other words continuously place adverts for him to see in *Progressive Grocer*, "the magazine of the grocery trade". The magazine thus plays a role of another invisible brand and another invisible enclosure, encircling all the others. *Progressive Grocer* presents itself as a place where competition meets, a place that exposes it, a place that shapes and directs it. "To you all, my dear readers, I will explain how to fight one another (for my greatest profit)." *Progressive Grocer* intends to brand the competition, *to make an impression*: printing the names of brands but also impressing them, relying on the press to apply pressure on its audience (of grocers) and the public (of consumers).[18]

However, one should not be deceived; once again, we should be careful not to stop at the image. Examining three adverts – a well-known brand, press magazine and *Progressive Grocer* – allows us to identify the actors involved in the game of pens and brands, but not to conclude that their positions were stable and hierarchical. If I look at the advertising game at this or that point, based on this or that advert, that advert will dominate, whilst at the same time mobilising the others. However, there are as many dominant places as there are actors. From this point of view, what is being played out in the space of the grocery store is analogous to what occurs on Escher's stairs (Figure 4.17). If I focus my attention on one of the characters on the stairs, those who are on his right are lower down and those on his left are higher up. However, since this observation is valid at any point, no actor, paradoxically, is at the top or bottom of the stairs.

In commerce we have the impression that the actor under consideration is always at the top of the stairs and that all the others are at the bottom. However, as all of them are in this position it is impossible to know who is at the top and bottom of the advertising chain, who dominates of the manufacturer,

Figure 4.17 M.C. Escher, "Ascending and Descending"
Source: © 2014 The M.C. Escher Company – The Netherlands. All rights reserved. www.mcescher.com

press, retailer and consumer. The actor controlling in one sequence is always being controlled in another.

The interlocking of brands and enclosures manages to "keep the market going" (as well as make heads spin – confusing them and directing them as appropriate). Everyone in turn defends his place, brand and territory: the press is seen as a public space, brands as a national space, small business as a local space, and *Progressive Grocer* as the central space where, in its own view, this round should be played out (clearly with its own competitors on the horizon, *Chain Store Age* and *Supermarket Merchandising*, which respectively promoted, from 1927 and 1936, chain stores and supermarkets). The juxtaposition and rotation of these identities and locations obviously poses an existential problem for the shopkeeper, who must take into consideration the movement of brands and enclosures, affixing its own brand and arranging his enclosure, even questioning his place and identity.

Re-penning commerce and being noticed

Over time, the permanent redefinition of enclosures (pens) and "fancy words" (brands) that made it possible to manage a grocery store caused it to redefine itself, spatially as well as morally. For a long time, whilst energetically modernising itself as we saw, independent commerce remained small commerce: although the furniture, decor and supply of products were considerably renewed, this was to better preserve the stabilities of these places, the permanence of the small shop, firmly planted within its four walls, immobile on the edge of the street. However, soon, with the increasing use of cars and the proliferation of other kinds of commerce on the edge of town, streets became too narrow and too cluttered to make it possible to park vehicles. This was why some became concerned to establish themselves elsewhere, on the edge of town (1946, 10, 54–55; 1953, 08, 48–52). The relocation of shops to outside town centres ended up making location a variable that was adjustable as well as recoverable in another way.

Regarding adjustment, the logic was that of expanding enclosures both inside and outside: inside the movement was of course one of increasing surfaces (1955, 02, 142–143); outside it was directed towards organising car parks, the "car enclosures" that little by little became the subject of the same kind of care given to "arranging", which had previously been reserved for the shop's "enclosure for products and customers". People took an interest in developing a city-wide inventory of parking possibilities (1956, 03, 62–63 sq.). They asked themselves about "the best arrangement parking areas" (1956, 05, 41), just as until then the concern, to the point of nausea,[19] had been the best shop layout (see above). They considered pooling car parks between companies where there was a lack of space, and their impact on the value of land as well as on turnover was measured (1956, 10, 160–163). Car parks were used as an extension of merchandising by using big signs outside the shop to point to certain products (1956, 09, 261). Parking places were invented especially for returning trolleys (see Figure 4.18).[20]

However, perhaps what is most important is found elsewhere, with the increasing value of the sales space which still made it possible – for the last time? – for the respective dynamics of pens and brands to come together and combine their properties to defend and extend commerce. The relegation of sales surfaces to the background of car parks in fact provoked problems of identification, and thus led to the invention of a new type of description for commercial identities, in the form of gigantic signs (brands) at the top of flagpoles planted in the middle of car parks (see Figure 4.19).

The extension of the brands and enclosures dynamic to outside the shop constituted a turning point, not only for the former because this movement came with a mutation to their size and thus their identity, but also, significantly, for the magazine *Progressive Grocer*, which had no other choice than to encourage and accompany this movement, first by adopting a larger format in 1950 (pen), then by equipping itself with increasingly large headlines (brand): *The magazine of mass food selling* in 1952, *The magazine of supermarkets and superettes* in 1953, *The magazine of supermarketing* in 1957.

This would be an appropriate place to stop: at the point when the grocery store and *Progressive Grocer* had a basis for the modern shape of the supermarket. Stopping, or rather going back in time: as always, the shopping universe incites us to go down the same path indefinitely. In addition, before leaving my readers to return to this same type of circular occupation themselves – armed, I

**Parking area
for shopping carts
saves time and money**

The new Supreme Market in South Weymouth, Mass. has many money saving features within its colorful walls, but the parking areas designated for shopping carts taken to automobiles have already paid their own way.

Wisely located throughout the parking lot with easily read signs, these locations have proved most successful in keeping carts from rolling loosely about the lot, and causing accidents and damage.

Designated employes make periodic trips through the lot and collect the carts which have been precollected by considerate customers.

MORE ▶

Figure 4.18 Shopping cart parks
Source: 1958, 04, 100

BECAUSE their sign had to be erected a certain distance back from the street to conform to a city ordinance, The Boys Market placed this striking, shopping basket-shaped sign on their parking lot.

Figure 4.19 Flagpole of the Boys Market
Source: 1956, 10, 172

hope, with new knowledge about the associated dynamics – I would like to look with them, in greater detail, at the tool, more than any other innovation, that accompanied, facilitated and transformed the grocery store. I would like to invite my readers to take a trip with our trolleys around the supermarket – or more precisely the "minimarket" – given how much the development and transformative power of this vehicle, which has become the symbol of today's supermarkets, owes to the cramped space of the grocery stores of yesteryear; more so than all the other innovations explored until now.

Acknowledgements

This chapter includes elements taken from "Reconnecting Marketing to 'Market-things': How Grocery Equipment Drove Modern Consumption (Progressive Grocer, 1929–1959)" by Franck Cochoy from "Reconnecting Marketing to Markets" edited by Araujo, Luis; Finch, John & Kjellberg, Hans (2010). Printed By permission of Oxford University Press.

This chapter also includes elements taken from "Market-things inside": Insights from Progressive Grocer (United States, 1929–1959) by Franck Cochoy from "Inside Marketing: Practices, Ideologies, Devices" edited by Zwick, Detlev & Cayla, Julien. Printed by permission of Oxford University Press.

Notes

1 I am not only referring to the imagery of the Western, with its cowboys, but also more fundamentally to the unification of the American mass market (Tedlow, 1990) and the subsequent development of mass marketing, in which the agricultural economy played a leading and pre-eminent role (Cochoy, 1999).
2 See studies on how self-service was received by distribution professionals in America, England and Sweden: Rachel Bowlby (2001), Paul Du Gay (2004) and Hans Kjellberg and Claes-Fredrik Helgesson (2007).
3 This drawing was not borrowed from *Progressive Grocer* but from a book written by its leading author, Carl Dipman, and published by the magazine (similar to a special edition).
4 Cardboard boxes bring together the properties of cellophane and food and beverage cans, given that they borrow a degree of flexibility from the former and the opaqueness of the latter. In the developments that follow, after a general contextualisation of technical progress in terms of packaging, I suggest examining the case of cans and cellophane more precisely, which allow us to understand, particularly clearly, how all packaging operates.
5 Nonetheless, a new risk emerged – that of theft – given that a small can slipped far more easily and discreetly between the equipment of commercial enclosures than a large cow between the strands of a barbed wire enclosure!
6 For a complementary perspective on other aspects involved in the standardisation of food cans in France, see Bruegel, 2003.
7 Perception specialists speak about "affordance" when referring to the skill of things themselves to prescribe particular uses (the shape of a handle inviting people to grasp and turn it; the colourful protuberance of a button urging us to press it; etc.) (Gibson, 1977).

8　Of course, the intervention of cans or cellophane was not exclusive; their contribution to the transformation of commerce was accompanied and supported by the use of glass jars and cardboard box packaging. For more information on these other innovations, see Cochoy, 2002, 2008a; Grandclément, 2008; Hine, 1995; Twede, 2012.

9　The importance of low furniture and tubular devices is vital: these elements provided maximum visual openness, useful to both the consumer (for scanning the products) and the grocer (for watching the shop).

10　The analogy is not coincidental: several commercial equipment manufacturers at the time – trolleys, turnstiles, metal shelves – were specialists of metal wire and/or metal, such as American Metal Products, Inc., American Wire Form Co., Boston Metal Products Corp., Lyon Metal Products Inc., or United Steel and Wire Co.

11　See the birth of merchandising as the art of efficient product presentation, a subject to which *Progressive Grocer* is very much dedicated (Barrey, 2007).

12　For more details on these two points see Chapter 5.

13　The advertising rhetoric consisting in highlighting all the media outlets in which one appears in order to make an impression, is endemic. We could mention dozens of examples of brands displaying coverage of their products in the magazine press (Cocomalt, 1929, 08, 125), but also in radio messages (Camay, 1939, 10, 76), and also in all these media simultaneously, to which we can add the daily press and urban posters (Kellogg's, 1940, 07, 79), and shortly afterwards, television (Simoniz, 1952, 08, 146–147); etc.

14　For a similar analysis, see Grandclément, 2008.

15　The practice of brands recommending merchandising is recurrent (including in the history of French commerce, see Barrey, 2007), to the extent that we would be justified in presenting manufacturers as the real inventors/promoters of self-service. See the National Cash Register, which literally sold and performed this kind of sale (1939, 01, 80–81); see the American Can Co. (1947, 11, 26; 1948, 03, 30; 1950, 10, 33), and Nescafé (1950, 01, 174–175), which suggested using trolleys as displays; see Coca-Cola, which suggested shelving tips (1950, 12, 130–131); see Texcel, which supplied micro-shelves that could be attached to tills for selling its sticky tape (1951, 02, 166–167), etc. On the one hand, brands promoted their enclosures; on the other, enclosure – and trolley – manufacturers suggested using their material as an advertising vector (1957, 04, 228).

16　The name *Progressive Grocer* is always featured on the left of the even-numbered pages: it is therefore visible on the double page of *Life*, but also in the bottom left-hand corner of the Coca-Cola advert we reproduced.

17　On the marketing use of Buridan's donkey, see Cochoy, 2002.

18　For an enlightening analysis of the role played by the trade press in the organisation of markets, see Kennedy, 2005.

19　Continuously featuring the restarted and renewed layout of the perfect shop was a recurrent theme in *Progressive Grocer*; there are almost countless references we could mention in this regard.

20　Even if it is more anecdotal, car parks were even used reflexively as a commercial space for selling cars (1958, 08, 68).

5 Rolling stores, or the tour of trolleys

The introduction of the shopping trolley truly played a key role in the transformation of the grocery store, and yet up to now I have only mentioned this
introduction in passing, indirectly and late on in the journey, when discussing
the problems with doors and turnstiles. If I proceeded in this way, it was not
through a lack of logic or a failure to do justice to this innovation, but because
I made the choice to adopt an approach that followed the movement of the
actors themselves, who took a long time before paying attention to the shopping trolley. Indeed, this vehicle holds a mystery. After its introduction in
1936, the trolley quickly invaded both advertising space in *Progressive Grocer*, in
various forms produced by no fewer than four manufacturers in the space of a
few years (American Wire Form Co.: 1936, 08, 107; United Steel & Wire Co.:
1938, 02, 182; Metwood MFG. Co.: 1938, 05, 163; Folding Carrier Co.:
1940, 06, 161), and photographs of points of sale reproduced by the magazine
(1937, 05, 45; 1938, 04, 94; 1939, 05, 43; 1939, 07, 43; 1939, 10, 77; 1940,
09, 83; etc.), by causing in passing – this is exactly the word – the transformations that I have just briefly mentioned, and many more that I shall present.
However, in spite of this presence and these effects, this innovation was to
continue being neglected by the magazine for a very long time, which devoted
almost no articles worthy of this name.[1] Shopping trolleys revolutionised things
and people, quite literally – they accompanied consumers' "tours" around
shops and encouraged stock "rotation" – and yet the grocers' magazine showed
them a disinterest that never ceases to be astonishing.[2]

More specifically, this disinterest focused on the trolley's direct and positive
contribution to the consumer and commercial change. However, the trolley
became an object of interest for the magazine when it discovered it could be
used as a display (1945, 06, 74–75; 1945, 07, 123; 1949, 12, 60; 1950, 01, 40–43;
1950, 02, 66–69; 1950, 03, 46 sq.; 1950, 08, 38–39),[3] a handling tool (see Chapter
4; 1944, 06, 211; 1945, 10, 94–95; 1946, 12, 46–47), or when, as time went on, it
became a cause for concern. It was discussed when it needed to be repainted
(1946, 06, 74–75), when it squeaked (1946, 02, 70), when it did not work
properly (1943, 09, 54),[4] or when, much later, it disappeared after starting to take
over time in car parks (1957, 11, 142–146).[5]

How can this mystery be explained? How could a magazine that made a profession out of supporting the tools for transforming commerce have failed so badly in drawing attention to the one tool that would end up becoming their symbol? Although no certain explanation is possible, I shall risk putting forward two hypotheses, both of which stem from the necessary distinction between the magazine and its readership that was underlined in the first chapter. Indeed, the clear contrast between the almost complete editorial absence of shopping trolleys and their advertising and pictorial ubiquity seems to show that what did not interest *Progressive Grocer*'s journalists nevertheless held the attention of its readers.

The mystery of trolleys

As we have seen, *Progressive Grocer* is a magazine that bet everything, at least initially, on the open display. Its journalists can be defined as merchandising enthusiasts who, like "commercial decorators", were above all attached to furniture, product placement, shop architecture, the high-quality organisation of sales space, much more than to commercial management and logistics. It is therefore highly likely that they found it difficult to become interested in this (dreadful?) trolley which did not fit very well (or too well!) into their frame of reference: this object "can't stay still" and therefore does not fall within the logic of planning and layout, except when asking ourselves – using blueprints with more general objectives – about the best way to park it (1944, 05, 59; 1946, 03, 58). In addition, the ownership of the trolley is variable (it belongs to the grocer but also to the consumer whilst they are shopping), as is its content (which is in the process of belonging to the consumer whilst still being the property of the grocer), and this complicates how it is understood: it is symptomatic that the magazine is only really interested in the trolley when the grocer controls it exclusively. Finally, and *a priori*, the trolley accepts choices more than it shapes them,[6] which undoubtedly endows it with less importance, in the eyes of specialists, than the merchandising that they were attempting to develop.

The second hypothesis concerns the more open attitude of users which, in my opinion, in order to be fully understood, must first be compared with the innovators' point of view. Thanks to the remarkable works by Catherine Grandclément (2006, 2008), we now have a better understanding of the industrial history of the supermarket trolley. This history was particularly marked by the grocer Sylvan N. Goldman who, drawing his inspiration from a folding chair, in 1936 invented a chassis with two seats, small wheels and a handle which could not only effortlessly move two baskets, but could also be folded back when not in use. The device was then perfected by an engineer, Orla E. Watson, who made the chassis baskets more solid and, above all, introduced the possibility of telescoping trolleys laterally when not in use, thanks to the ingenious addition of a hinge and small, mobile gate at the back of the trolley. Goldman, the first innovator, then copied his challenger's method and, following a lengthy copyright lawsuit, recovered the use of the patent on the condition he paid Watson the corresponding royalties. The entire[7] history is summed up in an advert in which the original trolley is relegated to the bottom left-hand corner, whilst the new telescoping trolley by Watson's Telescope Carts Inc. (1949, 04, 258), adapted by Goldman's Folding Carrier Corp. (thanks to the disappearance of one of the two baskets), is proudly presented at the top (Figure 5.1).

This history, far from being limited to the backstage of an industrial, technological and legal confrontation, took place continuously with reference to the public stage of the market (at its accompanying uses). The market intervened either as a restriction weighing on the temporal framework of the industrialisation process (Grandclément, 2006), or as a resource of which manufacturers tried to take advantage in order to move their businesses forward, via the shaping of commercial sales pitches. From reading the advertisements of trolley sellers – the list of which should not be restricted to the Goldman-Watson[8] pairing – one would think everything happened as though their product had been made "for" developing mass consumption. Every time that quantitative argument for "more" (more money, more volume, more sales, more profits …) is put forwards – in line with a trope that incidentally appears as one of the figures required for selling any kind of equipment to readers of *Progressive Grocer* – and this argument is completed by the promotion of the more qualitative benefits suitable for supporting the particular solution offered by the advertiser, according to a clear logic of differentiation. For example, American Wire Co. accompanied the promise borne by its trolleys of "bigger sales per customer" with the careful transposition of the health benefit that the company had used thus far to promote its metal baskets, meant to guarantee "no-germ[s]" (1936, 10, 180). United Steel & Wire Co. claimed that "United baskets and carts mean more of her money in your pocket at greater profit for you", whilst emphasising that its trolleys provided "the least amount of fatigue" (1938, 02, 182). A few months later, the same company associated the quantitative argument of sales volume with a new characteristic of its trolleys, that of foldability: "UNITED Folding Carts are designed to give your customer maximum purchasing capacity and at the same time take up only a minimum of your floor space" (1938, 05, 165), an argument used three pages later in the same edition by Metwood MFG Co. This manufacturer also presents trolleys that are both lucrative and foldable – they are deemed "the Most convenient, Practical and Profitable [shopping carts] on the Market!" – whilst nevertheless pointing out that they are different: the solid sides of the baskets will ensure they do not "bend, jam, catch together like nesting baskets" when they are stacked (1938, 05, 162), contrary to the defects thus implicitly attributed to the competition.

Therefore, everything occurred as though the trolley had been made "for" developing mass consumption, and as though it had happened thanks to the thousand improvements added step by step, as though the latter had responded to the needs of the grocer and his customers with regards to fulfilling their respective objectives. However, before yielding to the comfort of "socio-logical" interpretation, we could also ask ourselves whether or not trolleys had been initially manufactured "to sell trolleys", full stop! For if the arguments on their

Figure 5.1 From the folding cart to the telescoping cart
Source: 1947, 11, 225

potential contribution to increased sales, ergonomic improvement of purchases and optimisation of commercial logistics were commercial justifications given by their inventors, we do not know whether the main interested stakeholders – retailers and customers – adopted trolleys for these reasons and in this spirit. In fact, the users' viewpoint cannot necessarily be deduced from that of the inventors. The fact that trolleys were becoming widespread does not give us the reasons behind it, and it would therefore be hasty to conclude that the innovation's dissemination proves the performative effect of the sales pitches meant to justify it. Although the dissemination of trolleys could have been responding to a real "functional" interest, could it not also refer back to the concern to "follow the crowd", according to Tarde's logic of imitation (Tarde, 1903; Grandclément, 2006), or according to a more traditional mechanism of distinction (Bourdieu, 1984)? Could the trolley not have been to the small grocery store what the tractor was to small-scale agriculture – namely, a matter of pride and modernity which could not be reduced to the utilitarian dimension of the service rendered (Mendras, 1958)?[9] Or, put more simply, were not trolleys introduced "in passing", because they were available, were part of the equipment offered at the time, and would accompany and prolong current practices, without this being for all that the effect of precise calculations, a scrupulous reading of advertising, or beady-eyed attention being paid to their potential?

It is this last hypothesis that I would like to explore here (without, however, excluding the other two and their variations, or the idea of functional suitability). In fact, it seems to me, the adoption of trolleys arose at least in part from a mechanism of "negligent appropriation". In my opinion, this equipment belongs to a category of objects that were both new and trivial, which took their place in the world without necessarily causing a lot of noise, reflexivity or cross-perspectives from the actors at whom they were targeted.[10] If they permeated society, it is certainly because they were invited in, but above all it is due to their ability to insert themselves into practices that were already in use, to accompany existing movements, to assist an earlier flow in picking up speed, by following the steepest slope that was suddenly offered to them.[11] These action supports did not practise "determination", but rather "empowerment": they "allowed" current activities to follow other paths, often more easily; they offered shortcuts, or presented themselves as such.

Foldable trolleys

The partial validity of this hypothesis can be demonstrated with a close inspection of the fate of one of the most extolled functionalities of trolleys: their foldability. This foldability can be put back into the context of a rather general propensity of innovators to "stuff" their innovations with functions, undoubtedly in the hope that increasing the number of possible "use outlets" creates more chances that the object will be adopted in its entirety,[12] thus anticipating the Lancasterian rationale rather well, according to which the characteristics of objects rather than the objects themselves are the target of consumer preferences (Lancaster, 1966). As we have seen, foldability was, initially, one way among others to sell trolleys, along with cleanliness, the fight against tiredness, the increase in potential storage space, etc. Nonetheless, foldability took pride of place amongst all these arguments. I have already pointed out that it very quickly appeared as one of the main characteristics put forward by a wealth of suppliers, who were also ready to fight each other to ensure that their foldability was better than their competitors'. The reasoning behind such a strategy directly comes across when reading the manufacturers' commercial sales pitches. At a time when trolley use was still in its infancy (remember that the commercial arguments I am referring to appeared in the vehicle's early years), and when the main market for this type of equipment was still the small independent grocery store (in 1936 – the year when trolleys were introduced – this type of shop still accounted for two thirds of retail grocery turnover),[13] the primary target for trolley advertisers was neither the customer, nor the supermarket (even though this form of sales was expanding at this time; Zimmerman, 1955; Grandclément, 2008), but the small grocer. However, although it should be mentioned that the trolley would be useful to the latter because it would also be useful to its customers, it is important not to forget his interest and possible objections, particularly with regard to an object whose still uncertain contribution was matched only by its obvious bulk – a very annoying defect for something that was supposed to be used in a small space where it was beginning to be understood that each square centimetre lost was a missed opportunity for displaying and therefore selling.

This then is undoubtedly why some manufacturers made foldability their crucial selling point, and even their raison d'être. It is quite significant that the supposed inventor of the trolley, Sylvan N. Goldman, decided to name his business "The Folding Carrier Corp", rather than "The Doubling Basket Co." In these pioneering times, it was much better to highlight the space-saving offered to the grocer rather than the increase in volume promised to the consumer. In order to get trolleys into the shop, the best argument was that of being able to take them out again! This is also no doubt why the effort to find foldable solutions continued unabated, even after the initial introduction phase: the first attempts and solutions by United Steel & Wire Co., Metwood MFG Co. and Folding Carrier Co.,[14] already encountered, were joined by American Wire Form Co. (1940, 09, 214) and Tote-Cart Co.[15] (1942, 09, 133), and extended with the invention of other folding devices such as "Clipper-Carts" and "Stack-Away", with solid chassis and baskets that could be folded in one move by (respectively) Modern Store Equipment Co. (1945, 08, 145) and Plymouth Metal Products Corp. (1949, 01, 133), "convertible" trolleys from Tote-Cart (1945, 08, 224), etc. (see Figure 5.2).

All these versions and alternatives continued until the appearance of the telescopic trolleys by Orla E. Watson (1949, 02, 232), which were themselves quickly copied and promoted in *Progressive Grocer* by other manufacturers, long before poor Watson had showcased his own product in the magazine – see the

Figure 5.2 Variations of foldable trolleys
Source: From left to right: Metwood MFG Co., 1938, 05, 162; Modern Store Equipment
Co., 1945, 08, 145; Plymouth Metal Product Corp., 1949, 01, 133

copies by Folding Carrier Corp. that I have already mentioned (1947, 11, 225),
but also those by "E-Z" Glider and Basket Co. (1948, 09, 273), Boston Metal
Products Co. (1948, 10, 28), United Steel & Wire Co. (1948, 10, 246) and
Tote-Cart Co. (1948, 11, 148).

However, until Watson's key innovation, foldability as a selling point does
not seem to have produced the desired effect. I leafed through the pages of all
editions of *Progressive Grocer* between 1929 and 1959, one by one. On this
occasion, I found hundreds of photographs where trolleys were indeed a feature, but I never found a single photographic image of a folded chassis. At best,
I came across images of stacked baskets, but these baskets did not belong to
trolleys at all, either because the shop did not have any (1952, 04, 88–89), or
because the trolleys found there were all being used and were equipped with
their own baskets (1942, 03, 138). One could object that some of the trolleys
used were found in this state simply because they had been bought from
manufacturers that did not offer a foldable option. This is very likely: snapshots
are not always good enough to be able to recognise with certainty the various
makes and models, which are often quite similar, as well as whether there is a
folding device. However, the potential presence of non-folding trolleys already
shows that some grocers did not feel that "foldability" was a *sine qua non* condition for introducing the device into the nevertheless confined space of their
grocery store.

Over time, however, explaining the actual absence of folding by the non-
foldability of trolleys is an argument that does not stick, as we have seen that
almost all manufacturers integrated foldability quite quickly, and that moreover
it is identifiable in most of the shots, despite the absence of trolleys that are
actually folded (1939, 07, 43; 1944, 09, 84–85 sq.). The last reference
mentioned – where four of the Goldman company's "foldable trolleys", all
completely unfolded, can be seen very clearly in the foreground[16] – wholly
summarises the intriguing mystery of the absence of folding trolleys when not
in use, given that these open chassis clutter the space of a tiny shop … which,
however, was photographed to illustrate an example of good spatial

management when lacking space, in an article significantly entitled "Remodeling Narrow Store? Here Are Ideas" (Figure 5.3). *Progressive Grocer* deals with "small" business, where trolleys are more cumbersome than necessary, and yet, even in some of the smallest shops that demonstrate acute awareness of optimising the sales area, trolleys are used, scattered around and unfolded, much more than they are absent, stacked or folded away.

How can this mismatch between commercial sales pitch and actual practices be explained? First let us note that trolley foldability never drove out

Figure 5.3 Remodeling Narrow Store? Here Are Ideas
Source: 1944, 09, 85

competitors, and with good reason: it did not work! Folding trolleys required consumers to carry out too many operations, and there was too much maintenance for grocers. The consumer and the cashier were part of the technical device, and this hinge, which was needed to fold the chassis, worked very badly: once his trolley was empty, the consumer found his arms full of bags into which the grocer had transferred the merchandise; the grocer was obliged to remain in his place to serve the next customer, or to leave in order to help the first customer by accompanying him to his vehicle (see below). These two options left little time – or desire – to arrange trolleys, especially when this risked being done for no reason, as a new customer could at any moment unfold the trolley that had just been folded.

It is better (or worse), in my opinion, to take a very limited risk, in the absence of being able to verify it, and formulate the following hypothesis: if folding and stacking caused a problem, it was mainly because a folded chassis with small wheels on its base was more or less completely unable to stay upright for a long time,[17] especially if one had to repeatedly attach it to other chassis of the same type and in the same position, which in turn were in the same predicament. Even though they were equipped with braking devices, as we seem to discern in adverts by the Folding Carrier Co. and more clearly on trolleys by United Steel & Form Co.,[18] folded and vertically stacked chassis were no doubt highly likely to collapse with the least disturbance, like a "house of carts", and be thus unable to logically escape the frequent and well-known fate of folding chairs when stored in the same position! In addition, many of the adverts showing vertically folded chassis – generally seen as a cut-out,[19] without any support that might explain this miracle, and with good reason – are potentially misleading.[20] It is very probable that chassis could only be folded and stacked without risk horizontally, thus adding another problem to that of folding and reassembling the trolley – being that of the back of the poor person responsible for "reassembling" it.

In addition, advertisers of so-called foldable trolleys were perfectly aware of the problems caused by their innovation, as soon as they tried to go from the technical script of folding (Akrich, 1992) to the action of implementing actual folding. The clear proof of this is given to us by Goldman's almost immediate conversion, despite being the long-standing self-proclaimed king of the folding trolley, to the new stacking device. The fact that Goldman leapt onto his competitor's innovation without waiting, at the cost of plagiarism and thus taking a significant legal risk (Grandclément, 2006), demonstrates quite well his perception of the potential benefit of the new device, and above all, in contrast, the doubts he had most probably secretly been harbouring regarding the real merits of his own product. This is in fact demonstrated by the extraordinary admission of these doubts as soon as the alternative had been adopted. In the poster reproduced above, where the Folding Carrier Co. announces the launch of its new telescoping trolleys, the central commercial argument put forward is that with these new trolleys, there will be "NO MORE BASKET CARRIER PARKING PROBLEM!" And Goldman hammered the point (or rather, the hinged trolley) home a few

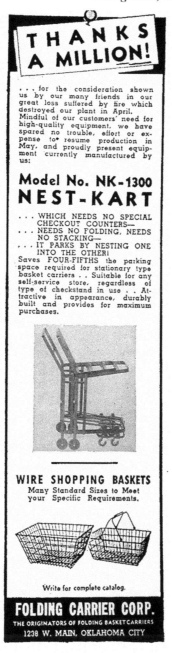

Figure 5.4 Needs no folding, needs no stacking
Source: 1948, 06, 207

months later in another advertisement specifying, with regards to basket devices that could now be stacked, "NEEDS NO FOLDING, NEEDS NO STACKING" (1948, 06, 207), no longer stigmatising a vague storage difficulty, but these specific operations, as numerous as they were tedious, that his former product required.

In other words, as soon as he adopted the "nesting" option, Goldman was no longer afraid of disowning trolley foldability (which he had presented proudly as his strategic advantage for ten years), suddenly presenting it as a dreadful defect that new telescoping equipment would thankfully overcome, thus recognising in passing that since the beginning his innovation had not worked, or had worked very badly! Last but not least, while abandoning his folding trolleys for his new telescoping frames, Goldman did not forget to praise the advantage of his own solution, "WHICH NEEDS NO SPECIAL CHECKOUT COUNTERS", in order to differentiate himself from his competitor, as if he was trying to appear again as a first mover rather than a miserable copier.

By contrast, the convenience of Watson's innovation was indeed clear: telescoping trolleys take up less space, no longer by requiring the repetitive and exhausting effort of disassembly and folding, then unfolding and reassembly,[21] but by interlocking almost "by themselves"[22] (thanks to replacing the deficient human hinge with an efficient technical one), thus finally making it possible to compact trolleys, socially as well as technically. Goldman's sentiment, far from being isolated, on the contrary received the implicit consent of all professionals in the sector, given that "nesting" was unanimously approved, to the point where within a few months – except for the time needed to sell off stocks of old models – it ousted all preceding foldable solutions and instituted the new reign of superb telescoping trolleys ("E-Z" Glider and Basket Co.: 1948, 09, 273; Boston Metal Products Corp.: 1948, 10, 28; United Steel and Wire Co.: 1946, 10, 246; Tote-Cart Co.: 1948, 11, 148; American Wire Form Co.: 1949, 02, 243; Plymouth Metal Products Corp.: 1949, 06, 161; United Steel and Wire Co.: 1949, 07, 215; Chatillon: 1950, 03, 213; etc.).

As soon as reducing the congestion of trolleys operated according to the principle of least effort, practices would flow once again, trolleys would fit into one another, initiating a virtuous circle almost by themselves, beginning with the consumer picking up a vehicle from the trolley pen, to returning the trolley to its pen when the customer left, and in the meantime, all the customer's "trolley shopping" – not to mention the checkout of course. By specifying that "[t]he new type of nesting carriages save a great amount of floor space", an article devoted to the new trolleys implicitly shows that in the old days there was nothing comparable that worked (1948, 12, 63).

Collapsible trolleys

However, if it now appears quite clearly that foldability did not work, can we really be sure that nesting worked any better? A contemporary reading of Watson's innovation could lead to a suspicion similar to the one Goldman's first trolley finally fell victim to: just as foldability does not guarantee folding, nesting does not necessarily guarantee trolleys will interlock. Indeed, who is to say consumers would put the trolleys away, whose usefulness in carrying shopping certainly did not stop at the shop door? We all know, from experience, that these contraptions have an annoying tendency to scattering outside shops, a tendency that only the implementation of a change machine managed over time to tidy.

Now, in Watson's time, the latter innovation did not yet exist … and indeed is hardly prevalent in the United States at the time of writing. Today, and in the absence of the change lock, nesting cannot completely guarantee trolleys will actually be interlocked, just as their foldability of yesteryear failed to lead to them being folded. It is difficult to see why today's problem would not have existed in the past. It had to be one or the other: either consumers put trolleys away in the shop and found themselves in difficulties with getting their shopping at least as far as their car, or they went to their car with the trolley, making it then the car park that risked being cluttered with abandoned trolleys.

However, a closer examination of commercial spaces at that time quickly shows that such a suspicion is curiously anachronistic: what did not work for Goldman's trolleys and what still does not work today, without an additional device, very quickly and on the whole, worked very well for Watson's trolleys: once they were empty, these trolleys were returned to their place and obediently stacked ready for the next customer. Herein lies a new mystery. Did obtaining this better result depend on the innovation's more efficient technical properties? Undoubtedly: as I have already noted, nesting removed the trolley disassembly-reassembly operation and reduced the effort required to put them away.[23] However, not only that: the success of the operation also depended on the more global use of trolleys and service in post-war America. Two points should be mentioned here.

The first point is that in the United States, trolleys were taken and kept inside the shop for a very long time, thanks to the implementation of ingenious devices designed to make this happen. The first device of this kind can be seen in Figure 5.5. This "automatic cart return", which the image's caption highlights so proudly in capitals, is nevertheless achieved at the cost of a few little additional adjustments (and actions), as is incidentally suggested by using the passive voice. The solution proposed for achieving this return efficiently is very elegant, discreet and subtle, as it relies on the installation of a simple rail. The latter, like a new boundary drawing its inspiration from the separating and organisational power of the original wire (but without the barbs – see Chapter 4), managed to guide incoming customers so as to put them in the path of the well-ordered line of available trolleys along the length of the "entry side" of the rail,[24] and separate customers from their trolleys upon leaving the checkout. Once empty, only the trolleys passed easily under the rail to rejoin the line on the "entry side", whilst customers remaining on the "exit side" only had to follow the rail to reach – with their arms full – the shop's exit.[25] An even easier and more convenient way of achieving the same result lay in the use of "tunnel checkouts", which "compulsorily" absorbed and arranged trolleys on one side,

AUTOMATIC CART RETURN is provided by this arrangement. Carriages are pushed through checkout lane, under the guide rail and into the path of incoming traffic. The new type nesting carriages save a great amount of floor space.

Figure 5.5 Automatic cart return
Source: 1948, 12, 63

while the customer left with the merchandise he had paid for in bags on the other (Figure 5.6).

Thanks to such sorting devices, trolleys thus remained almost "naturally" well arranged inside the shop; the trolley-customer hinge hybrid started to work just as easily as the technical hinge of the little back door, thus ensuring that, when all is said and done, the overall functionality of Watson's innovation, and of the trolleys that it inspired, was achieved. However, if the implementation of these devices gives a rather good explanation of what was happening technically upstream, it gives quite a bad clarification of the social acceptability of what was happening downstream – namely, that one needed to take away one's shopping with arms fully loaded, without the help of a trolley.

We now come to the second point, which no longer subordinates the telescoping of trolleys to the mobilisation of a technical sorting device for these vehicles (prior to the departure of customers), but instead to the intervention of a social device to assist customers (after the storage of the trolleys). Even in the 1950s, when the majority of grocery stores had become superettes and when car use was becoming widespread,[26] customers left the shop with their bags in their arms. Hence an umpteenth mystery: how could customers agree so easily to be separated from the trolley that had been so useful when doing their shopping, and then sometimes find themselves so encumbered when leaving the shop?

WALTER ONG, owner, Central Market, Phoenix, Ariz., shows the checkstands whicl eliminate the "battle of carts." Each stand is hollowed out so that baskets movi through the tunnel-like opening. Sackers or carry-out boys keep the carts moving

Figure 5.6 Tunnel check-out
Source: 1952, 09, 78–79

The fact that it was necessary to implement the technical filtering devices I have just described is a good indicator of the problem: why implement such stratagems, which have now disappeared, unless it was anticipated that customers might want to continue their journey outside the shop (at least as far as their vehicle if they had one) with the trolley that had been so useful to them up to the checkout, allowing them to forget the weight of their shopping, and whose sudden absence risked appearing all the more painful? In a world where customer service was still an essential component of the job, even at the time of "self-service", translating the moral injunction to return trolleys into the technical impossibility of keeping them beyond the checkout or the shop exit, according to the process of "delegation" so well described by Latour (1991b), was the best way of silently keeping trolleys inside the shop, without the risk of having constantly to call people to order and provide customers with impossible justifications.

However, if the tacit withholding of trolleys avoided certain discussions with customers, it definitely posed an unresolved problem of a "break in assistance" which, if not stressful, at least diminished the clientele's attachment to this "self-service" whose useful trolleys changed into cumbersome packages as soon as they passed through the checkout, rather like Cinderella's coach turning into an inert and heavy pumpkin on the last stroke of midnight. In order to prevent this problem and thus avoid the customer sharing Cinderella's disillusion, grocers generally seem to have endeavoured to assist their customers[27] physically in the long term by carrying their purchases to their vehicles (1950, 12, 35; 1952, 10, 172; 1958, 03, 168), or even delivering them to their home.[28] Even in 1959, at a time when customer assistance was starting to decline, a slightly sceptical and nostalgic editorial by R.W. Mueller, editor-in-chief of *Progressive Grocer*, questioned the reasons behind the disappearance of home delivery, which some increasingly regarded as a cost despite it also being, according to this author, an investment in customer loyalty (1959, 11, 6) – as if, for the first time in its long history, *Progressive Grocer* found that progress lay rather in the past.

As such, the neat interlocking of trolleys depended not only on the quality of their intrinsic hinge, but also on the technical filtering devices between trolley and customer installed in the shop, but even more so on the social devices for assisting customers put in place at the exit.

The last point carries a superb paradox: it is precisely service which enabled the spread of the trolley that would ruin it (or rather, reduce it); it is because Americans are attached to service that they allowed trolleys to function properly, to interlock correctly, and thus finally find their place in the commercial space. This point is difficult to understand for those who know little about the United States. Even today, in American supermarkets one generally still finds two people at checkouts (both always standing up), one for checking out the products and the other for packing bags. Consumers do not have to put their trolleys away, which since they do not have coin slots, generally hang around car parks until an employee comes to collect them. Thus self-service, even though it is presented as being absolute (contrary to the semi-self-service that continues in delicatessens, etc.) is never complete. In the United States, it was only at the end of the 1950s that trolleys were allowed to wander. This was probably because the gradual conversion of grocery stores into superettes and supermarkets, and the corresponding increase in turnover and thus the size but also the number of trolleys,[29] eventually congested the internal storage space in the shop, to the point where holding devices were rendered inoperable (1958, 04, 100; 1958, 07, 94). The break in the "seawall" of holding devices and the

6

WHEN MY SHOPPING is finished, the checker calls out the price of every item and doesn't do it so fast that it completely confuses me. How I hate the checkers who work like inhuman automatons! If my purchases are large, a clean, neatly dressed, courteous boy carries my groceries to the car. He carefully puts them on the floor and not on the back seat where they might stain the upholstery.

Figure 5.7 Permanence of service
Source: 1950, 12, 35

corresponding "abandonment" of trolleys outside shops thus gave rise to new corrective innovations and new enthusiasms – such as the creation of spaces just for trolleys, with a sign inviting customers to put them away themselves (1958, 04, 100) and the design of car parking spaces with enough room for a trolley next to the car (1956, 12, 98). However, the vagrancy of trolleys also gave rise to new set-backs, shown, as we have just seen, by the need to allocate staff to collect trolleys scattered around car parks (1957, 04, 146; 1958, 07, 94) and, worse still, the assessment that trolleys were disappearing beyond the confines of the shop (1957, 11, 142 sq.). In the final analysis, it is one of the main paradoxes of the history of shopping trolleys that, having been confined within the shops where there was the least amount of space, they were (relatively speaking) released into the outside world by the supermarkets.

Innovation is often considered in terms of need and functionalism, implying awareness, reflectivity and purpose on the part of those involved. On the other hand, it is also often thought of within the framework of culturalism, which, on the contrary, postulates resistance from those who are supposed to act rather than think, according to the constraints of behavioural routines acquired from previous experiences. Should these models be opposed, rejected or exceeded as so often happens? Not necessarily, nor completely. The metamorphoses of how the trolley could be tidied away – from being folded to telescoped – show that the functionalist blueprint is on the side of the innovators, who argue in its favour, who extol the services provided by their equipment (foldability, hygiene, robustness, capacity, etc.) but is completely absent from the side of the users. Users, however, are less resistant than negligent. Innovations appear in their sphere of activity, and their practices adjust to them or not, according to the principle of the least effort required.

The question here is not that of the opposition between rationality and routine, as the routine of adjustment is as much a reflex as it is rational. If the innovation is suited to previous practices and facilitates them – if it allows what has always been done to be done differently and more easily (Latour, 1993) – it then immediately becomes a method of action, as shown by the eventual, very rapid switch to trolleys.[30] If, in contrast, the innovation is unsuitable – like the foldability that demanded a costly increase in action – then it is abandoned, forgotten, bypassed.

The sociology of techniques has paid particular attention to the propensity of actors to cobble innovations together in order to fit them into the framework of their practices (Akrich et al., 1988a, 1988b). The history of trolleys shows us instead that, for some objects, this hypothesis is probably much too demanding. For a banal functionality such as the foldability of trolleys, the laziness of abandonment is widely preferred to the effort of adaptation. Or rather, the negligence of some offers itself as an opportunity for the invention of others. An adaptive makeshift job emerges, but it is often the product of neither the initial innovator, nor the end user, but of other inventors who understand the difficulties encountered by both to sometimes offer adaptations of the object (as shown by Watson's smart innovation), sometimes adaptations of its context of use which are likely to make it functional once again (as shown by the development of trolley rails and tunnels).[31] Thus the innovation process sometimes arises less from an adaptive whirlwind loop that unifies the continuous contributions of innovator and users behind evolutionary closed doors (ibid.), than from an incremental and shared process mobilising a crowd of independent agents who, by seeking both to adapt their innovations to those of others and promote their benefits, finally contribute to creating the conditions of a technical system and thus an efficient object.

From the consumer on foot to families on wheels

If the transformations to the technical equipment of commerce favoured the intrusion of trolleys into the grocery store world, this intrusion in turn also led to significant changes. The most well-known of these is of course the growth in the scale of operations: the appearance of trolleys coincided with the advent of supermarkets (Grandclément, 2006), and there is little doubt that the growth of the latter would not have been possible without the support of the former: how would consumers have travelled over a larger surface area and purchased more without the aid of a suitable tool to enable them to accomplish such operations? The trolley was as necessary to the advent of supermarkets as the ship (and later, the aeroplane) was to crossing oceans. As this effect is well known, I would prefer to focus on another, more qualitative impact, concerning the social reconfiguration of supermarket customers by stressing, on the one hand, their "collectivisation" – with trolleys, consumer unity would increasingly consist of more than one person – and on the other hand, their "universalisation" – with trolleys, consumers were less frequently isolated female consumers as in the past, but increasingly formed small composite and family groups, making room for men and above all children. Of course, this does not mean these transformations were restricted to the exclusive action of the trolley, but simply shows that the latter contributed, in its own way, to increasing the consumption "census" by welcoming into the commercial area categories of people who had previously barely frequented it ... or had done so differently (Cochoy, 2008b).

As I have already pointed out, children remained *persona non grata* in the commercial area for a very long time. Or rather, they were only tolerated on condition that they behave not as children, but as adults, and not as adult consumers but as adult workers. The working child of commerce was first the grocer's employee – often their own son – responsible for lending a hand in the shop or delivering to customers. Before the war, *Progressive Grocer* often chose to illustrate its cover with the figures of working children (1923, 03; 1929, 11; 1923, 05; 1926, 05; 1930, 07; 1941, 10). Some advertisers did not hesitate to depict a scene in their adverts where a smiling and dominating grocer congratulates a little boy in an apron on having properly arranged Duff's cereals (1947, 08, 8), or where a little girl, also in an apron, energetically scrubs a kitchen floor with the product Tavern (1947, 08, 42–43) or polishes the enamel of a toilet with Bab-O detergent (1930, 02, 122). Such practices are enough to show the extent to which child labour remained, for a long time, not only typical to the grocery sector, but also quite widely accepted.[32] In addition, the working child of commerce, far from only assisting the grocer, was also joined by the child running errands for his parents (1939, 01, 148; 1946, 12, 128; 1943, 05, 149). One statistic shows that in 1946, unaccompanied children represented 2.2% of shoppers – certainly a modest proportion, but one which, for all that, is not insignificant (1947, 07, 64).

It is as though child labour resulted in them not being considered potential consumers. *Progressive Grocer*, and undoubtedly the grocers behind it, distrusted child consumers, whom they considered as being more of a risk of loss than a potential source of profits: when children are portrayed, they are usually messing around (1925, 04; 1927, 08, 40), pilfering (1939, 02, 135), have no money (1924, 05; 1936, 09), are dirty[33] (1935, 09, 34–35) and constitute as much of a nuisance as dogs (1939, 10, 62).[34] Admittedly, children or childhood objects appeared here and there promoting the advertisers' point of view (1929, 09,

134; 1938, 04, 173), but they seemed limited to manufacturers whose products were aimed specifically at children (Libby's fruit juices: 1940, 05, 145; Quaker Oats cereals: 1937, 03, 110–111; 1937, 06, 82–82; etc.), and did not mean children constituted the target audience. Instead, advertisers gambled on the mechanism of buying out of love, so clearly identified by Daniel Miller (1998): if you show the figure of a child, it is more in the hope of attracting his mother,[35] as you would proffer honey to draw out a bear (1938, 11, 96–97).

Moreover, the childish figure that widely dominated advertising space in *Progressive Grocer* before the Second World War was less that of a child than of a baby (1926, 12, 36–37; 1932, 07, 35), whose access to the grocery store obviously involved the mediation of his mother.[36] Although we do find some more audacious initiatives here and there, such as a miniature grocery store especially for children (1932, 08, 21), a parking area for pushchairs (1924, 04, 23), the promotion of sweets as a source of profit (1924, 05, 29) or free toys to sell more of certain products (1935, 11, 1; 1936, 05, 13; 1938, 11, 96–97; 1936, 09, 122; 1936, 10, 19–20; 1938, 08, 78–79; 1942, 04, 166–167),[37] the audacity and the rarity of these initiatives uses irony to show more about ordinary practices, as children were somewhat neglected by, even kept at a distance from, the grocery shop at least until the war.

We cannot fully understand this exclusion unless we extend the notion of cultural resistance to that of material resistance. I am referring here to the height and delicate balance of certain piles (1931, 04, 24–25) which grocers saw as incompatible with the presence of boisterous, mischievous and clumsy youngsters. I am also referring to the physical layout of shops, which for a long time remained completely unsuitable for their presence. Children faced counters that were much too high for them, unless they sat on them: either their feet touched the ground but their head was too low to be able to see anything (see Figure 5.8, on the left), or their head was at the right height but at the cost of no longer being able to get down by themselves (see Figure 5.8, on the right)!

However, the arrival of the open display and its attendant furniture would be an opportunity for development. The new open display cases would prove more welcoming to children, without, however, this necessarily being a desirable attribute. Thus, in a passage in one of his books dedicated to the best way of presenting sweets in an open display case, Carl Dipman, the editor-in-chief of *Progressive Grocer*, recommends that they not be displayed on tables in order to avoid children stealing them (Dipman, 1935, p. 128), without fear of compromising their access to a product of which they are actually the symbolic target audience. However, two phenomena would combine to awaken increased demand on the part of the child consumer. First, the adoption of lower, more open units (1931, 09, 24 sq.; 1932, 02, 28–29; 1932, 08, 85) inherent in the implementation of the open display, then the growing use of floor-level displays (1937, 05, 44–45) and display shelving (1940, 02, 30–37; 1944, 07, 183; 1949, 05, 51) suitable for the development of self-service, meant that products were better adapted to the physical and sensory capacities of the

"WE DISPLAY JOLLY TIME
NEAR THE CASH REGISTER . . .

. . . because it makes bigger sales,"

Register Company, Dayton, Ohio   *says B. G. Penney of the Lamb Grocery, Portland, Ore.*

Figure 5.8 Children and counters
Source: 1930, 10, 39; 1930, 11, 123

youngest customers. Second, and more importantly, ever since the open display era, manufacturers of the glass-panelled furniture that were emblematic of this type of sale would find that the properties of their furniture were the means to establish children as crucial agents in the increase of sales, via their role as purchasing advisers. Here, everything relies on the implementation of a pictorial rhetoric designed to promote the dual benefit of "showcases", whose very accessible window proved capable of both reassuring the grocer – being able to close it avoided any undesirable activity by children – and of awakening his interest – the transparency of the same window allowed children to demonstrate their preferences very vigorously to their mothers, and thus also to demonstrate to professionals the advantages that they could gain from it (see Figure 5.9).

At the crossroads of the furniture that unintentionally welcomed children and the equipment that, in contrast, deliberately sought to do so, we naturally find the pairing formed by the trolley and the checkout. The checkout falls into the first category: it was only in order to facilitate the entry of trolleys that it was suggested the old counter be lowered, but this lowering allowed children to watch how operations unfolded (and perhaps even also participate in them). Whereas the trolley would slip from the first category to the second, to the point of finally becoming the tool that would almost definitively sanction, and even accept children be consumers in their own right.

Before trolleys were introduced, or rather before their use as a means to transport children became widespread, it was not particularly clear what should be done with them, especially very small children. People attempted one way

Figure 5.9 Weber glass display case
Source: 1930, 12, 29

or another to manage the dilemma of welcoming mothers, encumbered by their infant children, in order to ensure these precious consumers entered, but also to relieve these same mothers of their progeny once they had entered, so they would have their hands free for shopping. Various solutions were tried to overcome this dilemma, following a common penning logic, consisting less of welcoming children into the sales area than of keeping them at a distance: some offered to look after children in high-chairs that were placed near the checkouts, thus allowing mothers to attend to their shopping freely (1946, 04, 80); others created play areas at the shop entrance (1946, 07, 60–61).

However, these innovations seem to have arrived too late – they were chronicled in 1946[38] – and were easily overtaken by an alternative and clandestine solution organised by the parents themselves and used for the entire preceding decade, whereby trolleys (even though they were very narrow and unstable) were used to ferry their children around the shop. This use is all the more interesting as it first appeared in images devoted to other subjects (1940, 02, 86)[39] – something which has the advantage of attesting both its reality and the "ascendant" origin. Using trolleys as strollers indebted to customer initiative rather than the action of innovators and professionals, and was quickly adopted by these same professionals and innovators, first as an illustration on the cover of *Progressive Grocer* (1940, 05; 1941, 01[40]), then as a commercial sales argument for an advert by the trolley manufacturer American Wire & Form Co., which placed not one, but two children in its trolley (1941, 09, 165; see Figure 5.10). However, in this advert the manufacturer did not seize the opportunity to modify his equipment to take this new use into account: far from being concerned about lost sales space or related safety issues, it seems instead to have depicted the embarkation of children in a humorous fashion to illustrate both the storage capacity and solidity of its trolleys, thus anticipating a type of advertising rhetoric that would make Samsonite, the luggage manufacturer, famous (for example, when the latter depicted two teams of bulldozers playing football with a suitcase; Parasie, 2010).[41]

However, over the next few years, the hybrid use of trolleys as pushchairs and baskets on wheels would, on the contrary, become the subject of increasing concern on the part of the manufacturers, who, in dealing with it, resolved a new problem. Although placing children in trolleys had indeed resolved the previous conundrum of finding a way to welcome "child-clad" mothers whilst freeing their hands for handling products, it had also simultaneously introduced a new difficulty, consisting in finding a way to keep this maternal consumer and her trolley without losing the purchasing capacity occupied by the child. The solution to this problem would emerge after a long series of tentative experiments, a few of which are listed here.[42]

In 1947, the Tote-Cart Co. company offered "baby toters", a type of trolley whose upper level, fitted with an extension, allowed the upper basket to be moved forward, thus freeing up a space in the back where it was then possible to attach a small detachable folding seat that could accommodate a child (1947, 12, 196). Nevertheless, the second basket, now regained, was just an illusion;

American Wire Form "NO GERM" Gliders are welded, not once but twice, at every joint, first by an electric spot and then by electric arc.

If you want strong, rigid gliders and durable, long-wearing baskets that will last longer under severe abuse, send for catalog and prices on our latest models.

AMERICAN *Wire Form* **COMPANY, INC.**
269-273 Grant Ave.   Jersey City, N. J.

Figure 5.10 Double welded for double wear
Source: 1941, 09, 165

this double-basket, child-carrying trolley was actually only achieved by adding two accessories to a standard trolley – the first being a support for the extension that was usually used to hold a third basket, and the second being a seat for accommodating a child, which then replaced the extension normally available for a third basket (for a solution to the puzzle, see 1949, 10, 242). A trolley equipped in this way raised the additional problem (admittedly, relative) of an even more trying folding procedure.

The following year, another manufacturer (unidentifiable in the photo) replaced the usual folding chassis with a curved, tubular structure that appeared to be much sturdier, which allowed a small bench to be installed at the rear of the trolley, thanks to which a child could be transported whilst facing its mother, with his back turned to the shop. The caption that accompanied the presentation of this robust device also emphasised its ability to prevent accidents (1948, 02, 144).[43] In 1950, the W.R. Alexander Co. was not afraid of launching a foldable trolley with a single, large-capacity basket – thus attempting a kind of retroactive transition between the foldable double-basket trolleys and the telescoping single-basket trolleys that had already appeared by the time – furnished with a very uncomfortable seat in the form of a wire hammock, turning the child towards its mother,[44] but whose flexibility also allowed it to preserve the traditional principle of foldability[45] which, as we know, was a very theoretical benefit (1950, 05, 16).

By this time, however, telescoping trolleys were definitely starting to replace the original folding trolleys, which the manufacturer Chatillon was the first to spot, offering the addition of a seat overhanging the basket (1950, 03, 213), but without necessarily specifying whether this device would or would not hinder trolley nesting.[46] Shortly afterwards, the Folding Carrier Co. seized the opportunity to promote a very similar device, which certainly occupied a part of the basket when the trolley was in use, but which could be pushed backwards and thus preserve its interlocking capability (1951, 09, 251). However, it would be still several more years before the same company finally found (or re-adopted?) the solution we recognise today – in other words, the invention of a folding seat fitted to the trolley's back opening (1955, 03, 207), a method also launched by United Steel and Wire Co. (1955, 05, 267) and which was soon adopted by other manufacturers (American Metal Products, Inc.: 1956, 05, 212; Tyler: 1958, 05, 212; Tote-Cart Co.: 1958, 05, 246) (see Figure 5.11).

This unrelenting commitment shown by manufacturers in the highly intensive race to find the best way of opening up trolleys to children without thereby compromising their previous qualities in terms of storage capacity and stacking ability tends to confirm the existence of social pressure and a marketing opportunity for such solutions. Social pressure first led users to turn trolleys into pushchairs without waiting for technologists to help them in this innovation enterprise (Von Hippel, 2002); then the marketing opportunity encouraged manufacturers and distributors first to "put up with" the presence of children, then to organise it. In any event, it certainly seems as though the

Figure 5.11 Child seat variations
Source: 1947, 12, 196; 1948, 02, 144; 1950, 05, 16; 1950, 03, 213; 1951, 09, 251; 1955, 03, 207

generalisation of carrying children in trolleys, without and then with the help of a suitable device, coincided with their proliferation in the commercial space.

The few statistics supplied by *Progressive Grocer* reflect such a development. I previously mentioned a survey from 1947 showing that 2.2% of shop clientele consisted of unaccompanied children. This figure by no means includes the presence of children accompanying adults. This presence started in fact to become significant in relation to the frequency of visits. Indeed, the same survey highlighted the fact that, of all consumer types, it was children who made the most visits to shops per week (4.0 on average), ahead of women (3.9), men (3.1) and couples (2.8) (1947, 07, 64).[47] In fact, the post-war baby boom, economic growth and trolleys seem to have combined to accelerate this development.

Admittedly, trolleys equipped with seats initially only played a modest role, if we judge them in light of the small proportion of this type of equipment in a fleet that was on the whole modest. In 1956, and as Table 5.1 shows (already quoted in part), only supermarket trolleys were equipped in significant number with child seats and, even so, this type of equipment only represented a quarter of the average 58.5 trolleys owned by this type of shop. Nevertheless, the figures show that the number of trolleys and of those equipped with baby seats clearly depended on surface area, which tends to substantiate the idea of a functional utility (and thus use) of trolleys and their seats, when equipped with them. This equipment had, in fact, the extraordinary property of correcting physical and behavioural asymmetries between children and adults. More specifically, trolleys and seats offered a resting place for tired children – allowing their mothers to consider longer and more thorough trips in the commercial area than they would have been able to carry out without such a device – but the same trolleys also offered a play area for boisterous children – here again making it possible to continue purchasing operations in a negotiated manner.

The general introduction of trolleys and trolleys with child seats, although modest overall, was nevertheless enough to bring about a general shift towards a more deliberate and strategic welcoming of children, confirmed by the implementation of play areas (1951, 03, 82–83; 1953, 09, 138) or free magazines to read (1952, 10, 72; 1954, 12, 91; 1951, 09, 110–111; 1953, 09, 138; 1959, 01, 53), mini "educational" shops (1954, 05, 130–135), toys in the shop itself (1952, 10, 72), coin-operated mechanical horses (1953, 03, 92–93; 1959, 07, 126), toy departments (1953, 11, 180; 1954, 09, 78–79; 1959, 03, 80–81), specific displays (1954, 07, 126; 1959, 04, 81), entertainment (1952, 01, 74–75; 1953, 10, 100; 1957, 11, 84; 1959, 02, 168 sq.; 1959, 09, 97 sq.), ice cream stands (1957, 04, 162), and even the very early introduction of miniature trolleys especially for children (1953, 07, 95), without, however, shopkeepers and manufacturers neglecting the more traditional pursuit of seducing mothers via the depiction of children.

Above all, the growing use of trolleys unquestionably contributed to the change in morphology of the social entity that chose the supermarket, too often restricted, as we shall see, to the figure of the lone consumer. Admittedly, a previously quoted survey from 1947 showed that at the time, an overwhelming majority (86.6%) of people still did their shopping alone. Moreover, this individual consumer was usually a woman, given that more than two thirds of shoppers were single women (68.9%), compared with single men who accounted for 17.1%, with couples representing only 12% of the purchasing population. This survey said nothing about the possible presence of children with the couples, simply giving information about the number of children shopping on their own (2.2%) (1947, 07, 64).

Table 5.1 Distribution of trolley types

	Average no. total carts	*Average no. carts with baby seats*	*Ratio of regular carts to those with baby seats*
All shops	21.7	4.1	18.9
Supermarkets	58.5	14.8	25.3
Superettes	15.8	2.4	15.2
Small shops	8.6	0.7	8.1

Source: 1956, 04, 70

More than ten years later, things seem to have developed very clearly, as shown by a detailed survey on the composition of "clusters" – the results of which are shown in Table 5.2. No matter the type of shop, single women were now in the minority (39% on average). Although the lesser investment of single women was in no way translated into an increase in that of men (surprisingly stable at around 20%, in other words almost half as many as women), we can see a spectacular progression in "collective" shoppers. Admittedly, single adults still represented almost 60% of the clientele, but "groups" of consumers (namely couples or adults accompanied by children or not) made up almost all of the remaining 40%. By carrying out a few small additional calculations based on the overall figure shown in the first column of the table, we note that these couples (accompanied or not) now represented a quarter of customers (25.3%), while adults (on their own or in a couple) accompanied by children reached a similar proportion (23.2%). Lastly, note that the old figure of the child alone has practically disappeared: it is scarcely ever encountered, except in the country-side (1.2%), but in a proportion that was almost half of what it had been in the immediate post-war period (2.2%).

In other words, it really seems that the circulation of trolleys accompanied or joined a significant movement reconfiguring what we understand by the term "consumer". Whereas the consumers of yesteryear eventually corresponded quite often to what economics expected them to be – isolated entities, making choices and calculations alone or almost always on their own, in the commercial area – the trolley encouraged the conversion of this isolated unit into a "collective cluster" gathered around it, choosing together (1956, 01, 40 sq.), and thus for a while, giving a certain pre-eminence to the contemporary Parsonian family – in a much more egalitarian version – over the old egotistical figure dear to traditional economics.

Table 5.2 Distribution of customer types (%)

	All stores	City stores	Suburban stores	Country stores
Woman alone	39.0	40.0	44.0	36.7
Man alone	19.6	21.0	19.5	19.3
Couple	17.6	20.2	13.1	16.7
Couple with children	7.7	6.7	5.7	9.5
Man with child	3.1	2.9	2.7	3.4
Woman with child	12.4	9.0	14.8	13.2
Child	0.6	0.2	0.2	1.2
Total	100%	100%	100%	100%

Source: 1958, 08, S107

Shopping is a family affair

Figure 5.12 Shopping is a family affair
Source: 1958, 08, S106

Acknowledgements

This chapter includes elements taken from "Hansel and Gretel at the Grocery Store", Franck Cochoy, *Journal of Cultural Economy*, Vol. 1 Issue 2, pp. 145-163, Taylor and Francis Ltd., reprinted by permission of the publisher.

This chapter includes elements taken from "Driving a shopping cart from STS to business, and the other way round. On the introduction of shopping carts in American grocery stores (1936–1959)", *Organization*, Vol. 16, No. 1, pp. 31–55, reprinted by permission of the Publisher.

Notes

1 I noted some short items on the first trolleys made by the American Wire Co. (1936, 08, 107) and United Steel and Wire Co. (1938, 05, 130) which made do with reproducing sales pitches, undoubtedly provided by the relevant businesses, and two short paragraphs on the trial of shopping trolleys in the pioneering and remote self-service outlets of Seattle (1938, 01, 145).

2 An article from 1929 dedicated to the "success story" of a small grocer had the title "From a PUSHCART to a $300,000 Yearly Business" (1929, 08, 15–17). Such is the paradox of the trolley: it can fully encompass commerce in the figure of the transient trader, and cease being a concern as soon as it passes through the shop door.

3 The trolley's ability to act as a display was belatedly taken up by trolley manu-facturers themselves (1950, 06, 13), which went as far as suggesting special trolleys devoid of push bars (1951, 02, 228), but also by a whole series of advertisers which had encouraged displaying in trolleys was a way of increasing sales (1949, 05, 30–31; 1950, 06, 183; 1953, 10, 76).

4 This concern about the technical problems connected with trolleys can be read between the lines during the development of adverts which, over time, began to take into account the lessons learned from using trolleys and equipment ageing, and tried to take advantage of this in particular by focusing on the quality of the wheels (1950, 08, 135; 1950, 11, 214; 1953, 12, 51; 1954, 02, 166), durability of vehicles (Tote-Cart Co., 1948, 11, 148; Folding Carrier Co., 1950, 01, 141; American Wire Form Co., 1948, 12, 180), material quality and solidity, by boasting about the use of chrome (United Steel and Wire Co., 1948, 10, 246), construction of protective devices made from metal ("E-Z" Glider and Basket Co., 1948, 09, 273) or rubber (W.R. Alexander Co., 1950, 03, 229), load capability tests (John Chatillon & Sons, 1950, 06, 144), etc. Along the way, the sale of trolleys would be accompanied by the publication of maintenance manuals (1950, 10, 266; 1952, 03, 127).

5 Here, the trolley is only showing a rather general characteristic of innovations, which tend to disappear from view when they work, and in contrast attract much attention the moment they begin to malfunction, hence how differently they were "considered". "The arithmetic of technology is quite curious, as one can never calculate the elements involved: if it works well, it counts as one, or even nothing (if it is a simple intermediary), but if it breaks down, suddenly dozens or hundreds of people and skills appear" (Latour, 1996a, n.p.).

6 This statement, whilst valid at first glance, does not hold water upon closer inspection (Cochoy, 2008b).

7 Or almost: the legal arrangement between Watson and Goldman only occurred later, in August 1949 (Grandclément, 2006).

8 Goldman's primacy owes more to his own efforts to establish it (Goldman had a hagiographical thesis and then a book written about "his" invention, which he had also cleverly deposited at the Smithsonian Museum of American History) than to the reality of the situation. History instead seems to show the almost simultaneous emergence of similar solutions. Besides, Goldman did not advertise in *Progressive Grocer* until quite late, in 1940. Better still, American Wire Form Co. was already selling a trolley that was very similar to Goldman's in 1936 (1936, 08, 107), whilst Goldman's first market tests date to June 1937. Previous solutions that were more or less similar to Goldman's, meticulously inventoried by Catherine Grandclément, strengthen this view of the matter. Watson's innovation was certainly much clearer, different and decisive, but it does not exclude improvements made by other com-panies which all contributed to giving the trolley its modern shape, such as the child seat, protective parts for the wheels, and so on. Catherine Grandclément also points out that the Goldman-Watson lawsuit resurfaced following the extension of the copyright dispute to other manufacturers.

9 Although on the whole grocers carefully and modestly adopted the innovation (in 1956, groceries moving from "small stores" to "supermarkets", via "superettes", owned 21.7 trolleys on average), one is struck by the sight of so many micro-shops being invaded by trolleys, on a much larger scale than can be seen in similar sized businesses today (the "small shops" of 1956 owned 8.6 trolleys on average, a figure reflecting a definite over-equipping when compared to the mere 58.5 trolleys in supermarkets at the time) (1956, 04, 70).

10 The lack of knowledge about mechanisms linked to the dissemination of simple tools for everyday life no doubt stems from the fact that the sociology of innovation has always tended towards the study of much rarer, more noble and sophisticated techniques (Edgerton, 1999).

11 The way in which trolleys were introduced is reminiscent of the "propensity of things", so dear to François Jullien (1995), aside from the use of different metaphors – liquid for commerce, the wind for the Chinese – but in both cases it is indeed a matter of fluidity. We are admittedly the antithesis of the "planning logic" that I use on occasion, but the contradiction is only apparent: Martin Giraudeau (2008) clearly showed that plans follow types of logic other than mere composition, as they can also be used to support fluidity – as we have seen, in order for matters to run smoothly, they need to be arranged and directed in a certain way.

12 This strategy, which constitutes the basis of current engineering software, is therefore not strictly anything new.

13 A proportion that would hardly vary in the years to come (1944, 03, 38–39).

14 Also by Roll'er Basket Co. in 1937 (Grandclément, 2006).

15 This manufacturer did not mention foldability in its advertising pitches but an inspection of its trolleys leaves no doubt as to the presence of this functionality.

16 Two of them do not have their baskets, which supports the hypothesis of an "outside the framework" usage of these trolleys, according to the semblance that they have been forgotten amidst the very neat and tidy appearance of the rest of the image.

17 Admittedly, the chassis could be stored upside down, but as well as damaging the paintwork and guaranteeing only a very small increase in stability, one problem would merely be replaced by another, substituting the awkwardness of picking a horizontally folded chassis up from the ground with the effort to turn it the right way up. I could also envisage stock areas with notches that would block wheels, but as I have not come across this solution, I can prudently conclude that it did not exist.

18 This company offered a trolley that when folded, activated a small block behind the wheels (1940, 08, 154).

19 The only photo of this type that I know of can be found in an advert by the Folding Basket Carrier Co., reproduced by Catherine Grandclément (2006). In it, several piles of folded trolleys have been very carefully lined up and stacked slightly diagonally.

20 From this point of view, the manufacturer Roll'er Basket Co., whose advertisement was found and reproduced by Catherine Grandclément (2006), is undoubtedly one of the few to have acted honestly by presenting its folded in the only really viable position, namely horizontal.

21 These operations, as Catherine Grandclément (2006) incidentally reminds us, are almost as tedious as those imagined by Bruno Latour as a way of understanding what the lack of a hinged door would impose on those who nevertheless want a "hole-wall": placing a sledgehammer on each side of a partition to open it up, and breeze blocks and cement to close it back up again (Latour, 1988a).

22 The lateral interlocking of the trolleys consisted simply of reworking the principle of "easy" vertical piling of the old metal baskets that we have already encountered in a lateral fashion.

23 One pair can hide another. Even if there was no longer any need to separate and reattach the "chassis-basket" coupling, now the "trolley-customer" pair needs to be assembled and separated, and done on the spot. Or, in other words, if removing the turnstile got rid of the problem of filtering people (or rather, had delegated it to checkouts and, potentially, automatic doors), now collections of people-object hybrids need to be created and filtered.

24 The arrangement in the illustration is clumsy as the trolleys shown here are away from the rail, which makes the "automatic return" that they are trying to illustrate rather improbable. However, by placing the line of trolleys against the rail, the device is perfectly viable, as a more spontaneous photograph of this type of device shown elsewhere can attest (1941, 01, 46).

25 Such devices already existed with the former foldable models (1941, 01, 46; 1948, 02, 197), but without trolleys being folded properly, using them meant the sales space became cluttered (1941, 07, 64–65; 1946, 12, 69).

26 In 1947, a survey of supermarket customers conducted in the Boston area showed that 33.8% did their shopping by car, while 55.5% went on foot and 10.7% used public transport (1947, 07, 63). Another survey conducted in 1948 of 600 families in the small town of Knoxville, Tennessee, showed that shopping on foot and by car were neck and neck, at around 40% each (the remainder was distributed between taking the bus, for about 5% and … telephone orders for nearly 15%!) (1948, 12, 52). A final, more optimistic, survey in 1949 assessed the distribution between automobiles, walking and public transport at 69.2%, 25.9% and 4.0%, respectively. This last survey is interesting mainly because it shows how the mode of transport contributes to the variation in purchase volumes: unsurprisingly, shoppers with vehicles buy in larger quantities than the others (66.1% of the former buy more than 15 items, versus only 50% of the latter) (1949, 03, 86).

27 In an undoubtedly more anecdotal fashion, we can also note the invention of devices aimed at merchandising or organising the problem of merchandise reception in order to reconcile the maintenance of service with the withholding of trolleys that was common practice at the time: one of these devices appeared as a conveyor belt for carrying purchases from checkouts to a hatch interface between the shop and the car park, where customers could then go to pick them up (1951, 09, 109); another consisted of being given a ticket at the checkout for a delivery point that was installed in the car park to collect the corresponding purchases. In exchange for this ticket, an employee would both bring the customer's car to the delivery point and load it with the merchandise (1956, 12, 66).

28 Paradoxically, one of the arguments long used for promoting self-service was not its ability to replace service, but rather its ability to help maintain it. This can be seen in numerous articles, with titles such as "You Can Change to Self-Service Arrangement and Still Give Charge-And-Delivery" (1940, 08, 24–25); "Self-Service Works Well Combined With Service" (1942, 03, 42–43); "Egger Went Self-Service But Continued His Charge & Delivery Service" (1945, 08, 52–53); "Reconcile home payment and delivery with self-service organisation at the forefront: it works!" (1945, 10, 94–95); "Can I Adopt a Self-Service Layout – And Still Offer Home Payment and Delivery?" (1946, 12, 46 sq.).

29 However, the evolution was modest in comparison with today's standards: in 1956, American supermarkets only had 58.5 trolleys on average (1956, 04, 70).

30 Goldman never ceased talking about the so-called resistance of consumers to his innovation and putting forward a thousand ploys that he could have used in order to overcome it: "teaser" adverts, the use of extras, making demonstration films (Wilson, 1978). However, the very rapid appearance of trolleys in the American commercial arena – and not only Goldman's – raises very serious doubts about this heroic entrepreneurial activity. One could even ask whether the eminently "pro-active" dissemination logic that is usefully put forward by traditional technical

anthropology – Rudolf Diesel and his engine (Bryant, 1976); Eastman Kodak and amateur photography (Jenkins, 1975); Thomas Edison and the light bulb (Hughes, 1979); etc. – does not arise chiefly from the choice of method consisting, for this type of research, in promoting the point of view of the innovator rather than that of the market into which his innovation is to be introduced. Innovators inevitably give themselves the leading role, or at the very least stress the efforts that they had to deploy when the social acceptance of their products thus occurs in a more fluid and spontaneous fashion, according to a logic that, since it does not necessarily refer to expressing a "demand", does not necessarily always correspond to the direct actions of the entrepreneur.

31 Here we find the wonderful dynamic of the "prosthesis" (working directly on the body of the disabled person) and of "empowerment" (working in the sphere of activity of the disabled person to place it within his reach) described by Michel Callon (2008).

32 Child labour, endemic in the nineteenth century (Abbott, 1908), was still wide-spread in the United States at the start of the twentieth century (Barnhouse Walters and Briggs, 1993) and even beyond (Margolin, 1978).

33 According to Terry P. Wilson (1978), biographer of Goldman, the so-called inventor of the trolley, a citizen of Dallas, Texas, reportedly filed a complaint with the mayor of his town in July 1942 in order to obtain a ban on the presence of children and domestic animals in shopping trolleys when shopping, on the grounds that the children's damp nappies – not to mention the dogs and cats – compromised the hygiene of the trolley for the next customer. Considering this request to be well-founded and consistent with its remit, the Dallas Department of Health ruled in favour of the plaintiff's request. However, angry mothers then succeeded in mobilising to denounce the lack of heart and humanity of local bureaucrats, leading to the retreat and abandonment of the planned ban.

34 All these fears continued even after the presence of children in the commercial space was generally accepted, as can be seen by the child-trap turnstiles already presented (1958, 02, 128, see Chapter 4), but also in the recurring cartoons on the theme of silly behaviour (destroying merchandise: 1922, 05, 21; using packets as building blocks: 1927, 04, 40; tying an old man's beard to a trolley: 1946, 10, 178; mixing up price tags: 1946, 10, 182; balancing on a pile of cans: 1947, 01, 136; drawing on the shop floor: 1947, 02, 223; juggling with fruit: 1949, 01, 88; breaking half a dozen eggs to give his mother the half-dozen she wanted: 1952, 02, 195; candidly mentioning at the checkout the products eaten whilst shopping with his mother: 1952, 07, 139; using a pile of cans as a shooting gallery: 1952, 11, 130; not being able to climb down a pyramid of cans after having climbed up it: 1952, 12, 114; opening cans for the pleasure of hearing the pop of air rushing in: 1958, 03, 158).

35 We are given a clear illustration of the enticement of children via the seduction of their mother in an article from 1937 entitled "Try a 'Snack Shelf' for Children", with the proposal: "Now that physicians recommend between-meals snacks for active youngsters, mothers are watching your shelves and ads for energy-giving foods which are dietically right for the childhealth point of view. [...] All you need is a shelf or two, a few yards of colourful oilcloth from the dime store to make an attractive covering, a bright poster with youngster-appeal, and a list of foods that physician and mothers approve. Paste on your poster a picture from a magazine showing a child eating with great enjoyment. [...] then stock the shelf with different items each week so that it maintains interest [...] Mothers are always concerned about children's food, so a display like this should prove a 'hot spot'" (1937, 09, 136).

36 The main advertiser with this point of view was Gerber, the baby food manu-facturer (1929, 08, 86–87; 1930, 01, 74–75; 1936, 05, 13; 1936, 09, 122; 1937, 01, 114; etc.), but you can also find advertisements from Heinz (1935, 06, 5; 1940, 03, 142), American Can Co. (1935, 08, 64–65; 1939, 04, 12–120), Quaker Oats (1935,

09, 163; 1936, 09, 119; 1937, 03, 10; 1938, 08, 78–79; 1939, 01, 78–79), Pillsbury (1936, 09, 62–63; 1936, 10, 19–20; 1939, 03, 10–11), Clapp's Baby Foods (1937, 03, 106–107; 1938, 08, 92–93; 1938, 11, 96–97; 1939, 01, 124–125; 1940, 11, 132–133), etc. Mention should also be made here of the particular role of "National Baby Week", promoted both by the magazine (1938, 04, 45; 1939, 04, 40; 1940, 04, 46–47; 1941, 04, 48–49; 1942, 04, 48–49; 1942, 04, 55, etc.) and by certain advertisers such as American Can Co. (1939, 04, 120–121; etc.) and Gerber (1940, 04, 169; 1941, 04, 126–127; 1942, 04, 134–135; etc.).

37 These free small toys intended for children also included free baby utensils, aimed more at parents, as shown by a Gerber advert that not only relies on dolls but also metal cups, cutlery, dishes and bibs which the company's baby mascot extols whilst thus addressing his mother in a speech bubble: "Mother! Get these grand gifts for your baby" (1937, 01, 114).

38 However, Daniel Cook mentions that similar devices had been used in large shops throughout the inter-war period (Cook, 2003, p. 152).

39 This image would be followed and reinforced by others of the same type (1945, 10, 103; 1948, 07, 72; 1950, 02, 226).

40 This very strange illustration features a baby holding a can of food, sitting in the upper basket of a trolley that is being pushed by an old man with a long beard and a long scythe – clearly an allegory of death – probably to show that the universe of the grocery store was now open – thanks to the trolley? – to all human beings, from their birth until their demise.

41 This parallel could open up a fascinating extension to the history of the trolley. Suitcases were also gradually equipped with little wheels, then with telescopic handles. The obvious contrast that has emerged between the simplicity and utility of these innovations on the one hand and their extremely late appearance on the other, is an enigma whose resolution should logically attract all the attention of specialists in the anthropology of techniques.

42 The few solutions presented do not claim to exhaust the list of possible variations, which are probably more numerous than those I have been able to identify with any certainty. At least this is what is suggested, for example, by the presence of a drawing (too specific to have been invented) found in a rather more "adult"-themed cartoon, showing the father of the family, alone, enraptured by a bikini-clad starlet jumping out of a cake on top of a box of instant cake mix, on the left of which lies a single-basket trolley whose bow has been cut out to install a seat ... which here is ... empty (1955, 01, 113).

43 For a photograph of this device being used in real life, see 1949, 07, 71; for a similar device, see 1953, 04, 97.

44 The manufacturer presented this characteristic as an advantage that prevented children from grabbing products in the trolley or from the shelves.

45 The manufacturer emphasised the capacity benefits of this solution by pointing out that the telescoping trolleys equipped with seats that were available on the market "both reduce grocery capacity and interfere with nesting so that hoped-for economy of floor space is negligible".

46 A solution of the same kind, in the form of an adjustable shell in the upper part of the trolley (at the risk of a high loss of storage space), can be seen in a snapshot from 1952 (1952, 02, 79).

47 This figure also shows the significance of proximity or the absence of systematic car use at this time.

6 Conclusion

In this book, I decided to illustrate the marketing dynamic of self-service in the middle of the twentieth century based on examples in *Progressive Grocer*, which are *a priori* out of phase and from the grocery world, but which I hope have nonetheless finally proven appropriate. The choice was that of a "medial" focalisation – an approach consisting in wearing the spectacles of specialised media to observe the development of the world concerned. This way of doing things exposed me *a priori* to the dangers of using a single source and, worse still, the risk of a fictional approach to the reality of commerce. However, paradoxically it is precisely these two potential pitfalls that allowed me to get closest to the American grocery world and its transformations. Because *Progressive Grocer* was the central medium available to independent retailers to find out about the general state of their activity and collect information about possible innovations, the magazine's point of view is also their own. Regardless of the reality of the changes described, these changes imposed themselves as the way things were, as the movement to follow, to such an extent that this movement was eventually incidentally depicted in many more "constructed" representations.

Progressive Grocer's modernist rhetoric was actually even more effective as it closely linked the intellectual and the practical, the "performative" and the "performed". The magazine's astuteness consisted in presaging the trick of the French "Myriam" advert,[1] in other words accompanying the reference to new possible commercial situations by depicting those promised in the previous stage. Thus the magazine displayed a rhetoric that was both linguistic and pictorial, as well as the real effects of this rhetoric. *Progressive Grocer*'s articles and adverts are as intellectual as they are practical: both combine images and text; they mix a direct display of objects, facts and scenarios with comments and narratives aimed at giving them commercial meaning and appeal. The magazine does not exactly speak words that do things, but instead connects tangible words to meaningful things in order to change the way business is thought of and carried out – or more specifically, to demonstrate that commercial thoughts and actions have already been transformed and that there is no choice but to act in response.

In this mechanism, showing the competition, or rather its possible effects, what it will cost to remain immobile against the progress of business, plays a central role. The grocery store was in fact a competitive arena for two reasons: first, it displayed products where the coexistence of rival offers was carefully organised; but second, it was a place that itself faced strong competition – from other grocery stores but, above all, from large shops, from chain stores as soon as they appeared, and from supermarkets from the end of the 1930s.

Competition was also organised by the magazine in its own pages, between suppliers and factors promoting competition (brands, press, manufacturers of cans, shelves, tills, trolleys, etc.). Linking all of these actors eventually created a lot of competitive and spatial constraint, and shows us that the grocery world, which we might have thought was rigid and outdated, doomed to shrink and passively submit to the pressure of supermarkets, was on the contrary and against all expectations a fantastic laboratory for the "progression" of modern types of sales and relocation of goods and services. This was first as an improvement to service, assisted by improved hygiene, tools to help grocers in their work, telephone sales and motorised delivery; then as a more radical transformation in which the surreptitious and deliberate introduction of different equipment and packaged products finally proved complementary to or even replaced salespeople.

At the end of this investigation at the heart of the small American grocery store, but also inextricably of the stories that *Progressive Grocer* narrated and heard, we realise that the advent of "self-service" owed itself not to the brutal removal of all obstacles to the commercial relationship, in the hope of giving free rein to limitless choice, as with the "laissez-faire" ideology, but paradoxically to the moving and renewal of boundaries, through a "faire laissez-faire" approach aimed at pushing practices "in the appropriate direction". Within the narrow spaces of their confined premises, promoters of the modernist grocery shop were thus able continuously to reconfigure the boundaries necessary to the advent of "freer" and more efficient commerce. They changed their blueprints literally and figuratively, moved the counters and extended to the glass cases at the time of the open display, in order to invent a free view that respected product integrity; replaced display cases and counters with display shelving and checkouts in the era of self-service, in order to reconcile the increased traffic of free movement with the control needed to record payments. They also generalised the more discreet boundaries, such as adjustable shelves intended to separate products smoothly, or canned food and cellophane tasked with replacing the old boundary of the counter. They again played on the shop's outer enclosure by installing, more or less discreetly, turnstiles and "magic doors" able to free up and control the flow of customers in one move … and by introducing mobile spaces and enclosures, in the form of trolleys, which increased people's mobility whilst marking out in the clearest and most generous fashion the extent of the property they were in the process of acquiring.

This undertaking, intended at the outset to preserve small business, was so successful that the former immutable and narrow confines of family-run grocery stores became too narrow for the flow thus generated. Over time *Progressive Grocer* turned its interest in grocers to the superettes they became, then to the superettes-turned-supermarkets, and thus in the extension and corresponding relocation of a certain number of shops. The abandonment of "Main Street" in favour of more comfortable and advantageous locations (1931, 02, 14–15), which had been exceptional in the 1930s, became an important theme in the 1950s (1952, 01, 58; 1952, 01, 60; 1953, 08, 48–52; 1955, 02, 142 sq.). "Enlightened" (or rather enlightening) small businesses and their representatives thus also moved with the consumers and partially adopted the model of the largest supermarkets, as has so often been said. However, instead of being absorbed by a model imposed from outside, following a movement supposed to overcome the immobility of the past, *Progressive Grocer* also promoted a deliberate, inventive and intensive movement for modernising the retail grocer, at the end of which the transformation of small business also fully participated in defining, and often anticipating, the distinctive traits and devices of the large-scale distribution that succeeded it. This transformation was achieved through a process that looked like Pasteur's – in other words, a dynamic where local conditions (diffusion) and lateral contaminations (contagion) combined to generate and generalise jointly a new entity and its effects, here the original shapes and attributes of self-service and its ability to support the progress of the grocery store world.

This progress was entirely based on an interlocking logic. For a long time, economic sociology has focused on (and is sticking to) the related notion of embeddedness. Karl Polanyi was the first to find in this idea a way of describing two opposing worlds, where one is included in the other: the economic would be embedded in the social (Polanyi, 2001 [1944]). Mark Granovetter (1985) contested the "hypersocialised" idea of Polanyi's structural embeddedness, preferring instead a relational embeddedness: economic behaviours are caught in the web of concrete social relations. However, with both authors, the determinants of social action, whether structural or relational, are always of a strictly social order. On the contrary, by shifting from embeddedness to interlocking, by following the branding and enclosing dynamic, we have the means to understand the cross-cutting games of inclusion and designation, where observable links and dependencies are as material as they are human, as economic as they are social (Cochoy, 2012). Furthermore, the interlocking is reversible: it is as if we were building magic Russian dolls, in which the first doll contains the last. Every entity is penned and branded; the space for interlocking is both very confined and yet very fluid; locations are continuously reinvented and redefined; competition is both turned and performed.

In order to summarise the dynamic in question, there is nothing that beats the example of the trolley – one last time! Not only did trolleys fit into one another (initially with the vertical interlocking of baskets, then the lateral interlocking of baskets attached to their chassis), but above all they were also part of a generalised interlocking: cans were placed in the trolley, which was itself a box in a shop, which in turn was a box in the economy, and so on. These successive interlocking movements were only compatible with market flexibility by virtue of a sleight of hand making the nesting both articulated and reversible, thanks to the double device of pens and brands.

Branding and penning made it possible to implement a social project that was as crazy as it was real, making solids fluid, making boxes flow – finding a way of resolving the problem of "circling the square" rather than "squaring the circle". The trolley operates as a symbol of the entire process. It is both an enclosure and circulating location; it shakes yet also consolidates the property space. Besides the traditional elements of the door and bridge so dear to Simmel, the trolley introduces the most modern figure of the vehicle, capable of creating a different link between the inside and outside, thanks, in a way, to the temporary imposition of a "mobile space". As is shown in a surreal manner in Figure 6.1, the continuous alchemy of enclosures and brands runs through the entire history of the market, returning to us today like a "boomerang" (as a metaphor and a brand, see the name of the drink), with barbed-wire pens as the mythical origin and branding on merchandise as the horizon, via covered carts (from the old prairie) or wire fencing (of modern supermarkets). For a long time to come, these trolleys will create the link between them, in order to embark products in its infinite whirlwind.

Figure 6.1 Branding, penning … loading
Source: France, March 2008

Note

1 In this famous billposting campaign, a young woman in a bikini was undressed over three successive posters in which each time a new promise was made – "on September 2nd I'll take off the top"; "on September 4th I'll take off the bottoms" – featuring the fulfilment of the previous promise. The model is already in a swimsuit when she promises to move on to a monokini; she is in a monokini when she promises full nudity (Cochoy, 2011a). Fulfilling promises and performing commitments operates as a guarantee of the performative nature of the promises to come.

Bibliography

Abbott, E. (1908), "A study of the early history of child labor in America", *The American Journal of Sociology*, Vol. 14, No. 1, pp. 15–37.

Akrich, M. (1992), "The de-scription of technical objects", in Bijker, E. and Law, J., *Shaping Technology/Building Society: Studies in sociotechnical change*, MIT Press, pp. 205–224.

Akrich, M.,Callon, M. and Latour, B. (1988a), "À quoi tient le succès des innovations. Premier épisode: l'art de l'intéressement", *Annales des Mines, série "Gérer et comprendre"*, No. 11, juin, pp. 4–17.

Akrich, M., Callon, M. and Latour, B. (1988b), "À quoi tient le succès des innovations. Deuxième épisode: l'art de choisir les bons porte-parole", *Gérer et Comprendre*, No. 12, septembre, pp. 14–29.

Alexander, J. (2008), "Efficiencies of balance: Technical efficiency, popular efficiency, and arbitrary standards in the late Progressive Era", *Social Studies of Science*, Vol. 38, No. 3, pp. 323–349.

Anderson, O.E. Jr (1953), *Refrigeration in America*, Princeton, NJ: Princeton University Press.

Andreoni, J., Harbaugh, W. and Vesterlund, L. (2003), "The carrot or the stick: Rewards, punishments, and cooperation", *The American Economic Review*, Vol. 93, No. 3, pp. 893–902.

Austin, J.L. (1961), *Philosophical Papers*, London: Oxford University Press.

Bader, L. (1939), "A Survey of consumers' and independent store owners' reactions to recent price legislation", *The Journal of Marketing*, Vol. 4, No. 1, pp. 59–67.

Barnhouse Walters, P. and Briggs, C.M. (1993), "The family economy, child labor, and schooling: Evidence from the early twentieth-century South", *American Sociological Review*, Vol. 58, No. 2, pp. 163–181.

Barrey, S. (2007), "Struggling to be displayed at the point of purchase: The emergence of merchandising in French supermarkets", in Callon, M., Millo, Y. and Muniesa, F. (eds), *Market Devices*, Sociological Review Monographs, Vol. 55, Issue Supplement s2, pp. 92–108.

Bertrand-Dorléac, L., Delage, C. and Gunthert, A. (2001), "Présentation", *Vingtième siècle, revue d'histoire, dossier Image et histoire*, No. 72, pp. 3–4.

Bourdieu, P. (1984), Distinction; *A Social Critique of Judgement of Taste*, Cambridge, MA: Harvard University Press.

Bowlby, R. (2001), *Carried away: The Invention of Modern Shopping*, New York, NY: Columbia University Press.

Brooke (2010), "The sense of dissonance: An interview with David Stark", April 14, http://thesocietypages.org/economicsociology/2010/04/14/the-sense-of-dissonance-an-interview-with-david-stark/

Brown, M. and Philips, P. (1985), "The evolution of labor market structure: The California canning industry", *Industrial and Labor Relations Review*, Vol. 38, No. 3, pp. 392–407.

Bruegel, M. (2003), "Normaliser pour gagner la confiance des consommateurs? L'industrie française des conserves alimentaires dans l'entre-deux-guerres", in Stanziani, A. (ed.), *La qualité des produits en France, XVIIIe–XXe siècles*, Paris: Belin, pp. 151–173.

Bruno, I. (2012), "Quand s'associer, c'est concourir. Les paradoxes de la 'coopétition'", in Cochoy, F. (ed.), *Du lien marchand, Essai(s) de sociologie économique relationniste*, Toulouse: Presses Universitaires du Mirail, pp. 54–78.

Bryant, L. (1976), "The development of the diesel engine", *Technology and Culture*, Vol. 17, No. 3, pp. 432–446.

Buenker, J.D. and Kantowicz, E.R. (eds) (1988), *Historical dictionary of the Progressive Era, 1890–1920*, New York, NY: Greenwood Press.

Butler, J. (2010), "Performative agency", *Journal of Cultural Economy*, Vol. 3, No. 2, pp. 147–161.

Çalışkan, K. and Callon, M. (2010), "Economization, part 2: A research programme for the study of markets", *Economy and Society*, Vol. 39, No. 1, pp. 1–32.

Callon, M. (1986), "Some elements of a sociology of translation: Domestication of the scallops and the fishermen of St Brieuc Bay", in J. Law (ed.), *Power, Action and Belief: A New Sociology of Knowledge*, London: Routledge & Kegan Paul, pp. 196–233.

Callon, M. (1998), "Introduction: The embeddedness of economic markets in economics", in Callon, M. (ed.), *The Laws of the Markets*, Oxford: Blackwell, pp. 2–57.

Callon, M. (2005), "Why virtualism paves the way to political impotence: A reply to Daniel Miller's critique of The Laws of the Markets", *Economic Sociology: European Electronic Newsletter*, Vol. 6, No. 2, pp. 3–20, http://econsoc.mpifg.de/archive/esfeb05.pdf.

Callon, M. (2007), "What does it mean to say that economics is performative?" in MacKenzie, D., Muniesa, F. and Siu, L. (eds), *Do Economists Make Markets? On the Performativity of Economics*, Princeton, NJ: Princeton University Press, pp. 311–357.

Callon, M. (2008), "Economic markets and the rise of interactive agencements: From prosthetic agencies to habilitated agencies", in Pinch, T. and Swedberg, R. (eds), *Living in a Material World, Economic Sociology Meets Science and Technology Studies*, Cambridge, MA: MIT Press, pp. 29–56.

Callon, M. (2010), "Performativity, misfires and politics", *Journal of Cultural Economy*, Vol. 3, No. 2, pp. 163–169.

Callon, M. (2013), "Qu'est-ce qu'un agencement marchand?" in Callon, M. et al. (eds), *Sociologie des agencements marchands*, Paris: Presses des Mines, pp. 325–440.

Callon, M., Millo, Y. and Muniesa, F. (eds) (2007), *Market devices*, Oxford: Blackwell.

Campbell, D. and Wright, J. (2012), "The importance of peripheral vision in evaluative practice", http://ucanr.org/sites/UC_CCP/files/125957.pdf.

Canu, R. (2007), *Publicités et travail marchand, La manipulation des documents publicitaires sur le marché des télécommunications (2003–2007)*, thèse pour le doctorat de sociologie, Université Toulouse II, Toulouse, 11 décembre.

Canu, R. (2009), "La manipulation des documents publicitaires. Contribution à une sociologie du travail marchand", *Revue française de socio-économie*, No. 3, pp. 147–167.

Canu, R. (2010), "La magie des publicités. De l'enrobage des marchés à leur incarnation: les leçons du Magicien d'Oz", CERTOP, article de travail.

Carson, K.A. (2011), "Taylorism, progressivism, and rule by experts", *Freeman*, Vol. 61, No. 7, September.

Chandler, A.D. Jr (1977), *The Visible Hand: The Managerial Revolution in American Business*, Cambridge, MA: The Belknap Press of Harvard University Press.

Chatriot, A. and Chessel, M.-E. (2006), "L'histoire de la distribution: un chantier inachevé", *Histoire, économie et société*, No. 1, pp. 67–82.

Clarke, A.J. (1999), *Tupperware: The promise of plastic in 1950s America*, Washington: Smithsonian Institution Press.

Cochoy, F. (1994), "La gestion scientifique des marchés: marketing et taylorisme dans l'entre-deux-guerres", *Recherche et applications en marketing*, Vol. 9, No. 2, 1994, pp. 97–114.

Cochoy, F. (1998), "Another discipline for the market economy: Marketing as a performative knowledge and know-how for capitalism", in Callon, M. (ed.), *The Laws of the Markets*, Oxford: Blackwell, pp. 194–221.

Cochoy, F. (1999), *Une histoire du marketing, Discipliner l'économie de marché*, Paris: La Découverte.

Cochoy, F. (2002), *Une sociologie du packaging, ou l'âne de Buridan face au marché*, Paris: Presses Universitaires de France.

Cochoy, F. (2004), "La captation des publics entre dispositifs et dispositions, ou le petit Chaperon rouge revisité", in Cochoy, F. (ed.), *La captation des publics*, Toulouse: Presses Universitaires du Mirail, p. 11–68.

Cochoy, F. (2006), "Avant-Propos. Du Vaillant petit tailleur à la distribution d'aujourd'hui", *Réseaux*, Vol. 24, No. 135–136, pp. 19–31.

Cochoy, F. (2007a), "A brief theory of the 'captation' of the public: Understanding the market with Little Red Riding Hood", *Theory, Culture & Society*, Vol. 24, No. 7–8, pp. 213–233.

Cochoy, F. (2007b), "A sociology of market things: On tending the garden of choices in mass retailing", in Callon, M. et al. (eds), *Market devices*, Oxford: Blackwell, pp. 109–129.

Cochoy, F. (2008a), "Hansel and Gretel at the grocery store: *Progressive Grocer* and the little American consumers (1929–1959)", *Journal of Cultural Economy*, Vol. 1, No. 2, pp. 145–163.

Cochoy, F. (2008b), "Calculation, qualculation, calqulation: Shopping cart's arithmetic, equipped cognition and clustered consumers", *Marketing Theory*, Vol. 8, No. 1, pp. 15–44.

Cochoy, F. (2008c), "*Progressive Grocer*, ou la 'petite distribution' en mouvement (États-Unis, 1929–1959)", *Espaces et société*, No. 135/4, pp. 25–44.

Cochoy, F. (2008d), "Parquer et marquer les produits, ou comment gérer le territoire du petit commerce (*Progressive Grocer*, 1929–1959)", *Entreprises et histoire*, No. 53, décembre, pp. 34–53.

Cochoy, F. (2009), "Driving a shopping cart from STS to business, and the other way round. On the introduction of shopping carts in American grocery stores (1936–1959)", *Organization*, Vol. 16, No. 1, pp. 31–55.

Cochoy, F. (2010a), "Reconnecting marketing to 'market-things': How grocery equipments drove modern consumption", in Araujo, L., Finch, J. and Kjellberg, H. (eds), *Reconnecting Marketing to Markets: Practice-based Approaches*, Oxford: Oxford University Press, pp. 29–49.

Cochoy, F. (2010b), "'Market-things Inside': insights from *Progressive Grocer* (United States, 1929–1959)", in Cayla, J. and Zwick, D. (eds), *Inside Marketing*, Oxford: Oxford University Press, pp. 58–84.

Cochoy, F. (2010c), "Modernizing the grocery trade with cartoons in wartimes: Humor as a marketing weapon (*Progressive Grocer*, 1939–1945)", in McLean, C., Puyou, F.-R., Quattrone, P. and Thrift, N. (eds), *Imagining Organizations*, London and New York: Routledge, pp. 173–188.

Cochoy, F. (2010d), "Comment faire des affaires avec des mots-choses: politique de la performativité et presse commerciale (*Progressive Grocer*, 1929–1946)", *Réseaux*, No. 163 (août–septembre), pp. 75–103.

Cochoy, F. (2010e), "'How to build displays that sell': The politics of performativity in American grocery stores (*Progressive Grocer*, 1929–1946)", *Journal of Cultural Economy*, Vol. 3, No. 2, pp. 299–315.

Cochoy, F. (2011a), *De la curiosité, l'art de la séduction marchande*, Paris: Armand Colin.

Cochoy, F. (2011b), *Sociologie d'un "curiositif", Smartphone, code-barres 2D et self-marketing*, Lormont: Le Bord de l'Eau.

Cochoy, F. (2012), "La sociologie économique relationniste", in Cochoy, F. (ed.), *Du lien marchand, Essai(s) de sociologie économique relationniste*, Toulouse: Presses Universitaires du Mirail, pp. 19–54.

Cochoy, F. (2013), "La focalisation 'médiale': pour un regard post-constructiviste sur les outils de communication", *Études de communication*, No. 40, pp. 77–91.

Cochoy, F. (2014), "The American Marketing Association: A handrail for marketers and marketing history", *Journal of Historical Research in Marketing*, Vol. 6, No. 4, pp. 538–547.

Coll, S. (2012), "Le marketing relationnel et le lien marchand: le cas des cartes de fidélité suisses", in Cochoy, F. (ed.), *Du lien marchand, Essai(s) de sociologie économique relationniste*, Toulouse: Presses Universitaires du Mirail, pp. 197–218.

Cook, D.Th. (2003), "Spatial biographies of children's consumption. Market places and spaces of childhood in the 1930s and beyond", *Journal of Consumer Culture*, Vol. 3, No. 2, pp. 147–169.

Crossick, G. and Jaumain, S. (ed.) (1999), *Cathedrals of Consumption: The European Department Store, 1850–1939*, Aldershot: Ashgate.

Czarniawska, B. (2011), *Cyberfactories: How News Agencies Produce News*, Cheltenham: Edward Elgar.

Daumas, J.-C. (2006), "L'invention des usines à vendre. Carrefour et la révolution de l'hypermarché", *Réseaux*, Vol. 24, No. 135–136, pp. 59–92.

Denis, J. (2006), "Préface: les nouveaux visages de la performativité", *Études de communication*, No. 29, décembre, Performativité: relectures et usages d'une notion frontière, pp. 7–24.

Denis, J. and Pontille, D. (2010), "Performativité de l'écrit et travail de maintenance", *Réseaux*, No. 163, pp. 105–130.

Deutsch, T.A. (2001), *Making Change at the Grocery Store: Government, Grocers, and the Problem of Women's Autonomy in the Creation of Chicago's Supermarkets, 1920–1950*, PhD dissertation, University of Wisconsin-Madison.

Deutsch, T.A. (2010), *Building a housewife's paradise: Gender, politics, and American grocery stores in the twentieth century*, Chapel Hill: The University of North Carolina Press.

Deville, J. (2012), "Regenerating market attachments: Consumer credit debt collection and the capture of affect", *Journal of Cultural Economy*, Vol. 5, No. 4, pp. 423–439.

Didier, E. (2007), "Do statistics perform the economy?" in Callon, M., Millo, Y. and Muniesa, F. (eds), *Market Devices*, Oxford: Blackwell, pp. 276–310.

Diner, S.J. (1998), *A Very Different Age: Americans of the Progressive Era*, New York, NY: Hill and Wang.

Dipman, C.W. (1935), *The Modern Grocery Store*, New York, NY: The Progressive Grocer.

Du Gay, P. (2004), "Self-service: Retail, shopping and personhood", *Consumption, Markets & Culture*, Vol. 7, No. 2, pp. 149–163.

Dujarier, M.-A. (2014), "The three sociological types of consumer work", *Journal of Consumer Culture*, April, pp. 1–17.

Edgerton, D. (1999), "From innovation to use: Ten eclectic theses on the historiography of technology", *History and Technology*, Vol. 16, No. 2, pp. 111–136.

Emmet, B. and Jeuck, J.E. (1950), *Catalogues and Counters*, Chicago, IL: The University of Chicago Press.

Fellman, S. and Popp, A. (2013), "Lost in the archive: The business historian in distress", in Czarniawska, B. and Löfgren, O. (eds), *Coping with Excess: How Organizations, Communities and Individuals Manage Overflows*, Cheltenham, UK: Edward Elgar, pp. 216–243.

Fernie, S. and Metcalf, D. (1998), "(Not) hanging on the telephone: Payment systems in the new sweatshops", Center for Economic Performance, London School of Economics and Political Science, No. 390, http://eprints.lse.ac.uk/20275/1/%28Not%29Hanging_on_the_Telephone_Payment_systems_in_the_New_Sweatshops.pdf.

Fischer, C.S. (1988), "'Touch someone': The telephone industry discovers sociability", *Technology and Culture*, Vol. 29, No. 1, pp. 32–61.

Fischhoff, B. (1975), "Hindsight ≠ foresight: The effect of outcome knowledge on judgment under uncertainty", *Journal of Experimental Psychology: Human Perception and Performance*, Vol. 1, pp. 288–299.

Flink, J.J. (1972), "Three stages of American automobile consciousness", *American Quarterly*, Vol. 24, No. 4, pp. 451–473.

Genette, G. (1972), *Figures III*, Paris: Seuil.

Gibson, J.J. (1977), "The theory of affordances", in Shaw, R.E. and Bransford, J. (eds), *Perceiving, Acting, and Knowing*, Lawrence Erlbaum Associates, NJ: Hillsdale, pp. 67–82.

Ginzburg, C. and Poni, C. (1981), "La micro-histoire", *Le Débat*, No. 17, pp. 133–136.

Giraudeau, M. (2007), "Le travail entrepreneurial, ou l'entrepreneur schumpetérien performé", *Sociologie du travail*, Vol. 49, No. 3, pp. 330–350.

Giraudeau, M. (2008), "The drafts of strategy: Opening up plans and their uses", *Long Range Planning*, Vol. 41, No. 3, pp. 291–308.

Glad, Paul W. (1966), "Progressives and the business culture of the 1920s", *The Journal of American History*, Vol. 53, No. 1, pp. 75–89.

Godelier, M. (1989), *L'Idéel et le matériel: pensée, économies, sociétés*, Paris: Fayard.

Gould, L.L. (2001), "The Progressive era", in Finkelman, P. and Wallenstein, P. (eds), *The Encyclopedia of American Political History*, Washington, DC: CQ Press, pp. 310–312.

Gould, R.A. (1971), "The archaeologist as ethnographer: A case from the Western desert of Australia", *World Archaeology*, Vol. 3, No. 2, pp. 143–177.

Grandclément, C. (2006), "Wheeling food products around the store … and away: The invention of the shopping cart, 1936–1953", paper presented at the Food Chains Conference: Provisioning, Technology, and Science, Hagley Museum and Library, Wilmington, Delaware, November 2–4, www.csi.ensmp.fr/Items/WorkingPapers/Download/DLWP.php?wp=WP_CSI_006.pdf.

Grandclément, C. (2008), *Vendre sans vendeurs: sociologie des dispositifs d'achalandage en supermarché*, thèse pour le doctorat en socio-économie de l'innovation, Paris: École Nationale Supérieure des Mines de Paris.

Grandclément, C. (2011), "Le libre-service à ses origines: mettre au travail ou construire le consommateur?" *Entreprises et histoire*, No. 64/3, pp. 64–75.

Granovetter, M. (1985), "Economic action and social structure: The problem of embeddedness", *American Journal of Sociology*, Vol. 91, No. 3, November, pp. 481–510.

Haas, H.M. (1979), *Social and Economic Aspects of the Chain Store Movement*, New York, NY: Arno Press.

Hamilton, S. (2008), *Trucking Country: The Road to America's Wal-Mart Economy*, Princeton and Oxford: Princeton University Press.

Hine, T. (1995), *The Total Package: The Evolution and Secret Meanings of Boxes, Bottles, Cans, and Tubes*, Boston, MA: Little, Brown and Co.

Hofstadter, R. (1963), *The Progressive Movement, 1900–1915*, New York, NY: Prentice-Hall.

Horowitz, R. (2006), *Putting Meat on the American Table: Taste, Technology, Transformation*, Baltimore, MD: Johns Hopkins University Press.

Hughes, Th.P. (1983), *Networks of Power: Electrification in Western society, 1890–1930*, Baltimore, MD: Johns Hopkins University Press.

Hughes, Th.P. (1979), "The electrification of America: The system builders", *Technology and Culture*, Vol. 20, No. 1, pp. 124–161.

Hultén, B., Broweus, N. och and Van Dijk, M. (2009), *Sensory Marketing*, Basingstoke, UK: Palgrave Macmillan.

Jaycox, F. (2005), *The Progressive Era: Eyewitness History*, New York, NY: Facts On File.

Jeantet, A. (1998), "Les objets intermédiaires dans la conception. Éléments pour une sociologie des processus de conception", *Sociologie du Travail*, Vol. 40, No. 3, pp. 291–316.

Jenkins, R.V. (1975), "Technology and the market: George Eastman and the origins of mass amateur photography", *Technology and Culture*, Vol. 16, No. 1, pp. 1–19.

Jullien, F. (1995 [1992]), *The Propensity of Things: Toward a History of Efficacy in China*, Cambridge, MA: MIT Press.

Kennedy, M.T. (2005), "Behind the one-way mirror: Refraction in the construction of product market categories", *Poetics*, Vol. 33, pp. 201–226.

Kjellberg, H. and Helgesson, C.-F. (2007), "The mode of exchange and the shaping of markets: Introducing self-service in Swedish post-war food distribution", *Industrial Marketing Management*, Vol. 36, No. 7, pp. 861–878.

Kline, R.R. (2000), *Consumers in the Country: Technology and Social Change in Rural America*, Baltimore, MD: Johns Hopkins University Press.

Koch, S.L. (2012), *A Theory of Grocery Shopping: Food, Choice and Conflict*, London and New York: Berg.

Laïb, J. (1955), "The trade press", *The Public Opinion Quarterly*, Vol. 19, No. 1, pp. 31–44.

Lancaster, K.J. (1966), "A new approach to consumer theory", *Journal of Political Economy*, Vol. 74, No. 2, pp. 132–157.

Latour, B. (1988a), "Mixing humans and nonhumans together: The sociology of a doorcloser", *Social Problems*, Vol. 35, No. 3, pp. 298–310.

Latour, B. (1988b), *The Pasteurization of France*, Cambridge, MA: Harvard University Press.

Latour, B. (1991a), "The Berlin key or how to do words with things", in Graves-Brown, P.M. (ed.), *Matter, Materiality and Modern Culture*, London: Routledge, pp. 10–21.

Latour, B. (1991b), "Technology is society made durable", in Law, J. (ed.), *A Sociology of Monsters: Essays on Power, Technology and Domination*, London: Routledge, pp. 132–164.

Latour, B. (1992), "Where are the missing masses? The sociology of a few mundane artifacts", in Bijker, W.E. and Law, J. (eds), *Shaping Technology/Building Society: Studies in sociotechnical change*, Cambridge, MA: MIT Press, pp. 225–258.

Latour, B. (1993), *We Have Never Been Modern*, Cambridge, MA: Harvard University Press.

Latour, B. (1995), "The 'pedofil' of Boa Vista: A photo-philosophical montage", *Common Knowledge*, Vol. 4, No. 1, pp. 145–187.

Latour, B. (1996a), "On interobjectivity", *Mind, Culture, and Activity: An International Journal*, Vol. 3, No. 4, pp. 228–269.

Latour, B. (1996b), "Ces réseaux que la raison ignore: laboratoires, bibliothèques, collections", in Baratin, M. and Jacob, Ch. (eds), *Le pouvoir des bibliothèques: La mémoire des livres en Occident*, Paris: Albin Michel.

Latour, B. (1997), "Socrates' and Callicles' settlement – or, the invention of the impossible body politic", *Configurations*, Vol. 5, No. 2, pp. 189–240.

Latour, B. (1999), "Factures/fractures. From the concept of network to that of attachment", *Res*, No. 36, Autumn, pp. 20–31.

Latour, B. and Woolgar, S. (1979), *Laboratory Life. The Construction of Scientific Facts*, London, Beverly Hills: Sage.

Lave, J., Murtaugh, M. and de la Rocha, O. (1984), "The dialectic of arithmetic in grocery shopping", in Rogoff, B. and Lave, J. (eds), *Everyday Cognition. Its Development in Social Context*, Cambridge, MA: Harvard University Press, pp. 67–94.

Laycock, G. (1983), *The Kroger Story: A Century of Innovation*, Cincinnati, OH: The Kroger Co.

Lebhar, G.M. (1959), *Chain stores in America, 1859–1959*, New York, NY: Chain Store Publishing Co.

Levenstein H.A. (2003 [1993]), *Paradox of Plenty: A Social History of Eating in Modern America*, Berkeley, CA: University of California Press.

Leymonerie, C. (2006), "La vitrine d'appareils ménagers. Reflet des structures commerciales dans la France des années cinquante", *Réseaux*, Vol. 24, No. 135–136, pp. 93–124.

Leymonerie, C. (2011), "L'aluminium, matériau des arts décoratifs à l'Exposition Internationale de Paris en 1937", *Cahiers d'histoire de l'aluminium*, No. 46–47, pp. 9–49.

Licoppe, Ch. (2006), "La construction conversationnelle de l'activité commerciale. 'Rebondir' au téléphone pour placer des services", *Réseaux*, Vol. 24, No. 135–136, pp. 125–160.

Lippmann, W. (2008 [1925]), *Le public fantôme*, Paris: Demopolis (traduction en français présentée par Bruno Latour).

Longstreth, R.W. (1999), *The Drive-in, the Supermarket, and the Transformation of Commercial Space in Los Angeles, 1914–1941*, Cambridge, MA: MIT Press.

Longstreth, R.W. (2000), *The Buildings of Main Street: A Guide to American Commercial Architecture*, Walnut Creek, CA: AltaMira Press.

Loxley, J. (2006), *Performativity*, London: Routledge.

Lury, C. (2004), *Brands: The Logos of the Global Economy*, London and New York: Routledge.

McFall, L. (2008), "Rethinking economy: Pragmatics and politics", *Journal of Cultural Economy*, Vol. 1, No. 2, pp. 233–237.

MacKenzie, D. and Millo, Y. (2003), "Constructing a market, performing theory: The historical sociology of a financial derivatives exchange", *American Journal of Sociology*, Vol. 109, No. 1, pp. 107–145.

MacKenzie, D., Muniesa, F. and Siu, L. (eds) (2007), *Do Economists Make Markets? On the Performativity of Economics*, Princeton, NJ: Princeton University Press.

Mallard, A. (2002), "Les nouvelles technologies dans le travail relationnel: vers un traitement plus personnalisé de la figure du client?" *Sciences de la Société*, No. 56, mai, pp. 63–77.

Mallard, A. (2011), *Petit dans le marché, Une sociologie de la Très Petite Entreprise*, Paris: Presses des Mines.

Mallard, A. (2012), "Cadrer et encadrer la vente. Réflexion sur l'avenir des relations interpersonnelles dans une société d'organisations commerciales", in Cochoy, F. (ed.), *Du lien marchand, Essai(s) de sociologie économique relationniste*, Toulouse: Presses Universitaires du Mirail, pp. 81–106.

Margolin, C.R. (1978), "Salvation versus liberation: The movement for children's rights in a historical context", *Social Problems*, Vol. 25, No. 4, April, pp. 441–452.

Mayo, J.M. (1993), *The American Grocery Store: The Business Evolution of an Architectural Space*, Westport, CT: Greenwood Press.

McGerr, M. (2003), *A Fierce Discontent: The Rise and Fall of the Progressive Movement in America, 1870–1920*, New York, NY: Free Press.

Mellet, K. (2012), "Contagion, influence, communauté. Petite Socio-économie des agences de social media marketing", in Cochoy, F. (ed.), *Du lien marchand, Essai(s) de sociologie économique relationniste*, Toulouse: Presses Universitaires du Mirail, pp. 151–173.

Mendras, H. (1958), *Les Paysans et la modernisation de l'agriculture*, Paris: Édition du CNRS.

Miller, D. (1998), *A Theory of Shopping*, Ithaca, NY: Cornell University Press.

Monod, D. (1996), *Store Wars: Shopkeepers and the Culture of Mass Marketing, 1890–1939*, Toronto: University of Toronto Press.

Muniesa, F. (2011), *The Provoked Economy: Economic Reality and the Performative Turn*, London: Routledge.

Neville, H., and Lawson, D. (1987), "Attention to central and peripheral visual space in a movement detection task: An event-related potential and behavioral study", *Brain Research*, No. 405, pp. 253–294.

The New York Times (1926), "Butterick magazines to merge", *The New York Times*, June 17.

Norman, D.A. (1991), "Cognitive artefacts", in Carroll, J.M. (ed.), *Designing Interaction: Psychology at the Human-Computer Interface*, Cambridge: Cambridge University Press, pp. 17–38.

Parasie, S. (2010), *Et maintenant, une page de pub. Une histoire morale de la publicité à la télévision française (1968–2008)*, Paris: Ina éditions.

Péron, R. (2004), *Les boîtes: Les grandes surfaces dans la ville*, Paris: L'Atalante.

Pierce, Ch. (1934), *Collected Papers*, Cambridge, MA: Belknap Press of Harvard University Press.

Phillips, Ch.F. (1936), "A history of the Kroger Grocery & Baking Company", *National Marketing Review*, Vol. 1, No. 3, pp. 204–215.

Polanyi, K. (2001 [1944]), *The Great Transformation: The Political and Economic Origins of our Time*, Boston, MA: Beacon Press.

Presley, D.E. (1984), *Piggly Wiggly Southern Style: The Piggly Wiggly Southern story, 1919–1984*, Vidalia, GA: Piggly Wiggly Southern, Inc.

Ray, H. (2006), "Perceptions of working life in call centres", *Journal of Management Practice*, Vol. 7, No. 1, pp. 1–9.

Razac, O. (2002), *Barbed Wire: A Political History*, New York, NY: New Press.

Renfrew, C. and Bahn, P.G. (1991), *Archaeology: Theories, Methods, and Practice*, London: Thames and Hudson Ltd.

Revel, J. (2010), "Microstoria", in Delacroix, Ch., Dosset, F., Garcia, P. and Offenstadt, N. (ed.), *Historiographies, concepts et débats*, Paris: Gallimard, 2 vols, Folio Histoire, t. 1, pp. 529–534.

Rogers, E.M. (1962), *Diffusion of Innovations*, New York, NY: The Free Press of Glencoe.

Rolland, R. (1911 [1904]), *Jean-Christophe, Vol. I: Dawn*, trans. G. Cannan, www.gutenberg.org/cache/epub/7979/pg7979.html.

Serres, M. (1977), *Hermès IV: La distribution*, Paris: Minuit.

Seth, A. (2001), *The Grocers: The Rise and Rise of the Supermarket Chains*, Dover, NH: Kogan Page.

Shove, E., Pantzar, M. and Watson, M. (2012), *Dynamics of Social Practice*, London: Sage.

Shove, E. and Southerton, D. (2000), "Defrosting the freezer, from novelty to convenience: A story of normalization", *Journal of Material Culture*, Vol. 5, No. 3, pp. 301–319.

Smith, A. (2012), "The power of peripheral vision", http://coachingleaders.emotional-climate.com/the-power-of-peripheral-vision/.

Society for Historians of the Gilded Age and Progressive Era (n.d.), *Statement of Purpose*, www.historians.org/affiliates/SHGAPE.cfm.

Spellman, S.V. (2009), *Cornering the Market: Independent Grocers and Innovation in American Small Business, 1860–1940*, unpublished PhD dissertation, Carnegie Mellon University.

Stark, D. (2009), *The Sense of Dissonance. Accounts of Worth in Economic Life*, Princeton and Oxford: Princeton University Press.

Strasser, S. (1989), *Satisfaction Guaranteed: The Making of the American Mass Market*, New York, NY: Pantheon Books.

Tang, S. (2011), "History of the automobile: Ownership per household in US", Wikibook, http://en.wikibooks.org/wiki/Transportation_Deployment_Casebook/History_of_the_Automobile:_Ownership_per_Household_in_U.S.

Tarde, G. (1903), *The Laws of Imitation*, New York, NY: H. Holt and Company.

Tedlow, R.S. (1990), *New and Improved: The Story of Mass Marketing in America*, New York, NY: Basic Books.

Thoenig, J.-C. and Waldman, Ch. (2005), *De l'entreprise marchande à l'entreprise marquante*, Paris: Les Éditions d'Organisation.

Thompson, J.A. (1979), *Progressivism*, BAAS Pamphlets in American Studies 2, British Association for American Studies, South Shields: Peterson Printers.

Tolbert, L. (2009), "The aristocracy of the market basket: Self-service food shopping in the new South", in Belasco, W. and Horowitz, R. (eds), *Food Chains: From farmyard to Shopping Cart*, Philadelphia, PA: University of Pennsylvania Press.

Touraine, A. (1977), *The Self-Production of Society*, Chicago, IL: The University of Chicago Press.

Twede, D. (2012), "The birth of modern packaging: Cartons, cans and bottles", *Journal of Historical Research in Marketing*, Vol. 4, No. 2, pp. 245–272.

Vinck, D. (1999), "Ethnographie des activités de conception et d'innovation: le cas du maquettage numérique", *Management technologique, Impact de la technologie sur la gestion des personnes*, Grenoble, France, http://hal.archives-ouvertes.fr/docs/00/13/44/29/PDF/Cartier-99.pdf.

Von Hippel, E. (2002), "Horizontal innovation networks – by and for users", MIT Sloan School of Management, Working paper No. 4366–4302, June.

Weber, M. (1978 [1922]), *Economy and Society: An Outline of Interpretive Sociology*, 2 vols. Roth, G. and Wittich, C., eds, Berkeley, CA: University of California Press.

Wilson, J.A. (1942), "Archeology as a tool in humanistic and social studies", *Journal of Near Eastern Studies*, Vol. 1, No. 1, pp. 3–9.

Wilson, T.P. (1978), *The Cart that Changed the World. The Career of Sylvan N. Goldman*, Norman, OK: University of Oklahoma Press.

Worthington, W. Jr (1989), "Early risers", *American Heritage of Invention and Technology*, Vol. 4, No. 3, pp. 40–44.

Yates, J. and Orlikowski, W.J. (2007), "The PowerPoint presentation and its corollaries: How genres shape communicative action in organizations", in Zachary, M. and Thralls, C. (eds), *The Cultural Turn: Communicative Practices in Workplaces and the Professions*, Amityville, NY: Baywood Publishing, pp. 67–92.

Zimmerman, M.M. (1937), *Super Market: Spectacular Exponent of Mass distribution*, New York, NY: Super Market Publishing Co.

Zimmerman, M.M. (1955), *The Super Market: A Revolution in Distribution*, New York, NY: McGraw-Hill.

Zola, Émile (1886), *The Ladies' Paradise: A Realistic Novel*, translation, London: Vizetelly & Co.

Index

A-B-C Open Display Method (Dayton Display Company) 109
Abbott, E. 197n32
adjustable shelves 144–7
advertising 5; advertising rates in *Progressive Grocer* 21; advertising rhetoric 165n13, 187; advertising space, encouragement of consumption of 24–5; advertorial "Questions and Answers" 19–20, 24; growth of advertising in *Progressive Grocer* 26; lateral facility of advertisements 110–11; magazine advertising 17; in *Progressive Grocer* 19; success of *Progressive Grocer* with 25, 26, 27–8; turnover, exponential growth of *(Progressive Grocer)* 26
affordance 42, 48, 154, 164n7; predatory affordance 154
A.H. Fenske of Minneapolis 106
Akrich, M. 174
Akrich, M., Callon, M. and Latour, B. 182
Alexander, J. 8n5
aluminium lids (removable) 111
ambulatory advertising space, motorised delivery and 97, 99
American Can Company 139, 165n15; shopping trolleys 197–8nn36
American Grocer 21, 38n8
American Metal Products, Inc. 165n10; shopping trolleys 189
American Pop Corn Company 141
American Wire & Form Co. 108, 165n10; shopping trolleys 166, 171, 176, 187–8, 194n1, 194n4, 194n8
Ams, Charles 139
Anderson, O.E.Jr 119

Andreoni, J., Harbaugh, W. and Vesterlund, L. 50
anthropology of sciences and techniques 11
antivirus software 70
A&P 4, 8n9, 80
Appert, Nicolas 8n8
apron design, innovation in 72
Araujo, L. 38
Araujo, L., Finch, J. and Kjellberg, H.
archaeology 10; objects in 35; potential of 35
audience selection, selectivity of *(Progressive Grocer)* 20
Austin, J.L. 40, 42, 43, 59
automatic cart returns 177–8

Bab-O detergent 183
Bachelard, Gaston 11
Bader, L. 9n15, 39n13
Baker ice-making machines 103
bargain hunting females, canned goods and 120–21
Barnhouse Walters, P. and Briggs, C.M. 103
Barrey, S. 165n11, 165n15
baskets 144–7
batch sales 120–22
behavioural routines, use of shopping trolleys and 181–2
Bertrand-Dorléac, L., Delage, C. and Gunthert, A. 39n16
Better Grocery Stores (Progressive Grocer) 43
"Beware of Bugs" 70
Big Bear 6
Bjorkman, August 8n10
Blue Ribbon Malt Extract 141
Blue Streak can openers 117, 118
B&M Fish Flakes 141

Boston Metal Products Corp. 151, 152, 165n10; shopping trolleys 172, 176
bottled drinks distribution 115
boundaries, moving and renewal of 131–2, 137, 147, 151–2, 155, 177, 200
Bourdieu, Pierre 170
Bowlby, Rachel 1, 3, 144, 164n2
The Boys Market and flagpole 163
Brace Little Tailor disinfectant 70
brands: brand acceptance, telephone and brand loyalty 96; branding and "penning" (enclosing) goods 7, 131–2, 147, 149, 155, 160, 201, 202; enclosures and brands, redefinition of 161–4; identification by, use of 93–4; interlocking brands 155–61, 201; promotion of, telephone as instrument for 93–6
Brecht refrigerated furniture 103
Bruegel, M. 164n6
Bruno, I. 128
Bryant, L. 197n30
Buenker, J.D. and Kantowicz, E.R. 8n5
bulk products, supply of 69
Buridan's donkey 159, 165n17
Burns & Lutz Company of Kansas City 80, 84, 85–6, 86–7, 89
business, history of 3–4
Business Administration classes at University of Nevada 24
business flow, language, objects and images in organisation of 57–9
Butler, J. 50
Butterick, Ebenezer 15
Butterick, Ellen 15
Butterick Publishing Company 15–16, 17–19, 79, 129n7
Buy-at-Home News 15–17, 18

Çalişkan, K. and Callon, M. 38n1, 59
Callon, M., Millo, Y. and Muniesa, F. 42, 59
Callon, Michel 30, 35, 41, 50, 59n1, 88, 197n31
Camay 165n13
Campbell, D. and Wright, J. 13
Campbell Soups 139
cans, progressive merchandising with 114–28; bargain hunting females, canned goods and 120–21; batch sales 120–22; can containers, invention of 139; can pyramids 143; canned food fair, promotion of *(Progressive Grocer)* 24–5; canned foods sales, growth of

119, 120; Canned Foods Week 116, 118 122–8; canned goods, role in change for 115–16; canned goods, safety of 116; canned goods, seasonality and 118–19; canned goods, vitamins and 116; canned goods sales, telephone promotion of 92–3; fresh food substitutes, acceptance of 119; Levenstein paradox 116; National Van Camp Campaign 127; social differences, canned goods and 119–20; stack displays 122; technical qualities of cans 120; tin openers 116–18
Canu, Roland 24, 29, 34, 41, 42
Carson, K.A. 8n5, 75
cartoons, recurrent use of 40, 41, 51–4, 58, 197n34, 198n42
cash and carry: cash and carry system 64–5; operating costs for 66–7
cash registers 5, 9n14, 21, 36, 77, 111
causal imputation, problem of 57–8
Cellophane 144, 145
cellophane, introduction of 138, 144–5, 164n4, 165n8, 200
Central Market, Phoenix, Arizona 179
Chain Store Age 2, 9n11, 33, 161
chain stores: changing conditions and competition from 102–3; competition from, references to 4, 25, 45, 62, 102; management principles of 69
Chandler, A.D.Jr 1, 80
John Chatillon & Sons 176, 189, 194n4
Chatriot, A. and Chessel, M.-E. 7n1
checkouts, mobile barriers 147–9
Chevrolet Motor Company 101
child consumers, distrust of *(Progressive Grocer)* 183–4
children and use of shopping trolleys 185–91
Chiles, W. Brown 124
Clapp's Baby Foods 197–8n36
Clarke, A.J. 142
cleaning, need for regularity in 72
Coates, Harriet Ellsworth 127
Coca Cola 139; interlocking brands 155–7, 165n15, 165n16
Cochoy, Franck 1, 51, 59, 60n4, 60n7, 183, 193, 194n6, 201, 203; commerce, transformation of 133, 139, 144, 158, 164, 164n1, 165n8, 165n17; improvement before transformation of commerce 66, 75, 82, 90, 111, 119, 121, 129n7, 129n14; reading *Progressive Grocer* 14, 16, 28, 35, 38, 38n9

Cocomalt 165n13
cold-calling off-peak 84
Coll, S. 88, 90
collapsible trolleys 176–82
Columbus Show Case Co. 108
commerce, transformation of 1, 131–64;
    adjustable shelves 144–7; baskets
    144–7; can containers, invention of
    139; cellophane 138, 144–5, 164n4,
    165n8, 200; checkouts, mobile barriers
    147–9; customer flow channels 145–6;
    divisions within stores, mobility of 146,
    148–9; enclosures and brands,
    redefinition of 161–4; erratic nature of
    commerce 75–6; food cans 123, 139,
    140–42, 144, 164n6; furniture,
    adjustable shelves and baskets 144–7;
    glass packaging, innovations in 139;
    hands-free doors 151–5, 200;
    innovations in packaging 138–44;
    interlocking brands 155–61, 201;
    merchandising techniques, innovations
    in 140–44; metal wire, use of 146–7;
    minimarkets 164; mobile counters,
    checkouts as 148–9; Monarch Foods
    (and the Monarch way) 140–41,
    142–3, 144; open display glass cases
    139–40; packaged products, growth in
    value of (1870–1920) 140; packaging
    138–44; parking areas 162–4; parking
    areas, expansion of enclosures and
    162–4; pyramid displays 142, 143,
    197n34; real estate 132–3; retail
    furniture 144–7; self-service, move
    from "open display" to 133–8; spatial
    redefinition of grocery stores 161–2;
    turnstiles, magic doors and 149–55
commercial equipment 2–3
commercial innovation, Pasteurian
    concept of 3, 8n8
commercial relationship, (re-)organisation
    of 63–4
commercial uses for telephone,
    imagination in 90–91
community ties and service improvement
    63
competition 70, 72, 81, 94, 97, 110, 119,
    131, 159–60, 199–201; chain stores,
    references to competition from 4, 25,
    45, 62, 102; competitive pressures 32;
    distributive innovation and 2; joint
    initiatives and 126–7; mail order
    competition 17; merchandising
    innovation and 5–6

competitions, organisation of *(Progressive
    Grocer)* 22–4, 59–60n2, 123–5, 128,
    130n28
Computing Cheese Cutter Co. 112,
    113
consumers on foot, transformation to
    families on wheels 182–92
contemporary history, world of 35
Continental Paper & Bag Mills Co. 75
continuous improvement, potential for 63
Cook, Daniel Th. 198n38
copy writing 27, 110
Coshocton Glove Co. 73
cost implications of motorised delivery
    97–8
cost reduction, telephone's positive
    contribution to 83–4
counter displays 112–14
counterfeit testimonies, avoidance of
    25
credit and delivery: operating costs for
    66–7; by "service stores" 64
Crossick, G. and Jaumain, S. 129n4
customers: base knowledge of, effective
    use of 86–8, 89; customer satisfaction
    surveys 63; flow channels for 145–6;
    management of, telephone and 84;
    types of, distribution of (1958)
    192
cylindrical cardboard packages 73
Czarniawska, Barbara 11

daily life in retailing, rules for 71–2
Dallas Department of Health 197n33
Daumas, J.-C. 1
Dayton Display Company 109–10
Dayton Scale Company 77–8
The Delineator 15, 16–17, 18, 19
delivery systems: delivery and telephone,
    association between 96–7; sales
    back-up by efficiency of 88
demand side concerns 33
Denis, J. 43, 59
Denis, J. and Pontille, D. 58
The Designer 15
Deutsch, Tracey A. 2, 4, 9n12, 64, 110,
    129n2, 130n25
Deville, Joe 91
Didier, Emmanuel 57
Diesel, Rudolf 197n30
Diner, S.J. 8n5
Dipman, Carl 45, 76, 77, 80, 84, 85, 102,
    103, 105, 107, 108, 110, 111, 114,
    130n20, 135, 137, 164n3, 184

discourse 32, 35, 58, 92; absence of 44; effects of 11; performativity of 22, 111; power of 50
disinfection, modern methods of 72
displays: A-B-C Open Display Method (Dayton Display Company) 109; counter displays 112–14; glass display cases 107–8; models, display of potential in 47–8; open display glass cases 139–40; open displays 105, 107–10; open displays, children and 184–5; open displays, development of 135–8; open displays, idea of 45; pyramid displays 142, 143, 197n34; self-service, move from "open display" to 133–8; shopping trolleys as 166, 194n3; stack displays 122; that sell, building of *(Progressive Grocer)* 41–4; visual display 107–8; *see also* island displays
distance selling, concerns for 80–81
distribution spaces, transformation of 3
division of labour, telephone and 84
divisions within stores, mobility of 146, 148–9
The Doubling Basket Co. 171
driver-deliverer, link to salesperson 98
Du Gay, Paul 60n10, 164n2
dual identity of *Progressive Grocer* 62
Duff's cereals 183
Dujarier, M.-A. 60n7
Duluth Show Case Co. 108
Dun's and Bradstreet telephone directories 19

"E-Z" Glider and Basket Co. 172, 176
economic model of *Progressive Grocer* 19–29
economic sociology 201
Edgerton, D. 195n11
Edison, Thomas 197n30
electric lights 110
embeddedness, notion of 201
Emmet, B. and Jeuck, J.E. 18
employees: head-to-toe approach to 73; labour force, panoptic monitoring of 85; labour force training and productivity 7; staff performance, importance of 7, 72–3; staff recruitment 73; work of, physical and performance improvements in 72–3
enclosures (pens) 140, 143, 144–5, 149, 151, 158, 159–60, 165n15, 200; brands and 131–2, 161–2, 201–2; brands and,

redefinition of 161–4; commercial enclosures 144, 155, 164n5; flexible enclosures 131; mobile enclosures 147
equipment: acquisition of 73; equipment optimisation 73–8; improvements in 7; investment in 77; labour-saving equipment 76; shop equipment and optimisation of work of grocers 76
The M.C. Escher Company 160–61

facts, manufacture of 11
fallibility 10
false-bottom baskets 111
families on wheels, transformation from consumers on foot to 182–92
family affair, shopping as 193
Fanestil Store of Hoisington, Kansas 88
felicity conditions, notion of 58–9
Fellman, S. and Popp, A. 11
Fenske, A.H. 106
Fernie, S. and Metcalf, D. 85
Finch, J. and Kjellberg, H. 38, 164
Fischer, C.S. 91
Fischhoff, B. 62
Flamingo paper 75
flexibility of models 47
Flink, J.J. 130n18
Flit insecticide 70
flour beetle damage 69–70
Fly-Tox insecticide 70, 71
focalisation 12; clarity through medial focalisation 12–13, 13–14
foldable trolleys 170–76
Folding Basket Carrier Co. 195n19
Folding Carrier Corp. 166, 168, 169, 171, 172–3, 174–6, 189, 194n4
food cans 123, 139, 140–42, 144, 164n6
food industry, small businesses in 2
Ford Motor Company, delivery costs and 98, 100–101
free press principle of *Progressive Grocer* 21
fresh food substitutes, acceptance of 119
Frigidaire Refrigeration 103
furniture: adjustable shelves and baskets 144–7; blueprints of equipment and furniture rearrangements displayed by *Progressive Grocer* 133; *see also* equipment
future, analysis of past and knowledge of 54, 61–2, 64

Gair, Robert 138
Garford Motor Company 101
Genette, Gérard 12

George Reuter, Rochester, New York
72–3
Gerber Foods 144, 197–8n36
*Getting Down to Real Facts in the Grocery
Business (Progressive Grocer)* 43
Giant Lye miracle product 70
Gibson, J.J. 164n7
Giraudeau, Martin 47, 195n11
Glad, Paul W. 8n5
glass cabinets 108
glass display cases 107–8
glass packaging, innovations in 139
Glider and Basket Co. 194n4
globular glass containers (Panay
Company) 112
Goldberg, Bowen & Co. in San Francisco
98
Goldman, Sylvan N. 167, 171, 172, 174,
176, 194n8, 196n30, 197n33
Good Hardware 16
good practices, description of 75
Google Analytics 25
Gould, R.A. 8n5, 35
Graham Brothers Motors 101
Grandclément, Catherine 1, 4, 5, 6,
39n17, 41, 42, 48, 60n10; commerce,
improvements in 61, 64, 77, 94, 107,
111; commerce, transformation of 144,
148, 153, 165n8, 165n14; shopping
trolleys 167, 168, 170, 171, 174, 182,
194n7, 194n8, 195n14, 195n19,
195n20, 195n21
Granovetter, Mark 201
Great Depression, effects of 4, 5, 28–9
grocery world 200
The Grocery World 38n8
Gruendler Refrigeration 103

Haas, H.M. 2, 4
Hamilton, S. 1
hands-free doors 151–5, 200
Harvard Bureau of Business Research 66
Heinz Corporation 139, 197–8n36
Hine, Thomas 139, 165n8
history: of commerce from point of view
of *Progressive Grocer* 13, 14; difficulties
in presentation of 29–34; historical
documentation 34–5; historical
perspectives 5; historical research,
problem of abundance of data in
11–12; of self-service, *Progressive Grocer*
as source of 10
Hofstadter, R. 8n5
Holcomb and Hoke Refrigeration 103

Horowitz, R. 144
"How to Run a Retail Store" 23–4
Hughes, Thomas P. 6, 197n30
Hultén, B., Broweus, N. och and Van
Dijk, M. 107
humour and the funny war 51–9
humour in society, role of 51–2
humourous speech, joint performativity of
54
Hunt Grocery Company of Texas 91
Hunt Show Case Co. 108
Hussmann Refrigeration 103
hygiene and getting rid of vermin 7,
69–72, 200; bulk products, supply of
69; cleaning, regularity of 72; daily life
in retailing, rules for 71–2; disinfection,
modern methods of 72; flour beetle
damage 69–70; insect damage, dealing
with 69–70; insecticides,
advertisements for 70–71; merchandise
inspection, recommendation for 71–2;
preventative strategies 71; rat poisons,
advertisements for 70–71; small
quantities, purchasing in 72
hypersocialisation 201

IBM 77–8, 108
ideal shop model, building business with
45–8
independent grocers: comparative success
of 4–5, 6; re-presentation of grocer
economy in *Progressive Grocer* 30–32;
service promotion for 68–9; shop
layout advice for 134, 136; shop routes,
development of 137; spatial
redefinition of grocery stores 161–2;
store remodelling to accommodate
shopping trolleys 173–4
Indianapolis Gloves 73
Inland MFG. Co., Inc. 111–12
innovations: apron design, innovation in
72; chronology of 29; commercial
innovation, Pasteurian concept of 3,
8n8; diffusion of 3; existing
environment and 110–11; glass
packaging, innovations in 139; logic of
68; market place and competition as
stimuli for 131; merchandising
techniques, innovations in 5–6, 30, 31,
140–44; in packaging 138–44;
promotion of 6; technical innovations
3, 7
insect damage, dealing with 69–70
insecticides, advertisements for 70–71

intellectual content *(Progressive Grocer)* 199
intelligibility 10
interlocking brands 155–61, 201
interlocking of trolleys 176–7, 180, 189, 195n22
International Harvester Company 101
International Paper Company 150
introspection/interpretation, traditional methods of 35
introspective brilliance *(Progressive Grocer)* 44
island displays: appearance of 135; effectiveness of 136; "islands" as showcases 45

Jabobs Bros. Company 130n21
James Kirk & Company of Chicago 93
Jap Rose Bags 75
Jap Rose Soap 93
Jaycox, F. 8n5
Jean-Christophe (Rolland, R.) 57
Jeantet, A. 45
Jenkins, R.V. 197n30
Johns, Edward S. 73
joint initiatives, competition and 126–7
Journal of Marketing 28–9
journalists for *Progressive Grocer,* travels of 19
Jullien, François 195n11

Kamper, M. 85
Keener, Pop 63
Kennedy, M.T. 165n18
Kjellberg, H. and Helgesson, C.-F. 60n10, 164n2
Kline, R.R. 129n16
Koch, S.L. 60n7, 130n26
Kodak 33
Kroger 3, 4, 5, 6, 8n9, 9n16

labour force, panoptic monitoring of 85
labour-saving equipment 76
The Ladies' Paradise (Zola, É.) 1–2, 47
Ladies' Quarterly of Broadway Fashions 15
Laïb, J. 58
Lancaster, K.J. 171
language: action and, widening of gap between 43; acts of language, extension to language of acts 44; business flow, language, objects and images in organisation of 57–9; in gesture 44; linguistic rhetoric 199; skills in use of 40, 45, 48–9, 51, 52–3, 57–9

language performativity 40; marketing use of 75
Latour, B. and Woolgar, S. 11
Latour, Bruno 3, 11, 30, 35, 61; business with words 40, 41–2, 44, 51, 58, 61; commerce, transformation of 151, 152, 153; shopping trolleys and progressive retail 180, 182, 194n5, 195n21
Lave, J., Murtaugh, M. and de la Rocha, O. 72
Laycock, G. 3
Lebhar, G.M 4, 9n11
Levenstein, H.A. 116, 130n24
Levenstein paradox 116
Leymonerie, Claire 2, 38n3
Libby Foods 127, 139, 144, 184
Licoppe, Christine 89
Life magazine 157–8, 165n16
Ligonier Refrigeration 103
linguistic rhetoric 199
Lipman ice-making machines 103
Lippmann, W. 30
The Liquid Carbonic Co. 112
Lira, Jaciara Topley 38n2
local-level micro mail-order companies 80
location, mobility and 201
longitudinal improvement, logic of 98
Longstreth, R.W. 1, 6, 132
Loxley, J. 43
Luis, Araujo 38, 164
Lury, C. 94
Lyon Metal Products Inc. 165n10

McClelland Grocer Company, Decatur, Illinois 17
McCray Refrigeration 103, 104
McFall, L. 59
McGerr, M. 8n5
MacKenzie, D. and Millo, Y. 59
MacKenzie, D., Muniesa, F. and Siu, L. 59
McLean, C. 59
Macy's 80
magazine advertising 17
mail order: local-level micro mail-order companies 80; mail order companies, boycott of 17–18; turnover of mail order companies 17–18
Mallard, Alexandre 78, 88, 90
Margolin, C.R. 197n32
marketing devices 7, 58
mass consumption, shopping trolleys and 168–70

Mayo, James M. 8n3, 17, 119, 132
medial focalisation 10–14, 32, 199; visual distortions of 29
Mendras, H. 170
merchandise inspection, recommendation for 71–2
merchandising 5–6; equipment for, operation of 42; techniques of, encouragement of innovation in 30, 31; techniques of, innovations in 140–44
metal wire, use of 146–7
metallic shelving 108–9
The Metropolitan Monthly 15
Metwood MFG. Co. 166, 168, 169, 171, 172
Mike Cullen shops 6
Miller, Daniel 184
minimarkets 164
mobile counters, checkouts as 148–9
mobile space, temporary imposition of 200, 202
models: display of potential in 47–8; flexibility of models 47; ideal shop model, building business with 45–8; modernisation through modelling 47–8; organisational set-ups, modelling of 47–8; self-service, models of origins of 3–4, 9n16
The Modern Grocery Store(Progressive Grocer) 43
Modern Store Equipment Co. 171
modernisation: arrangements for modernising shops 133–5; modernising movement, inventiveness of 201; paths to, service improvement and 68–9; process of, transformation and improvement in 7, 62, 199–200, 201; of service, proctectivity within 63; telephone and 83; through modelling 47–8; transformatory and improvement aspects of 62
modernist rhetoric of *Progressive Grocer* 199
modernity of service, support for 66, 67–8
Monarch Foods (and the Monarch way) 140–41, 142–3, 144
Monod, David 2
monographs published by *Progressive Grocer* 43
Montgomery Ward 80
"More Money Every Year" 26–8
motorised customers 101–2

motorised delivery 7, 96–101; ambulatory advertising space and 97, 99; cost implications of 97–8; delivery and telephone, association between 96–7; driver-deliverer, link to salesperson 98; Ford Motor Company, delivery costs and 98, 100–101; longitudinal improvement, logic of 98; vehicle maintenance 98
moveable partitions 148–9
Mueller, R.W. 180
multiples, methods of 4–5; *see also* chain stores
Muniesa, Fabian 22

Nashua gummed and coated paper 75
National Association of Retail Grocers 66
National Canners' Association 116
National Cash Register (NCR) 9n14, 47, 165n15
National Cloak and Suit Company 17–18
National Grocers Bulletin 38n8
"National magazine of the Grocery Trade" 43, 158–9
National Retail Grocers' Association 38n12, 81, 85
National Van Camp Campaign 127
National Wholesale Grocers' Association 81
negligent appropriation, mechanism of 170
neoclassical economics 131
Nescafé 165n15
nesting of shopping trolleys 176
Neville, H. and Lawson, D. 13
New England Grocer 38n8
New York Times 15
Norman, D.A. 73
Northern Regional Library Facility (NRLF) 36
Norton, Edwin 139

Ong, Walter 179
open displays 105, 107–10; children and 184–5; development of 135–8; "open display," idea of 45; open display glass cases 139–40
organisational set-ups, modelling of 47–8
over-equipment 76
Owens, Michael 139

packaging and packaged products 110; commerce, transformation of 138–44; growth in value of (1870–1920) 140;

package wrapping, instructions for 73–6

PalmPilot 37

Panay Sectional Show Case Company 24, 112, 114

paper-folding techniques 73–4

"paraffined boxes" 75

Parasie, S. 54, 187

parking areas, expansion of enclosures and 162–4

Pasteur, Louis 3, 8n8, 201

perception, directed vision and 13

performative logic: generalisation of 50; suspension and extension of 43–4

performativity: aporia of 43; performative equipment 41; "performative" utterances 40, 42–3, 58–9; photography and power of 50; of *Progressive Grocer* 22, 40, 41–4; *Progressive Grocer* policies of 54–7; techniques of, empirical examination of 58–9

peripheral vision, promotion of 13–14

Péron, R. 132

Pet Milk Company 141

Phillips, Ch.F. 4

'phone as front page news 78–80

phone-based commercial relationships 84; *see also* telephone sales

"Phone for Food" campaign 81–3, 97, 122

photo stories, use of 49–51

photonovelas 49, 50–51, 58

pictorial elements within *Progressive Grocer*, concentration of 35–6

pictorial externalities in *Progressive Grocer* 32

pictorial rhetoric of *Progressive Grocer* 199

Pierce, Ch. 40

Piggly Wiggly 3–4, 5, 8n9, 9n16

Pillsbury 197–8n36

Plymouth Metal Products Corp. 176

"pocket tool" magazine, idea of 33–4

Polanyi, Karl 201

PowerPoint 58

pragmatics devices of "words-things" 40, 41–4

present times, archaeology of 34–7

Presley, D.E. 3

press and trade magazines, quotations in *Progressive Grocer* 25

preventative strategies, hygiene and 71

pricing aggression 68

pricing policy of *Progressive Grocer* 21

Printer's Ink 33

product distribution, industrialisation of 1

progress: associations and consolidation of 61–2; "Progressive Era," modernist rhetoric of 2, 8n5, 15, 61, 75; at time of Great Depression 28–9

Progressive Grocer 2, 4–5, 6, 7, 8n5, 8n7, 9n12, 79, 199; acts of language, extension to language of acts 44; advertising growth of advertising in 26; advertising in 19; advertising rates 21; advertising space, encouragement of consumption of 24–5; advertising success of 25, 26, 27–8; advertising turnover, exponential growth of 26; advertorial "Questions and Answers" 19–20, 24; arrangements for modernising shops 133–5; audience selection, selectivity of 20; "Beware of Bugs" 70; blueprints of equipment and furniture rearrangements displayed by 133; boundaries, moving and renewal of 200; business flow, language, objects and images in organisation of 57–9; canned food fair, promotion of 24–5; cans, progressive merchandising with 114–28; cartoons, recurrent use of 40, 41, 51–4, 58, 197n34, 198n42; causal imputation, problem of 57–8; child consumers, distrust of 183–4; competition 199; competition from chains, references to 4; competitions, organisation of 22–4; competitive pressures developed in 32; counterfeit testimonies, avoidance of 25; customer types, distribution of (1958) 192; demand side concerns 33; displays that sell, building of 41–4; dual identity of 62; economic model of 19–29; equipment optimisation 73–8; family affair, shopping as 193; felicity conditions, notion of 58–9; first issue (January, 1922) 16–17; flexibility of models 47; foundations of 2–3; founding objectives 18–19; free press principle of 21; history, difficulties in presentation of 29–34; history of commerce from point of view of 13, 14; history of self-service, source of 10; "How to Run a Retail Store" 23–4; humour and the funny war 51–9; humourous speech. joint performativity of 54; hygiene and getting rid of vermin 7, 69–72, 200; ideal shop model, building business with 45–8; identity of, bases for 19; innovations, promotion of 6; intellectual content 199; introspective brilliance 44; island displays, effectiveness of 136; "islands," appearance of 135; "islands" as showcases 45; journalists for, travels of 19; language, skills in use of 40, 45, 48–9, 51, 52–3, 57–9; language and action, widening of gap between 43; language in gesture 44; linguistic rhetoric 199; location, mobility and 201; material and conceptual, avoidance of gap between 32–3; medial focalisation 10–14, 32, 199; mediation through, targeted nature of 13–14; merchandising techniques, encouragement of innovation in 30, 31; models, display of potential in 47–8; modernisation process, transformation and improvement in 7, 62, 199–200, 201; modernisation through modelling 47–8; modernising movement, inventiveness of 201; modernist rhetoric 199; monographs published by 43; 'More Money Every Year' 26–8; motorisation 7, 96–101; 'National magazine of the Grocery Trade' 43, 158–9; objective causes, understanding and 44; open display, children and 184–5; open display, development of 135–8; "open display," idea of 45; organisational set-ups, modelling of 47–8; original cover (April 1923 issue) 23, 59–60n2; origins of 15–19; package wrapping, instructions for 73–6; performative logic, generalisation of 50; performative logic, suspension and extension of 43–4; performativity, photography and power of 50; performativity, policies of 54–7; performativity of 22, 40, 41–4; performativity techniques of, empirical examination of 58–9; photo stories, use of 49–51; pictorial elements within, concentration of 35–6; pictorial externalities in 32; pictorial rhetoric 199; "pocket tool" magazine, idea of 33–4; point of view, particulality in 12–13; pragmatics devices of "words-things" of 40, 41–4; present times, archaeology of 34–7; press and trade magazines, quotations in 25; pricing policy 21; progress,

consolidation and 61–2; progress at time of Great Depression 28–9; progressive modernisation 61–2; progressive stance, dual attachment to traditional and modern forms of retail grocery in 61–2; re-presentation of grocer economy in 30–32; reach of 21; readership map (1924) 20; readership measurement, competitions and 24; readership of (and growth of) 19–21, 21–2; sales at counter, disappearance from 29–30; self-promotional advertising 24–5, 26–7; "self publicity" 24; self-service, audiences reluctance to introduce 138; self-service, declaration of coming of 57; service improvement 62–9; service improvements, transformative aspects of 7, 101–14, 200; shop layout advice 134, 136; shop routes, development of 137; shopping trolleys, interest in, appearance of 166–8; shopping trolleys, neglect of innovation of use of 32, 166; staff performance, importance of 7, 72–3; strategic perspective of 19–29; suppliers to grocers as clients 21; supply side concerns 33; systematic states of business, tensions between magazine articles and realities of 32; target audience 19–20; Taylorism and 62, 72–8; telephone sales, development of 7, 78–96; testimonies, use of 48–9; "world's finest grocery store" 5–6, 8–9n10

promises, fulfillment of 199, 203n1
purchasing habits, recording of 88–9
Puyou, F.-R. 59
pyramid displays 142, 143, 197n34

Quaker Oats 94–6, 184, 197–8n36
Quattrone, P. 59

rat poisons, advertisements for 70–71
Rat-Tox poison 70
rationality, curiosity and 14
Razac, Olivier 131
real estate 132–3
real-time competitions 22–4
recovering credit, telephone as instrument for 91
refrigeration 103–5, 107
Register Company, Dayton, Ohio 185
relational capital, telephone sales use of 88
Render Grocery in Texas 124

Renfrew, C. and Bahn, P.G. 35
research: historical research, problem of
    abundance of data in 11–12; material
    constraints on 35–7, 39n15;
    serendipity, research and 14
Retail Association 81
retail furniture 2–3, 144–7
Robinson-Patman Act (1936) 9n12,
    38–9n13
Rogers, E.M. 3
Rolland, Romain 57
Roll'er Basket Co. 195n14, 195n20

salary costs, optimisation of 76–7
sales at counter, disappearance from
    Progressive Grocer 29–30
sales methods, development of 29–30
sales pitches 98, 110, 122, 130n17, 168,
    170, 171, 194n1
sales system organisation 77–8
sales without salespeople, evolution
    towards 62–3
Sanitary Can Company 139
Sanitary Cover Co. 112
Sears, Roebuck & Company 1, 17–18, 80
selectivity 11, 42
self-promotional advertising 24–5, 26–7
self-service: branding and "penning"
    (enclosing) goods 7, 131–2, 147, 149,
    155, 160, 161, 201, 202; declaration of
    coming of 57; devices for,
    shortcomings (and advantages) of 42;
    emergence of 6–7; as expression of
    modernity 68–9; female employment
    and idea of 55–6; grocery development
    and extension towards 54;
    interobjectivity of 50–51; labour
    shortage in wartime and 54–6; models
    of origins of 3–4, 9n16; modern
    arrangements of semi-self-service and
    29; move from "open display" to
    133–8; *Progressive Grocer* audiences
    reluctance to introduce 138; sales
    without salespeople, evolution towards
    62–3; symbols of 111; war, role in
    conversion to 54–5, 55–7
"sell telephone sales" endeavour 81
selling methods, alternative possibilities
    63–4
selling service to customers 68
The Sense of Dissonance (Stark, D.) 13–14
serendipity, research and 14
Serres, Michel 38n2
service, housewives' demand for 65

service costs, optimisation of 83–4
Service Grocers' Association 68
service improvement 62–9; cash and
    carry, operating costs for 66–7; cash
    and carry system 64–5; chains,
    management principles of 69;
    commercial relationship,
    (re-)organisation of 63–4; community
    ties and 63; continuous improvement,
    potential for 63; credit and delivery,
    operating costs for 66–7; customer
    satisfaction surveys 63; development of
    service, best practice awards for 67–8;
    independent grocers, service promotion
    for 68–9; innovation, logic of 68;
    intensification of service, societal trend
    towards 64–5; means for 72–8;
    modernisation, paths to 68–9;
    modernisation and 62; modernisation
    of service, productivity within 63;
    modernity of service, support for 66,
    67–8; pricing aggression 68; sales
    without salespeople, evolution towards
    62–3; self-service as expression of
    modernity 68–9; selling methods,
    alternative possibilities 63–4; selling
    service to customers 68; service,
    housewives' demand for 65; service
    promotion, group logic for 68; "service
    stores," credit and delivery by 64;
    telephone technology and 65;
    transformative aspects of 7, 101–14,
    200
service promotion, group logic for 68
"service stores," credit and delivery by 64
Seth, A. 2
S.F. Bower & Co., Inc 98
shopping cart parks 162
shopping trolleys 166–93, 201–2;
    abandonment of 181; American Can
    Company 197–8nn36; American Metal
    Products, Inc. 189; American Wire &
    Form Co. 166, 171, 176, 187–8,
    194n1, 194n4, 194n8; automatic cart
    returns 177–8; behavioural routines
    and use of 181–2; Boston Metal
    Products Corp. 172, 176; John
    Chatillon & Sons 176, 189, 194n4;
    children and use of 185–91; collapsible
    trolleys 176–82; consumers on foot,
    transformation to families on wheels
    182–92; display use for 166, 194n3;
    The Doubling Basket Co. 171; "E-Z"
    Glider and Basket Co. 172, 176;

foldable trolleys 170–76; Folding Basket Carrier Co. 195n19; Folding Carrier Corp. 166, 168, 169, 171, 172–3, 174–6, 189, 194n4; Glider and Basket Co 194n4; interest in, appearance of 166–8; interlocking of trolleys 176–7, 180, 189, 195n22; introduction of 166; manufacturers of 166; market and appearance of 168; mass consumption and 168–70; Metwood MFG. Co. 166, 168, 169, 171, 172; mobile space, temporary imposition of 200, 202; Modern Store Equipment Co. 171; neglect of innovation of use of *(Progressive Grocer)* 32, 166; negligent appropriation, mechanism of 170; nesting of 176; Plymouth Metal Products Corp. 176; Roll'er Basket Co. 195n14, 195n20; spread of use of, service and 180–81; stacking and folding, problems of 174–6; store remodelling to accommodate 173–4; supermarket customers, social reconfiguration of 183; technical problems, concerns about 166, 194n4; techniques, sociology of 182; telescopic trolleys 171–2, 176, 189; Tote-Cart Co. 171, 172, 176, 187, 189, 194n4; trolley types, distribution of 191–2; tunnel check-outs 178–80; UNITED Folding Carts 168; United Steel & Form Co. 174; United Steel & Wire Co. 166, 168, 171, 172, 176, 189, 194n1, 194n4; Watson's Telescope Carts Inc. 168; W.R. Alexander Co. 189, 194n4
Shove, E. and Southerton, D. 119
Shove, E., Pantzar, M. and Watson, M. 63
Simmel, Georg 202
small quantities, purchasing in 72
Smith, A. 13
Smith, T.W. 48
Smithsonian Museum of American History 194n8
social action, material elements in understandings of 35
social activity, Weber's perspective on 50
social differences, canned goods and 119–20
Spellman, Susan 2, 3, 4, 5, 8n9, 8n10, 9n14, 9n16, 32, 38n7, 38n8, 39n13, 63, 69, 129n16
Springfield Tea Co. 96

stack displays 122
stacking and folding shopping trolleys, problems of 174–6
staff performance, importance of 7, 72–3
staff recruitment 73
staging telephone sales 87
Standard Oil Co. 70
Stanley Magic Doors (hands-free) 152
Star Can Opener 117
Stark, David 13, 14
Steiden Stores 46, 47
Step-in-and-shop Serve Self Store 130n23
stereoscopic view, advantages of 13–14
sticky tape reels 73
Strasser, Susan 1, 2, 4, 17, 27, 42; commerce, transformation of 75, 80, 123, 131, 139, 143, 144, 155
strategic perspective of *Progressive Grocer* 19–29
superettes 200–201
supermarket customers, social reconfiguration of 183
Supermarket Merchandising 2, 6, 161
supermarket trolleys 111; *see also* shopping trolleys
supermarkets, progress of 6
suppliers 5; to grocers as clients for *Progressive Grocer* 21
supply side concerns 33

Tanglefoot insecticide 70
Tarde, G. 170
target audience *(Progressive Grocer)* 19–20
Tavern 183
Taylorian improvements, recommendations for 62, 72–8; apron design, innovation in 72; commerce, erratic nature of 75–6; cylindrical cardboard packages 73; employees' work, physical and performance improvements in 72–3; equipment, acquisition of 73; equipment, investment in 77; good practices, description of 75; head-to-toe approach to employees 73; labour-saving equipment 76; optimisation of work of grocers 76; over-equipment 76; paper-folding techniques 73–4; "paraffined boxes" 75; salary costs, optimisation of 76–7; sales system organisation 77–8; service improvement, means for 72–8; shop

equipment and optimisation of work of grocers 76; staff recruitment 73; sticky tape reels 73; training staff operations 73; under-equipment 76; voucher system with to-do list for shop 73; work-study comparisons 76–7; wrapping purchases at point of sale 73

technical devices: delegation of selling to 105; use of 37

technical innovations 3, 7

techniques, sociology of 182

Tedlow, Richard S. 1, 2, 4, 9n11, 17, 32, 80, 121, 144, 164n1

telephone sales, development of 7, 78–96; brand acceptance, telephone and brand loyalty 96; brand identification, use of 93–4; brand promotion, telephone as instrument for 93–6; Burns & Lutz Company of Kansas City 80, 84, 85–6, 86–7, 89; canned goods sales, telephone promotion of 92–3; cold-calling off-peak 84; commercial uses for telephone, imagination in 90–91; cost reduction, telephone's positive contribution to 83–4; customer base knowledge, effective use of 86–8; customer "captation" 90–91; customer details, recording of 89; customer management, telephone and 84; delivery systems, back-up by efficiency of 88; distance selling, concerns for 80–81; division of labour, telephone and 84; gender-based division between housewife and "male breadwinner" in telephone shopping 89; labour force, panoptic monitoring of 85; local-level micro mail-order companies 80; modernisation, telephone and 83; 'phone as front page news 78–80; phone-based commercial relationships 84; "Phone for Food" campaign 81–3, 97, 122; purchasing habits, recording of 88–9; recovering credit, telephone as instrument for 91; relational capital, telephone sales use of 88; "sell telephone sales" endeavour 81; service costs, optimisation of 83–4; staging telephone sales 87; telephone as market research tool 80; telephone-assisted sales, merits of 82–3; telephone-assisted sales, organisation of 80; "telephone rebound," visionary codification of 89–90; telephone sales systems, effective organisation of 84–6;

telephones per inhabitant (US, 1880–1940) 91

telephones: per inhabitant (US, 1880–1940) 91; telephone technology, service improvement and 65

telescopic trolleys 171–2, 176, 189

Terry, Dr. 17

testimonies, use of *(Progressive Grocer)* 48–9

Texcel micro-shelves 165n15

textile industry, small businesses in 2

theft, risk (and avoidance) of 131, 149, 151, 164n5

Thesco Refrigeration 103

Thoenig, J.-C. and Waldman, C. 131

Thoenig, Jean-Claude 131

Thompson, J.A. 8n5

Thrift, N. 59

tin openers 116–18

Tolbert, L. 3

Tom Smith Grocary, Miami, Florida 48

Tote-Cart Co. 146–7; shopping trolleys 171, 172, 176, 187, 189, 194n4

Touraine, Alain 7n2

traditional retailers 1, 47

training staff operations 73

trolleys *see* shopping trolleys

tunnel check-outs 178–80

turnstiles, magic doors and 149–55

Twede, Diana 5, 8n8, 117, 138, 140, 165n8

Twin-seam Leather Palm Work Gloves 73

Typer Corp. 189

under-equipment 76

Union Steel Products Co. 108

UNITED Folding Carts 168

United States: Bureau of Labor Statistics 120; Census Bureau 130n18, 140; Public Health Service 116; Transport Department Federal Highway Administration 130n18

United Steel & Form Co. 174

United Steel & Wire Co. 108, 165n10; shopping trolleys 166, 168, 171, 172, 176, 189, 194n1, 194n4

University of Chicago 116

US Slicing Machine Company 105, 106

vehicle maintenance 98

Vingtième siècle 39n16

visual display 107–8

Vogue magazine 15

Von Hippel, E. 189

voucher system with to-do list for shop 73

Waldman, Charles 131
Walker Bin Co. 108
Walters, Barnhouse and Briggs, C.M. 197n32
Watson, O.E. and Goldman, S.N. 194n7
Watson, Orla E. 167, 171, 172, 176, 177, 178, 182, 194n8
Watson's Telescope Carts Inc. 168
Weber, Max 50, 60n6, 103
Weber of Kansas 96–7
Weber Showcase & Fixture Co. 108, 186
Wilson, Terry P. 10, 196n30, 197n33
Wolferman's in Kansas City 85, 86
Woolworth 80, 107
work-study comparisons 76–7

World Exhibition (1937) 38n3
"world's finest grocery store" *(Progressive Grocer)* 5–6, 8–9n10
Worthington, W.Jr 1
W.R. Alexander Co. 189, 194n4
wrapping purchases at point of sale 73

Yates, J. and Orlikowski, W.J. 58
Young's Market Company of Los Angeles 6, 85

Zephyr System check-outs 147–8
Zimmerman, Max M. 6, 171
Zola, Émile 1–2, 47
Zwick, D. and Cayla, J. 164

For Product Safety Concerns and Information please contact our EU
representative GPSR@taylorandfrancis.com
Taylor & Francis Verlag GmbH, Kaufingerstraße 24, 80331 München, Germany

www.ingramcontent.com/pod-product-compliance
Ingram Content Group UK Ltd.
Pitfield, Milton Keynes, MK11 3LW, UK
UKHW021000180425
457613UK00019B/761